CU00920259

The Window Glass of the Order of St Gilbert of Sempringham:

A York-based study

By C. Pamela Graves

Published for the York Archaeological Trust
by the Council for British Archaeology   2000

Contents

List of Figures

List of Tables

Volume 11 Fascicule 3

The Window Glass of the Order of St Gilbert of Sempringham: A York-based Study

By C. Pamela Graves

With contributions by H.I. Alten, J.E. Burton, G.A. Cox, R.L. Kemp, J.F. De Laperouse, M.A. Little, J.P. Maish, S. Rees, N.S.H. Rogers and J.A. Spriggs

Key words: conservation, Gilbertine Order, glass, Haverholme, medieval, Sempringham, York

General Introduction

The Order of St Gilbert of Sempringham is of significant interest to the study of medieval England. It is the one peculiarly English monastic Order and the glazing evidence is of primary archaeological importance to the study and understanding of this community. The mother house for the Order was established at St Mary's Priory, Sempringham, Lincolnshire, by 1131, with a second house established at Haverholme, Lincolnshire, by 1139. During the height of the Order's popularity the Gilbertine Priory of St Andrew, York, was founded, in 1195. The glass collections from each of these monastic houses is presented and reviewed in this fascicule. The window glass from 46–54 Fishergate, recovered from excavations undertaken by York Archaeological Trust during 1984–6, is the largest assemblage of medieval window glass from a Gilbertine priory. There are approximately 50,000 fragments of glass, equivalent to c.6·25m^2. The collections from Sempringham and Haverholme are considerably smaller. However, despite the various limitations placed on the evidence, this study examines the dating and stylistic affinities of these assemblages as a means of identifying consistencies in the glazing preferences of Gilbertine priories. To this end a comprehensive review of all known glazing evidence from Gilbertine sites in England is included.

It would not have been possible to study this glass had not a great deal of time and effort been spent on the conservation of the assemblage. Waterlogged glass deposits form a sparsely investigated area of archaeological research, and successful recovery is rare in such conditions. An extensive and successful programme of innovatory work has been undertaken by the Trust's Conservation Laboratory and under its supervision a series of investigations were devised and carried out. The conservation of such a quantity of waterlogged glass was a huge problem within which new ground was broken. This work will be of interest not only to conservators, but to museums and archaeological units faced with the problems of storing quantities of glass, since the packaging was specially devised to allow for both access for study and long-term storage.

With the collaboration of Dr G.A. Cox, then of the Department of Physics, University of York, a programme of scientific analysis into the composition and corrosion patterns of some samples of the Fishergate glass was carried out. The volume of scientific research into archaeological glasses, and medieval glass in particular, is still limited and every contribution enhances our understanding of the subject matter. The sampling strategy of the Fishergate excavations created the opportunity to study the decay of medieval glass in specific soil environments. A research programme was devised but, given funding limitations, it proved impossible to put this into effect. The strategy and questions to be posed have been formulated and the material is available for experimentation in the future should the opportunity arise.

The fascicule begins with a review of the development of window glass production techniques during the medieval period. The construction methods used in the design and manufacture of a complete window are then outlined, information returned to during the description and discussion of the actual glass fragments. This summary of background information concludes with the documentary evidence for glazing and glass-painting in York.

Description of the glass from each of the Gilbertine houses is preceded by an historical and, where applicable, archaeological introduction. After presentation of the evidence the discussion looks at possible reconstructions of the glazing schemes and analyses the effect of the Gilbertine rule upon style, interpretation and execution. Accounts of the conservation strategies and a technical report into the examination of the glass follow. The report concludes with a catalogue of illustrated glass fragments (pp.543–54), a quantification list for the entire Fishergate corpus (pp.555–8), and a glossary of technical terms (given in italics on their first appearance in the text) used throughout the report (pp.566–8).

The production of medieval window glass

Some aspects of the construction of a painted and leaded window have changed little since medieval times. One of our main sources for understanding medieval practices is the treatise *De Diversis Artibus*, probably written in Germany in the early 12th century by the monk Theophilus (Dodwell 1961; Hawthorne and Smith 1963). To begin with, however, it is necessary to describe the kind of glass used. The main constituents of glass are silica, usually derived from sand, an alkali such as potassium or soda as a fluxing agent, and lime as a stabilising agent. Almost all Roman glass was made from soda, and withstands corrosion. High potassium glasses are known from at least the 9th century, from excavations at Flaxengate, Lincoln, and a production site at Szczecin Castle, Poland (Hunter 1981, 145; Dekòwna 1974). Early 10th century deposits at Winchester Old Minster contained non-durable window glass (Biddle and Hunter 1990, 362). This tradition is known as *potash* or *forest* glass because the main source of alkali was plant or wood ash with a high potassium content (hence potash, K_2O). The most common source of ash was probably beechwood, as recommended by Theophilus (Dodwell 1961, 37, 39), but it is possible that bracken or even seaweed might have been used at various times (cf. the suggestion by Cramp 1970, 335).

Potash reduced the melting point of the silica to a temperature easily obtainable in a medieval furnace. It is doubtful whether the medieval glass makers intentionally added lime, as it may have already been present in the batch constituents (cf. Turner 1956). A more detailed consideration of the chemical composition of potash glass is given below (pp.531–4). Potash glass is particularly susceptible to corrosion in damp environments, resulting in a wide range of appearances from opacity to opalescence (see Cox et al. 1979; Gillies and Cox 1988a, 1988b). These processes and conditions are also described below (pp.512–15, 534–5).

Coloured glass was obtained by the addition of metal oxides to the *melt* or molten glass mixture. This coloured glass was known as *pot-metal*. In medieval window glass the addition of ferrous oxides produced blue and ferric oxides produced amber or yellow. The addition of copper, dependent on a number of contingent factors, could produce blue, green or red. Similarly, cobalt could produce blue, but under certain conditions, green (Newton and Davison 1989, 7). The contingencies included the presence of manganese and other oxides in the melt, impurities and trace elements in the batch constituents, the temperature at which the glass was melted, and whether a reducing or oxidising atmosphere was present in the kiln (ibid.). A more thorough discussion of colouring factors in the Fishergate glass, in the context of other glass of York provenance, and based on analyses, can be found below (pp.415–19, 534–5, 538, Table 8).

Neither the available technology nor the essentially fragmented and individual nature of the craft organisation in the medieval period allowed any standardisation of processes and as a consequence colour, depth and tone of glass could vary not just between production sites, but from batch to batch. It is also clear that the length of time the glass was exposed to the heat contributed to variability in colour. Theophilus, in fact, describes how three different colours can be achieved from the same basic melt, depending on how long the glass is maintained in the kiln (Dodwell 1961, 42).

Most post-Roman window glass, until the late 17th century, was mouth-blown (for later technologies of flat glass production see Burgoyne and Scoble 1989). Of the two manufacturing processes known to have been used to make window glass, Theophilus describes only one: the *cylinder* or *muff* method (Dodwell 1961, 40–1; Harden 1961, 42; Newton and Davison 1989, 91–2). This process began with the collection of a blob or gather of molten glass on the end of a hollow blowing iron. The glass blower would inflate the gather and then manipulate it into a long cylindrical shape by swinging the glass suspended on the end of the iron. A process of alternate blowing and swinging would bring the cylinder to the desired size. The far end of the cylinder would be pierced and opened to match the diameter of the cylinder. Two edges would be pinched together to allow a *pontil* or iron rod to be attached with a small amount of glass. The blowing iron could then be knocked off from the other end of the cylinder, and this end opened out. The cylinder would then be placed in an annealing oven. When cold, it would be split longitudinally and replaced in an oven where the heat would allow it to open out on to a flat surface. The flattening process would be assisted by manipulation with smooth wood and tongs (Harden 1961, 42).

It is sometimes possible to identify cylinder blown glass by linear formations of air and gas bubbles, and by the elliptical or attenuated form of the *seeds* themselves. Other impurities in the melt would sometimes be drawn into striations by the cylinder process. The edges of the opened ends of the cylinder often developed a fire-rounded, thickened edge (what Harden calls a 'thumb' edge; Harden 1961, 43). Early cylinder blown glass had one matt side and one glossy surface, because it had been opened out on to a sanded or ash-covered table in the kiln. Later methods could produce a glossy surface on both sides. In the 14th century an improved technique of cylinder production was developed, probably in Bohemia, but imported to Lorraine, consequently giving the name *Lorraine* glass (Newton and Davison 1989, 92–3).

A glazier's workshop excavated by York Archaeological Trust on the site formerly known as City Garage, 9 Blake Street, off Stonegate, York (YAT 1975.6), produced over 300 thumb edge pieces from cylinder glass, a high proportion of the total glass fragments (O'Connor 1975, 13). Although it is unlikely that the glass was produced in the workshop, this find attests the use of cylinder glass in York in the 15th century.

The second method of flat glass manufacture was that known as *crown* or *spun* glass. In this the gather of molten glass was blown into a globular bulb, transferred to a pontil, manually opened out and flattened into a disc. The artisan then spun the disc, by means of the pontil to which it was attached, until by centrifugal force it attained the desired diameter (Harden 1961, 39). It is sometimes possible to identify crown glass by its varying thickness, tending towards its greatest thickness in the centre where the pontil rod was attached. If the edges of the circular table had been left untouched these would be thickened and fire-rounded (ibid., 40). As there was no necessity to open the disc against a flat surface, both surfaces of the crown disc could remain glossy. In the 17th century French scholars had thought that glass of this kind was invented in Normandy following the royal appointment of a manufacturing site in 1330 (Lafond 1969, 37). Consequently, it has been known as *Normandy* glass. The technique, however, must have been in use centuries before: the earliest examples known date to the 4th century, from Jerash and Samaria in Jordan

(Harden 1959; 1961). The date of its introduction to England is still uncertain, although Roman crown glass was discovered at Chichester (Charlesworth 1978; cf. Biddle and Hunter 1990, 350). The centre, or bull's eye, of a disc of crown glass was also found in the debris from the glazier's workshop at 9 Blake Street (O'Connor 1975, 14). It measured 155 × 105mm, with a thickness ranging from 8mm at the edge to 20mm at the central pontil mark (ibid.). The origins and supply of glass to the York glass-painters are discussed below (pp.352–3).

Apart from the pot-metal colouring of glass, mentioned above, two other techniques for colouring glass were known to medieval glaziers. Pot-metal red, or *ruby* glasses, were so intensely coloured that little light would be transmitted through them. In order to achieve a translucent colour, ruby glasses of the 12th to early 14th centuries were made with *multi-layered* red and white glass alternating in fine sheets (see pp.534–5; Newton and Davison 1990, 95; Spitzer-Aronson 1979).

The second technique was the application of a silver nitrate or silver sulphide to the exterior surface of a glass pane in order to produce a *yellow stain* when fired. Different depths of yellow could be achieved with varying amounts and applications of stain (Newton and Davison 1989, 99).

The construction of a window

The design for the window or panel would first be drawn to full-scale on a *cartoon* which would then be marked out on a board or table whitewashed with chalk and used as a template for construction. The only medieval tables to survive were found at Girona Cathedral, Catalonia, Spain, where the actual glass panel made from the table can be seen. The design for each independent shape of glass to be cut (known as the *cut-line*) was painted in a vegetable dye (Holden 1990, 9), although Theophilus suggests that lead or tin should be used (Dodwell 1961, 47). The glazier chose the piece or colour of glass required for each position and traced the shape through from the cut-line with a chalk solution (ibid., 48). The glass would be cut by drawing a hot iron across the surface and adding water or spittle to the crack (ibid., 48–9; Hawthorne and Smith 1963, 62–3). It would depend on the skill of the artisan how crude or controlled this cutting might be (cf. Biddle and Hunter 1990, 359, fragment 756; Kerr and Biddle 1990, 387, same fragment). To make a more precise shape the glazier might either cut the glass or groze it. *Grozing* was a method of paring the glass to an exact shape by small controllable bites (Dodwell 1961, 49). A sort of metal hook or grozing iron would be the tool used. A representation of medieval grozing irons can be seen in the arms of the Glass-Painters' Gild on the weather-vane of the prison in the 'St Peter in prison' scene of the Bowet window in the north aisle of York Minster choir (nX), c.1423, in the 'St John the Baptist in prison' panel in the Martyrdom window in the south aisle of the choir (sX), c.1420 (Knowles 1936, 241, fig.77, pl.XIV), and in St Helen's, Stonegate. (Where reference is made to glass in situ or comparative features of an extant window, the Corpus Vitrearum Medii Aevi numbering system has been used; see Newton 1979.)

The design of each piece of glass was painted on to the glass with natural hair brushes. The details, known as *trace lines*, would be traced through from the cartoon. For the *paint* itself Theophilus recommended copper calcined in an iron pan and ground green and Greek blue glass, bound together with wine or urine (Dodwell 1961, 49). Whilst most coloured glass was imported to York (see p.352), the paint was most probably made in the glazier's workshop. Records from Westminster Palace identify *geet* (black lead glass) and gum arabic for painting glass (Steane 1985, 254). Analyses have shown that there is often a large lead and iron oxide component to the paint (Graves 1995, 111). Varying sizes of natural hair brush would be used to make thick lines, area washes or fine detail. After painting, the pieces of glass would be returned to the kiln for firing until the glass and paint fused (Hunter 1981, 146).

Various techniques were developed for adding depth and modelling to glass painting, as well as some techniques for relieving the density of paint (see Marks 1993, 36). After the main outlines were drawn on the glass, dilute washes were used to give some measure of a three-dimensional effect. Washes can be seen on the 13th century head (*267*, Figs.183–4), emphasising the chin and shadow on the neck beneath, and also on the robed torso (*282*, Fig.189). Washes were often applied to the external surface of the glass, for example, to emphasise the folds of drapery (Fig.189, *286;* Fig.190, *293*). This technique was used from the 12th century (ibid.).

Two distinctive surface textures can be seen amongst the fragments of shading; in the first, linear strokes and smearing, for example on sf111, a yellow stained fragment; by contrast, from the 14th century and particularly in the 15th century, a *stipple* effect was produced by dabbing a soft brush over a wet wash, as found on sf9175 (amongst the miscellaneous painted fragments).

Highlights might be picked out by either a wash or a more solid band of paint with a stick, perhaps the end of a brush handle. This technique produced the effects seen in common edging patterns of the 14th century (Fig.195, p.407) and the diaphanous contemporary *rinceaux* used as background patterns (Fig.178, p.382). In the later 14th and 15th centuries, highlights might be scratched out from washes in a less geometric fashion in order to emphasise the three-dimensional effect desired in modelling human forms.

The cut and painted pieces of glass would be assembled on the board according to the detail of the original cartoon painted on the table. The H-sectioned lead *cames* (for discussion of production see pp.429–31) were bent to shape around the glass and cut to the required length. The pieces would be held in place with nails. Medieval representations of glaziers' nails show them to be broad- perhaps flat-headed (see the Gild of Glass-Painters' Arms in the Bowet window (nX), and in the Martyrdom window (sX) of York Minster referred to above, Knowles 1936, 241, fig.77, pl.XIV). Medieval glaziers' nails may have been excavated at the Augustinian hospital at Soutra, Lothian, possibly dating to the 14th century (A. Chisholm, pers. comm.). Nowadays farriers' nails are often used. The leaves of the lead came would be gently prized open to receive the glass, the glass tapped into place and the lead closed over it. Pieces of glass on either side would then be put in place. It can be inferred from Theophilus' instructions that the medieval practice was to start from the middle of a panel and work out, although nowadays glass artists start from a corner (Dodwell 1961).

The joints between the lead cames then had to be soldered, first on one side, then on the other, using a hot iron and tin rods for solder (ibid., 56–7). Although not prescribed by Theophilus, a kind of putty or cement would probably be used to seal the glass in the came, samples of which from York Minster have proved to be 'composed essentially of whiting (calcium carbonate)' (Gillies and Cox 1982, 182).

Four techniques of applying or inserting small pieces of pot-metal glass to a panel are detailed by Newton and Davison (1989, 96), of which three are known or thought to have been practised in York in the medieval period. The first was described by Theophilus and simply required a *jewel* of coloured glass to be attached to the glass beneath with a ring of the same paint used to draw details on the glass (Dodwell 1961; Hawthorne and Smith 1963). This would be fired to hold it in place. Examples of this technique are found in the St Cuthbert window (sVII, c.1445), York Minster, and St Michael's parish church, Spurriergate (sII).

The second technique, *annealing*, used a green or white glass as a solder between the coloured glass and the base glass, again fixed with firing (Newton and Davison 1989, 98). O'Connor and Haselock (1977, 377) suggest that there are examples of this type of jewel in York Minster. The third method was to lead the coloured glass into a drilled hole in the base glass. This was by far the most skilled method of introducing another colour, and, correspondingly, the most expensive method, but did not appear in England until the early 15th century (Marks 1993, 38–9). The fourth method was to incorporate the small piece of coloured glass into the overall design of the leadwork in the normal way, and an example can be found in window nXV of the North Transept, York Minster (Newton and Davison 1990).

The completed panels would then be placed in the stonework of the window embrasure. Sometimes the glaziers painted or scratched marks on the completed panels in order to help them place the panels in the correct location. Marks (1993, 36–7) compares this to other medieval craft practices. It may be that the symbols picked out from the paint washes of *375* and *376* (Fig.202, p.414) performed this function. The form of window jambs and mullions will often inform us of glazing techniques. In the 12th and early 13th centuries glazed panels were often set into wooden frames, which were lodged in a broad rebate of stonework. The lancets of the Five Sisters window (nXVI) of the North Transept, York Minster, have been treated in this way (Gibson 1979, 9). Generally, from the 13th century, the stonework of the jambs and mullions had V-shaped grooves or small, flat-bottomed rebates. Reyntiens (1977, 109) found the latter to be most common in the 15th and 16th centuries, but there would obviously be a degree of variability in local masonry practices (Fig.139, pp.276–9, *AY* 11/2).

The panels would be supported by iron bars, usually square-sectioned or flat, and sunk into the stonework. Horizontal bars are known as *saddle-bars*. Depending on the design of the window, it may have been more appropriate to bend the saddle-bars to follow the shapes of the panels. The collective term for the ironwork bracing a window is *ferramenta*. Rarely has any trace of ferramenta been excavated from Dissolution debris on monastic sites; the problem may, in some cases, be one of recognition if corrosion has fragmented the iron. The glass panels were attached to the bars with lead *ties* (Brown and O'Connor 1991; see also below p.429). Several of these strips would be soldered on to the lead of the panels in a horizontal line, or following the curve of the ironwork. The ties would then be twisted together around the iron bars. The panels might be finally pointed into place with a mortar or putty mix.

Glass-painting in York

York has a large amount of surviving documentation to illustrate the organisation of glazing and glass-painting in the city in the late medieval period (Knowles 1936; Swanson 1989, 92–5). Few glazing contracts survive in Britain, and ideas about the practices and movement of workshops are most often built on study and comparison of the painting styles of extant glass (but see Marks 1993, 40–51 and *passim,* on the organisation of the craft).

An extensive quantity of painted glass survives in York from the Minster and the parish churches (see RCHMY **2**, **4**, **5**; and a growing quantity of literature, e.g. Browne 1847, 1859; Winston 1848; Harrison 1922, 1927; Knowles 1936, 1956; Milner-White 1952, 1959; Gee 1969; French 1971, 1975; Gibson 1972; O'Connor and Haselock 1977; Routh 1986; French and O'Connor 1987). Some idea of lost images can be gained from antiquarian sources (e.g. Torre 1690–1; Gent 1730; Drake 1736; Allen 1828; Browne 1859; Davidson and O'Connor 1978). Documents, in particular wills, exist from the 1320s, but are more prolific from the 1390s onwards (Swanson 1983, 2). In addition, the building accounts or fabric rolls of York Minster exist for 1360 onwards.

The first major glazing period at St Andrew's Gilbertine Priory in York was in the first half of the 13th century, but no names of glass-painters in York have been found for any date in the 13th century (Marks 1991, 277; Swanson 1983, 39). The first named York glazier is recorded in 1313 as Walter le Verrour, and the number of named glaziers working in York and/or admitted to the freedom of the City of York rises sharply in the course of the 14th century, with numbers in the low twenties during most of the 15th century (Swanson 1983, 39–41; Knowles 1936, 11–12). In the first 30 years of the 16th century glaziers were being recruited at the 'rate . . . of five per decade' (Palliser 1979, 172). The Reformation affected this group of craftsmen badly and the craft can only have survived through taking commissions for domestic glazing (ibid.; Swanson 1983, 24).

The glaziers and glass-painters lived in the area around Stonegate, and the lower part of the street around St Helen's parish church. This was the church associated with the

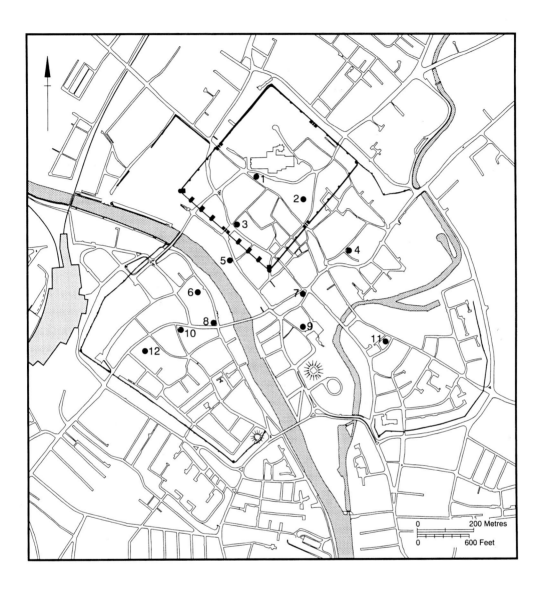

Fig. 164   *Map of York showing location of parish churches mentioned in the text*

1   *St Michael-le-Belfrey, High Petergate*
2   *Holy Trinity, Goodramgate*
3   *St Helen, Stonegate*
4   *St Saviour, St Saviourgate*
5   *St Martin-le-Grand, Coney Street*
6   *All Saints, North Street*

7   *All Saints, Pavement*
8   *St John, Ousebridge*
9   *St Mary, Castlegate*
10   *St Martin-cum-Gregory*
11   *St Denys, Walmgate*
12   *Holy Trinity, Micklegate*

Gild of Glaziers, and a number were buried here (Harrison 1927, 67–8; see the plaque erected by Knowles in 1922). The York glaziers had their own craft guild, whereas in other cities, apart from London, the glass-painters shared a gild with other crafts (Marks 1991, 277). The arms of the York gild remain in the east window of the north aisle of St Helen's church. Glass debris excavated at Blake Street, just off Stonegate, bears physical witness to the documented association between this quarter and the glaziers. The debris consisted of raw materials, a substantial quantity of fire-rounded edges suggesting the glazing equivalent of offcuts, with few painted pieces and no lead. This combination of charac-teristics suggests that the material was dumped from a workshop in the immediate vicinity (O'Connor 1975, 17).

The archaeological evidence from the Fishergate Gilbertine priory shows that there was a second major glazing programme in the first half of the 14th century, probably in the 1320s and 1330s. The surviving designs include architectural details from canopies, merlons from castellated structures, details of human figures, and patterns from the backgrounds of such scenes which show an awareness of the designs being produced in the Minster nave aisles and culminating in the work of the west window in 1338–9. A Chapter Act book for 1314–39 referred to contracts for the west wall windows, and, although all the originals have been lost, summaries of the contents of these documents were made by the Minster historian James Torre in about 1690 (French and O'Connor 1987, 4). The glazier for the west window was named as Robert, and Knowles identified him as Robert Ketelbarn (Knowles 1936, 31; French and O'Connor 1987, 4). Ketelbarn, a freeman of the city in 1324, was responsible for glazing projects in York and a number of sites in the surrounding district in the 1320s and 1330s (French 1975, 82–3). A contract also existed for the two smaller windows which flank the west window in the Minster nave aisles, and it named the glazier as Thomas de Bouesdun (French and O'Connor 1987, 4).

As has been said, 'any survey of stylistic developments in York during the second quarter of the 14th century is bound to be somewhat speculative' (French and O'Connor 1987, 18). The work of the Master Robert/Thomas workshop which has been identified in the Minster has been distinguished, however, from the work of another contemporary work-shop which was responsible for the glazing of All Saints' church, North Street, York. At the time of the major rebuilding and reglazing of the Fishergate Gilbertine Priory, there were at least two influential workshops practising in York and the north of England, as far as Cartmel in Cumbria, Morpeth in Northumberland, and Beverley in the East Riding of Yorkshire (French and O'Connor 1987, 18–23). These two groups shared much in the way of technique, style, ornamental repertoire and iconography. The extent of the work of these groups, or of the influence they had on other craftsmen, has not been explored fully to date. These groups, in turn, were part of a wider milieu of glass-painting with shared traits of ornament, style and composition. Other centres of glass-painting in this tradition were found across the country, from the West Country (based in Bristol, Gloucester, Tewkesbury and Wells) to East Anglia, where the main example was that of the Lady Chapel of Ely Cathedral (French and O'Connor 1987, 22, n.42–3). Comparisons have also been drawn between the glazing styles of York and Normandy in the 1320s and 1330s.

Within ten to fifteen years of the west wall glass of York Minster being contracted glass-painters and glaziers were being summonsed to work on the windows of St Stephen's Chapel, Westminster. This was a major royal work which spanned the middle to late years of the 14th century. The glass was recorded in the early 1800s, and, according to French and O'Connor:

> . . . *they show pieces of figures, backgrounds, canopies and borders which are close to York work in style, design, colour and technique. To find the 'court style' of Edward III anticipated at York is not so surprising given the wealth and status of the donor [Archbishop Melton], and the fact that Master Robert had almost certainly worked on a number of royal glazing schemes in the York area* (1987, 22 n.44 and 45).

The presence of Parliament in York on several occasions in the 1320s and 1330s would have brought many court figures into contact with the work then being carried out in the Minster and in surrounding churches. The major court figures and their retinues were billeted in the precincts of the numerous religious houses in York, as well as the castle. Because of the destruction of the Dissolution, 200 years later, the glazing schemes of most of these houses in the first half of the 14th century remain lacunae in our knowledge, although they may have been influential. The evidence is limited to excavated fragments of broken glass (collections, for example, in the Yorkshire Museum; see also D. O'Connor in *AY* 10/5 forthcoming for glazing from the College of Vicars Choral at Bedern). This is the context in which the glazing of the small, relatively poor, suburban religious house at Fishergate should be considered.

A master glazier would run his own workshop, but the size of his staff depended upon his reputation and how successful he was in securing patronage and contracts. Swanson details the personnel in a mid 15th century workshop, that of John Chambre junior, who was admitted to the freedom of the city in 1415. The workshop consisted of Chambre's son, who became free by patrimony as a glazier in 1449, William Inglish, Robert Hudson, Thomas Coverham and John Witton (Swanson 1983, 23; YML, D/C Wills 1 fo.266, 1450). The most interesting and characteristic aspect of this group is the way in which many were either born of glass-painting families, carried on as glaziers themselves, or married into glaziers' families. William Inglish became a famous glazier in York, and his own son followed him in the craft. Coverham's father had been a glazier before him. Both Coverhams and Hudson worked for the Minster (Swanson 1983, 23; YML, E3.9 m.1, 1420; E3.25 m.2, 1471). Chambre's sister married into the Petty family of glaziers. Swanson suggests that it was connections such as these that facilitated the sharing and dissemination of stylistic traits and techniques from workshop to workshop (Swanson 1983, 23).

The design of a window or set of windows would be arrived at from discussion between the master glass-painter and the patron. We know from observation of a series of figure panels, for example, that particular cartoons would be re-used, reversed or slightly altered to provide several images, e.g. the figures of bishops and archbishops in the nave west window of York Minster, of 1338/9 (French and O'Connor 1987, 5); two depictions of the Holy Trinity of c.1470 appear in St Martin-le-Grand, Coney Street (sIV), York, and Holy Trinity, Goodramgate (I), York (Marks 1993, 35, fig.26). It is probable that master glaziers would price their work according to the different scenes required, whether old cartoons could be re-used or entirely fresh scenes had to be devised. Figures of the regular run of saints in stock sizes, painted from old cartoons when trade was slack, could be bought at a cheap rate in York (Knowles 1936, 47). Costs for glass at the time of the initial glazing of St Andrew's Priory in the early 13th century cannot be arrived at exactly. Salzman calculated costs of new work in plain glass to the Dean and Chapter of Chichester in 1240 as slightly under 3d per square foot for a contracted glazier and 4d for irregular staff. This, he concluded, worked out as 1½d for the glass, and 2½d for the labour (Salzman 1967, 175). In 1286, the glazing of a chapel in the Tower of London worked out at 8d per square foot for coloured glass and still 4d for white glass (ibid., 175–6). Whilst the cost of coloured glass varied between 6d and 10d per square foot including labour, the cost of white glass seems to have stayed remarkably consistent in the south of England between the 1240s and 1280s. One of the factors which would affect the price of glass would be transportation, as will be discussed below. Perhaps a better idea of approximate costs for the second major period of glazing at St Andrew's Priory, York, can be gained by looking at contemporary costs to patrons in York itself in the first half of the 14th century. The Exchequer Accounts for 1327 contain an entry for glazing work carried out for the Archbishop's Palace in York. Twenty-three feet of white (or uncoloured) glass were 'worked up' (presumably painted and assembled) and bought from Robert the glazier at 5d a foot, making 9s 7d (Salzman 1928, 119). Thirty-seven feet of coloured glass, similarly 'worked up', cost 30s 10d, at 10d a foot. The costs of glass for the Minster west window in 1338/9 are recorded as 6d per foot for white glass and 12d per foot for the coloured glass (French and O'Connor 1987, 4).

Probably the primary reason why coloured glass was more expensive was that most of it, if not all, was imported from the Continent. Indeed, survey of the Minster Fabric Rolls and wills made by York glaziers indicates that most of the white glass used in York was of English origin (*vitri Anglicani*) (O'Connor 1975, 14). The importation of glass was made possible through contacts between the merchants and shippers of York and both Germany and Flanders. The Hanse trading confederation had depots at both York and Hull, whilst the York Merchant Adventurers were present in Germany, Cologne and Danzig (Knowles 1936, 9). Three types of glass, known according to their origins as 'Renysshe', 'Hessian' ('Hass' glass) and 'Burgundy' (*vitri Borgandie*), were bought by York glass-painters from Germans (known as 'Dutchmen') (ibid.; O'Connor 1975, 14; Raine 1858, *passim*) in transactions recorded in the customs particulars at Hull (Swanson 1983, 36, n.111). Glass was also bought from Normandy (Knowles 1936; O'Connor 1975, 14). Prices varied with time and the vicissitudes of political and trading relations with these areas. On the whole, imported coloured glass was about twice the price of white glass because the white glass could be blown in England. White glass was manufactured in England, particularly around the area of Chiddingfold on the Surrey-Sussex border, from at least the first half of the 14th century, if not before. A furnace at Blunden's Wood, Hambledon, Surrey, has been dated by pottery and archaeomagnetic dating to the second quarter of the 14th century, about 1330, and has produced pale green crown window glass as well as vessel glass (Wood 1965; Kenyon 1967, 68; Charleston 1991, 248). The composition of the glass was potash, consistent with local sand and wood ash (Wood 1965). Large quantities of white glass were supplied for the building of St Stephen's Chapel, Westminster, by John Allemayne of Chiddingfold in 1351 and by glassmakers in Shropshire and Staffordshire in 1349 (Kenyon 1967, 27–9; Marks 1991, 263). In 1418 the Dean and Chapter of York Minster bought over 72lb of glass from John Glasman of Rugeley in Staffordshire (Salzman 1967, 183, citing York Fabric Rolls; Knowles 1936, 199–200, gives the date as 1417). The only furnaces known so far in North Yorkshire are those excavated at Hutton and Rosedale; they are of different design to the medieval furnaces and date to the immediate post-medieval period, 1580–1600 (Crossley and Aberg 1972).

The medieval glaziers of York were amongst the most prosperous of the building craftsmen in the city in the 15th to early 16th centuries, second only to the masons, a conclusion supported by the proportion who made wills, entered the freedom and even took civic office (Swanson 1983, 23, 28; Palliser 1979, 172). Almost all those listed in Chambre's workshop (see p.351) were admitted to the freedom of the city at some time, as indeed were most of the glaziers working in York. This does not, however, seem to have been a requirement of those who worked solely in the Minster's workshop (Swanson 1983, 23). Individuals could be brought in for specific contracts or commissions at the Minster. John Thornton, a man with a well-established reputation and workshops in Coventry, was contracted to make the Great East Window in 1405, but waited five years before taking out the freedom (ibid.). The evidence for contract work in York has been cited, and was possibly 'more readily available to the glass-painters than it was to other craftsmen' (Swanson 1983, 24). There is little indication of how work for the parish churches or other religious houses was commissioned; Marks supposes that it was mostly carried out by contract (Marks 1993, 94). Swanson concluded, however, that a great deal of work for the religious institutions in the city, and possibly the suburbs such as St Andrew's, may have been paid on the basis of a daily wage (Swanson 1983, 24). It is probable that small-scale glazing was carried out in the (sub)urban priories and friaries in accordance with secular bequests, and repairs might have been paid for by individual donors.

The Gilbertine Priory of St Andrew, Fishergate

Historical evidence for the Gilbertine priory

By J.E. Burton

The foundation of the Gilbertine priory

The priory of St Andrew, Fishergate, was one of a group of four religious houses in the diocese of York belonging to the Gilbertine Order, which was established in the mid 12th century by St Gilbert of Sempringham to provide for women who wished to enter the religious life. The Order enjoyed considerable popularity in Gilbert's lifetime, particularly in the eastern counties of England (see Fig.228, p.485). Gilbertine houses were of two types: houses for both nuns and canons (which also included provision for lay brothers and sisters), and houses for canons only. The two major priories in Yorkshire, the 'double' house of Watton and its sister priory, Malton, established for canons only, were founded by Eustace FitzJohn in the middle years of the 12th century. The smaller houses of Ellerton and St Andrew, Fishergate, date from some 50 years later; like all but one of the Gilbertine priories founded in the late 12th century, they were for canons only (Foreville and Keir 1987, xxxvi–xxxix). In the 13th century an attempt was made to settle the Gilbertines in Scotland. Before 1228 canons from Sixhills occupied a site at Dalmilling (Ayrshire), granted by Walter FitzAlan, but by 1238 it had been transferred to the Cluniacs of Paisley (Cowan and Easson 1976, 105–6; Foreville and Keir 1987, xxxviii–xxxix).

The founder of St Andrew's, Fishergate, was Hugh Murdac, prebendary of Driffield, rector of Bamburgh, king's justice and, between 1201 and 1204, disputed archdeacon of Cleveland (*YMF* 2, 20–1; Clay 1944–7, 429). Hugh evidently intended his new priory to accommodate twelve canons: his foundation charter explicitly granted the church of St Andrew's to 'God and twelve canons of the order of Sempringham' (Dugdale 1846, **6**, 962). The size of the priory was thus in line with the establishment of a house of the Cistercian Order, whose constitution laid down that each new colony should comprise twelve monks (the number of the apostles) and an abbot. The statutes of the Gilbertine Order, however, which in their surviving form date from the early 13th century, tied the numbers in a priory to its resources, with a minimum of seven canons in a double house. It was envisaged that in normal circumstances the number of men would not exceed 30 (ibid., xlii). In fact, by 1200 several Gilbertine priories, notably Sempringham, Haverholme and Watton, surpassed this number (Foreville and Keir 1987, xxxii–xxxiii). St Andrew's Priory, therefore, with an initial complement of twelve canons, would have been one of the smaller Gilbertine houses. As with all religious houses, the York Gilbertine community contracted in the later medieval period.

The date of foundation lies between February 1195, when Simon de Apulia who witnessed the foundation charter was received as dean of York, and 1202, when an agreement was reached between the priory and the dean and chapter of York Minster (*YMF* **1**, 1; Dugdale 1846, **6**, 962).

The priory church and buildings

The priory occupied a site of 5½ acres between the River Foss and Fishergate (*VCHY*, 360). The OS map of 1852 shows the precinct plan which it calls Stone Wall Close (ibid.), the name given to the site by Drake (1736, 249). The southern boundary of the site was Blue Bridge Lane and the northern boundary the glassworks which still occupied the site in 1944 (Knight 1944, 172). The same map also shows a spring well (covered) within the site, and remains of the priory walls surviving to the north, on the southern edge of the glassworks, and at the south of the site in Blue Bridge Lane. The southern boundary wall was still visible in 1995 (*VCHY*, 360).

There is little written evidence for the priory church and buildings. In general, medieval wills can be a valuable source for references to the fabric of a religious house, and to its internal furnishings and altars. However, the evidence for St Andrew's is disappointingly meagre, as the priory did not figure prominently among the testamentary dispositions of the people of York. No wills have been located which leave bequests for the fabric of the church, and only one testator has been identified who indicated a desire to be buried at the priory. This was Marion Redmane, whose will of 1428 left one mark to the priory for her burial, and appointed the sub-prior, Robert Canon, as her executor (BI Prob. Reg. **2**, fo 534v; I am grateful to Dr P.J.P. Goldberg for this reference).

Some building and restoration of houses in the immediate vicinity of the priory evidently took place in the 1330s, financed by the gifts of Henry Burghersh, bishop of Lincoln, who announced his intention of repairing more buildings as well as the priory cloister (PRO C66/185, m.19–20; *Cal. Pat. 1334–8*, 102–3; see p.365). The fullest description of the priory buildings, however, comes from the Dissolution accounts of William Blitheman, one of the official receivers who took the surrender of the priory in 1538. Blitheman noted that the vestments in the vestry, which were sold to Richard Goldthorpe, were worth 34s 4d, and that the ornaments in the church, all of which (except for one clock reserved for the king) were also sold to Goldthorpe, were worth 29s. The sale of utensils from the kitchen and brewhouse brought 33s 4d and 16s 8d respectively, while eight bushels of corn in the granary were valued at 8s. Blitheman found vessels in the 'law [lower] buttry' and in the kiln house (*domus ustrina*), furnishings in the prior's dining chamber and stores in the 'upper buttery'. There was a mattress in the inner chamber, furniture in the guest chamber, and an old mattress in the 'law [lower] parlour', which was sold to the late prior's butler for 8d. Three fothers of lead from that part of the roof over the 'ielez' were reserved for the king. Where this lead came from and how much it represented is difficult to estimate. A fother is defined as a cartload of lead, or an unspecified measure which could vary a great deal. The 'ielez' could have been the enclosed walkway around the cloister, since the church itself had no aisles. Three bells in the bell tower, as well as 32oz of jewels and a chalice, were reserved for the king (PRO SC6/Henry VIII 7452; Clay 1912, 177–8).

Like most of the Gilbertine houses established after the death of the Order's founder in 1189, St Andrew's was never a wealthy house. The *Taxatio Ecclesiastica* of 1291 indicates that it was valued at £59 (*Taxatio*, 305, 325). When Bishop Henry Burghersh of Lincoln made grants towards the repair of the priory buildings in 1335 he did so because the priory was impoverished at that time: *prioratus, qui deprimatur multipliciter his diebus* ('the priory, which these days is burdened in many ways'). In 1360 the king granted protection for one year for the prior and canons of St Andrew's, which was then in considerable distress because of the withdrawal of rents and services by its tenants (*Cal. Pat. 1358–61*, 471–2). In 1463, 1464, 1468, 1487, 1489 and 1496 St Andrew's was excepted from the payment of the tenth on account of its 'notorious poverty' or 'impoverishment' (*Cal. Fine 1461–71*, 120, 136, 227; *Cal. Fine 1485–1509*, 75, 111, 178, 238). In 1504/5, the canons once again referred to their great poverty.

The Dissolution

St Andrew's is one of a number of religious houses whose assessment is missing from the *Valor Ecclesiasticus* of 1535. However, from other sources it is evident that the value of the priory was £59 5s 11d, £43 6s 8d clear (BL Cotton MS Cleopatra Eiv, fos 357v–8). It was thus far outstripped by the larger Yorkshire Gilbertine houses of Watton and Malton, valued at £240 17s 6d and £170 respectively, and even by the least wealthy of the Yorkshire Augustinian houses, Warter Priory (£143 7s 8d). In terms of its value, St Andrew's ranks with the middle range of Yorkshire nunneries, houses such as Marrick (£64 18s 9d), Sinningthwaite (£62 6s) and Nunkeeling (£50 17s 2d) (Burton 1979, 45). St Andrew's thus fell below the critical value of £200 per annum needed to avoid closure, and the priory was threatened with suppression in 1536 as a 'lesser monastery'. It survived, however, following the appeal made to the king by Robert Holgate, master of the Order of Sempringham, on behalf of all the Gilbertine houses, and Leland, in his itinerary of York, probably in 1536, remarked on St Andrew's 'a house of chanons Gilbertines by Owse without Fisschargate' (Toulmin Smith 1907, 55–6). The reprieve was short-lived and St Andrew's was surrendered to the king's commissioners in November 1538 by the prior, John Lepington, and three canons (*Eighth Report*, app.II, 51). The following month Sir George Lawson and others notified the king that they had taken the surrenders of a number of houses including St Andrew's (PRO SP5/3, fos 92–4; BL Cotton MS Cleopatra Eiv, fo 242; *L and P Henry VIII* 13, 387, 454; Clay 1912, 66). In 1539 the prior was awarded a pension of £10 and the three canons, William Bysset, Leonard Sharpe and John Hodgeson, £4 each (*L and P Henry VIII* 14, 67, 601; in BL Cotton MS Cleopatra Eiv, fo 242, the pension for the prior was given as £8, but the figure was later altered). Palliser (1971, 13) suggests that one of the canons may have become the incumbent of one of the Bishophill parishes and another the incumbent of Ellerton. Cross and Vickers have identified John Hodgeson as vicar of St Mary Bishophill Junior and Leonard Sharpe as vicar of Ellerton (Cross and Vickers 1995, 410).

For the full discussion of the documentation relating to the history of the priory itself, its estates and economy, see pp.49–65, *AY* 11/2.

The site at 46–54 Fishergate

By R.L. Kemp

The site lay directly east of the confluence of the Rivers Ouse and Foss, south of the Walmgate section of the medieval defences, and to the west of the main road linking the city to the village of Fulford and the south (SE60655115; Fig.165). It was on relatively high ground (c.10·7m OD) and shows no signs of ever having been flooded. The site occupied the point where the east-west morainic ridge across the Vale of York meets the River Ouse, and forms a natural crossing point. The moraine served as an important, well-defined prehistoric route linking East Yorkshire and the Wolds with the west. The crossing point was probably moved north from the rivers' confluence by the Romans to serve the legionary fortress, located for tactical reasons in the acute angle between the rivers (RCHMY 3, xxxvii–xxxviii).

Numerous commentators on York from the 17th century onwards have regarded Fishergate as the site of St Andrew's church and priory (e.g. Drake 1736, facing p.244). On the first edition of the Ordnance Survey map of York, published in 1852, the site was called 'Stone Wall Close' which contained the 'Site of St Andrew's Church, and of the Priory of St Andrew (Gilbertine Canons), founded 1202'. Also marked to the north and south of Stone Wall Close were 'Remains of Priory Wall'. Parts of this southern wall are still visible today in a rebuilt form. The 1931 edition of the Ordnance Survey map indicates 'Stone coffins found AD 1928' near Fishergate itself. Professor David Palliser has argued convincingly that the eastern limit of St Andrew's precinct corresponded with the medieval line of Fishergate (now called Fawcett Street) that ran up to Fishergate Bar. Speed's map of 1610 corroborates this; modern Fishergate first appears on James Archer's map of 1682.

From the early 18th century the site was occupied by a glassworks, and it was the closure of the 2ha Redfearn National Glass Co. Ltd factory at 46–54 Fishergate in 1984 that prompted the archaeological investigation.

The excavation

Archaeological work was begun after the factory site became vacant in early 1985, and in advance of redevelopment for housing and a hotel which began in 1986. Work was directed throughout for York Archaeological Trust by R.L. Kemp. The decision to undertake a programme of investigation was based on an expectation that the site would reveal a medieval priory and, possibly, earlier deposits of the Anglian period.

On the basis of analysis of the results from trial excavations it became clear that a wide strip on the western part of the site, parallel to the River Foss, and most of the northern part of the site had been destroyed by modern factory buildings (c.55% of the available site). However, the work also revealed that in the south-eastern quarter deposits had survived beneath late Victorian factory structures built on shallow foundations c.0·5m deep at maximum. In this undisturbed area highly complex floor deposits were revealed with

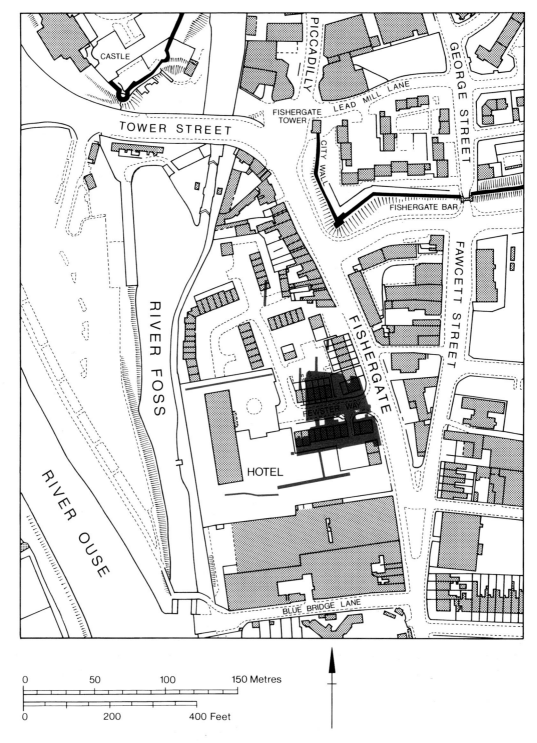

Fig. 165   Plan showing position of excavations (in red) at 46–54 Fishergate. (Reproduced from the Ordnance Survey map with the permission of Her Majesty's Stationery Office, © Crown Copyright. MC 10001225). Scale 1:2500

extensive associated deposits of medieval window glass, some inhumations and a number of masonry walls and robber trenches taken to represent the main priory buildings. These deposits were remarkably well preserved, and were protected by between 0·05m and 0·5m of later rubble or soil; only occasionally had modern services disturbed the medieval levels. The outline plan of the priory was clear.

In areas outside the priory (particularly to the south) a deep layer of medieval agricultural soil was encountered and removed down to natural. Pits and structural traces were found, dated by pottery and other artefacts to the Anglian period (c.700–860). These features had been slightly truncated by later medieval activity.

An area of c.2,500m^2, corresponding to the main priory buildings, was chosen for total excavation. The foundations and graves of the priory, while disturbing some of the Anglian deposits below, had at least protected these earlier levels from truncation by medieval agricultural activities. Owing to time restrictions, the medieval deposits were afforded a lesser level of data recovery than those of Anglian date. Regrettably, there was no opportunity to examine the post-medieval deposits and deposits associated with the early phases of the glass factory, which were cleared by machine to within 0·2m of the surviving walls and floors of the priory. Furthermore, during the excavation of the priory the complex floor deposits encountered during the trial excavations were removed rapidly in groups down to major floor surfaces. A less comprehensive programme of sieving was also adopted for medieval deposits.

The unthreatened southern area was left for posterity and now lies beneath the modern hotel car park. Trial trenches showed that this area contains further (truncated) settlement traces of the Anglian period, and the outer court and the southern fringes of the cemetery of the monastic complex. Parts of the narrow strip under the south pavement of Fewster Way also remain unexcavated (see Fig.165), and contain small areas of the chapter house and south cloister alley of the priory. Approximately 0·25ha (c.11%) of the total monastic precinct was excavated, which represents 50% of the threatened, available and surviving deposits.

The stratigraphic data were ordered into 'periods' and 'phases'. Periods are chronological units covering the entire site. They are divided into sub-periods (e.g. 6a, 6b), representing identifiable stages of development within each major division. Phases are smaller divisions, usually reflecting a chronological progression, and are numbered sequentially within each area of the site. Each phase may be defined as a collective unit of closely related activities taking place within a specific area or room. A list of phases containing window glass appears on pp.559–60, and a full list of phases can be found on pp.329–32, *AY* 11/2. Details of each phase and period are contained in the Level III archive report, available for consultation at York Archaeological Trust.

The excavation accounts for the few Roman deposits encountered will be published in *AY* 6, 8th/9th century (Anglian period) deposits are published in *AY* 7/1, and those of the medieval period and the architectural fragments from all periods are published in *AY* 11/2.

Table 5 Summary of archaeological development at 46–54 Fishergate

Period	Description	Characteristics
1	Natural subsoil	Till and fluvio-glacial sands, and clays with gravel
2 1st–4th century	Roman agricultural activity	Plough scores, minor ditches, mixed natural deposit containing abraded Roman pottery
3a Late 7th/early 8th–early 9th century	Part of Anglian trading settlement	Properties delineated by ditches and lines of pits and containing structures, pit groups, ?middens
3b Later 8th or early 9th century	?Levelling of first settlement	Period 3a pits and structures covered by distinctive horizontal charcoal-laden deposit spread; site possibly re-organised
3c Within 1st half of 9th century	Re-occupation of settlement area	Major ditch and a few pit groups (no discernible structures)
3z Late 7th/early 8th–mid 9th century	Features not linked to 3a–c	Pits, ditches etc. (probably belongs to Period 3a)
4a late 10th/1st half of 11th century	New settlement established	Structure in south-eastern corner and pits/post-holes to south-west. Latest pottery in fills is Stamford ware
4b Mid 11th–?mid 12th century	Cemetery and church (south-west), new building (south-east)	Burials and possible timber church in south-west, replacement structure to south-east
4c ?Later 11th or 12th century	Church possibly rebuilt in stone (south-west)	Construction deposits over Period 4b burials
4d 12th century	Continued use of cemetery and settlement	Burials in cemetery area and pits and post-holes over structures in the south-east
4z 11th–12th century	Features not linked to 4a–d	Pits, burials etc.
5 1142/3–1195	St Andrew's in the possession of Newburgh Priory	Historical reference only. Period not distinguished archaeologically

Table 5 (*contd*)

Period	Description	Characteristics
6a 1195–late 13th century	Gilbertine priory in original form	New monastic complex built in stone. Burials
6b Late 13th–early 14th century	First modifications to priory	Minor adjustments within church and rebuilding of cloister alley. Road/yard south of nave. Burials
6c Early–mid 14th century	Substantial alterations to priory	Complete rebuilding of church and east range, substantial changes in north range. Burials
6d Late 14th–15th century	Further modifications to priory	New fittings in church, alterations in east and north ranges, buttresses in cloister alley
6e 15th/16th century	Continued use and modifications to site	Adjustments to north range. Well, cess pit etc. in southern part of site
6f 16th century	Final modifications in north range	Adjustments to partitions in north range
6z 13th–16th century	Features not linked to 6a–f	Pits, burials, agricultural/horticultural deposits, hearths etc. Ditches north of priory area
7a c.1538	Demolition of church, cloisters and east range	Robbed wall foundations, heavy layer of rubble, window glass, limekiln
7b c.1540	Demolition of north range	Partially robbed wall cores
7c 2nd half of 16th century	Secular occupation of west range	Pits containing much animal bone, artefacts and pottery cut through robbed walls of north range
8 c.17th–19th centuries	Orchards	Extensive layer of dark loam
9 c.1870–1900	Early glass factory	Brick foundations
10 c.1900–1984	Modern glass factory	Modern buildings, concrete floors, services, pipes etc.

The few post-medieval remains from the site were not worthy of full publication but the archive report is available for consultation at York Archaeological Trust. The pottery from all periods appears in *AY* 16/6. Anglian and other finds are published in *AY* 17/9, and the medieval finds appear in *AY* 17/12 and *AY* 17/15 in prep. The coins will appear in *AY* 18. The anthroplogy of the 402 excavated burials is published in *AY* 12/2. The animal bones appear in *AY* 15/4, while all other biological remains were scarce and are therefore reported in brief in the appropriate excavation account.

All finds and site records are deposited with the Yorkshire Museum, York, under the site and accession number 1985–6.9.

Period summaries

The full sequence of development on the site is summarised in Table 5. Period summaries relating to the life, dissolution, demolition and later use of the priory site is given below. Summaries of all periods (1–10) appear on pp.68–73, *AY* 11/2.

Periods 6 and 7 (1195 to later 16th century) (Figs.166–7)

Levels attributed to both Periods 3 and 4 were sealed beneath a single deposit of imported earth interpreted as the remains of a foundation platform for the new priory of St Andrew of the Order of St Gilbert of Sempringham, begun in 1195 and dedicated in 1202.

Although evidence for the priory buildings, in the form of foundations, window glass, floor tiles, wall plaster and architectural fragments, was well represented, little of the refuse of everyday life such as animal bones, organic debris, pottery and personal objects was found. Presumably such material had all been regularly disposed of, possibly into the adjacent rivers (see *AY* 15/4, *AY* 16/6, *AY* 17/12 and *AY* 17/15 in prep.).

The original structures (Period 6a) comprised a cruciform church to the south of the cloister, probably with a low central tower, north and south transepts with eastern chapels, a presbytery and an aisleless nave, a chapter house with possible western vestibule, an eastern dormitory with latrines to the north and a northern refectory. All were linked by a continuous alley around the cloister garth. A presumed western range had been destroyed by the modern factory. Architectural fragments and an extensive assemblage of window glass broadly confirmed the historical date of construction and both showed some Cistercian influence. There was evidence that both the church and chapter house were glazed from the outset.

The priory underwent certain modifications (Period 6b) including the rebuilding of the cloister arcade and minor works in the church, which can be tentatively dated by coins and pottery to the late 13th or early 14th century (*AY* 16/6; *AY* 18 in prep.).

In the 14th century there was an extensive programme of alterations in which the church, east range and chapter house were rebuilt, and the undercroft of the north range,

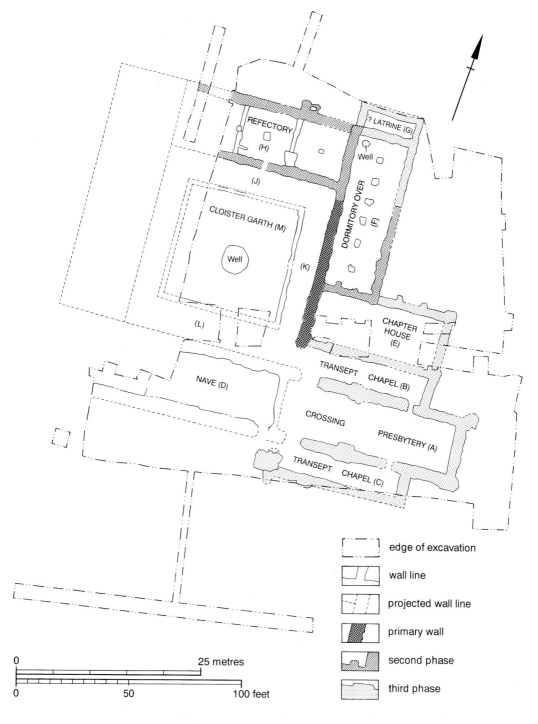

REFECTORY

(H)

? LATRINE (G)

Well

(J)

DORMITORY OVER

CLOISTER GARTH (M)

(F)

Well

(K)

(L)

CHAPTER
HOUSE
(E)

NAVE (D)

TRANSEPT CHAPEL (B)

CROSSING

PRESBYTERY (A)

TRANSEPT CHAPEL (C)

edge of excavation

wall line

projected wall line

primary wall

second phase

third phase

0   25 metres

0   50   100 feet

Fig. 166   *Order of construction of the original (Period 6a) priory and reconstructed plan of the west range at 46–54 Fishergate. (Room notation explained in AY 11/2.) Scale 1:500*

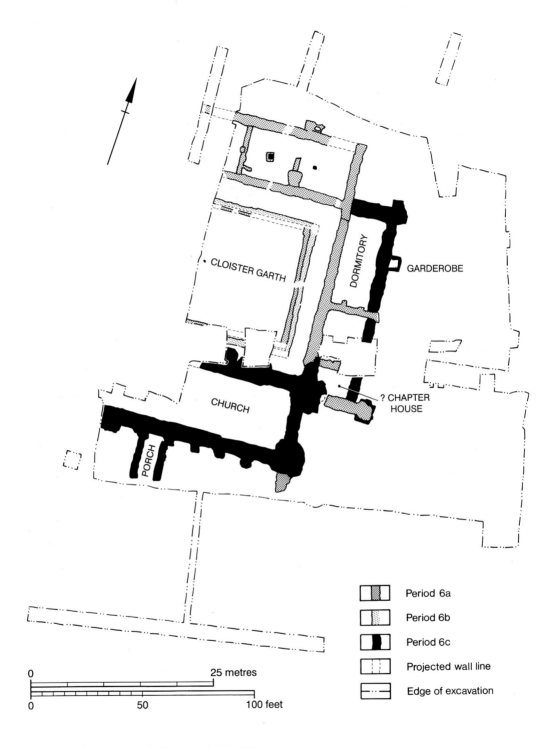

CLOISTER GARTH

DORMITORY

GARDEROBE

CHURCH

PORCH

? CHAPTER HOUSE

Period 6a

Period 6b

Period 6c

Projected wall line

Edge of excavation

0   25 metres

0   50   100 feet

Fig. 167   Plan of the priory in Period 6c. Scale 1:500

previously used for storage, was possibly converted for use as a ground-floor refectory or as domestic apartments (Period 6c) (Fig.167). An historical reference to the funding of certain building works at the priory in c.1335 by Henry Burghersh, bishop of Lincoln, may provide a context for these alterations. This rebuilding in the latest architectural style inevitably necessitated the re-fenestration of the church, and extensive reference is made to this episode in the main discussion.

The priory continued to be altered and adapted in minor ways (Periods 6d–f), until its dissolution in 1538 (Period 7a). The buildings were demolished and a limekiln was built in the cloister garth using elements of the cloister arcade. This heralded the wholesale robbing of the entire complex for building materials, including the customary interest in lead from both roofs and windows.

The windows of the priory had been stripped primarily for their lead came, and a considerable assemblage of glass fragments was excavated from a heap in the nave of the final phase of the church. It was the absence of came that suggested this was a lead-robber's working area, and that the glass represented waste following this process.

The northern range may have been used as stables and/or a store during early demolition operations until it was also demolished and robbed of all usable building materials (Period 7b). The final period of occupation is marked by rubbish pits, cut through the western end of the north range, which can be dated to the later 16th century; it is possible that the missing west range provided living quarters at this time (Period 7c).

Periods 8, 9, and 10 (c.17th–20th century)

The site was virtually abandoned and used as an orchard (Period 8) until it was partly occupied by an extension of the adjacent glass factory in the later 19th century (Period 9). By the 20th century the entire area of the site was under intensive industrial use (Period 10).

The Glass from St Andrew's Priory, York

Types of glass

Introduction

Nearly every excavation of a monastic site yields quantities of window glass, usually derived from Dissolution destruction debris, and this was the case at Fishergate (pp.436–41). Almost half the painted glass falls into the category of mid 13th century *grisaille*, the term applied to white glass painted with designs in monochrome (in this case red/brown paint). The word derives from the French verb *grisailler* — to paint grey, and refers to the overall impression of grey, interspersed with very little pot-metal colour, which a window of this type gives. Evidence of figures directly contemporary with this material is limited. There are, however, some figural details of the late 13th–early 14th century which were probably set on oak leaf grisaille. The second large group of glass has definite evidence of figures — human features and drapery — as well as the indirect evidence of architectural details from canopies, and decorated backgrounds (*diapers* and *rinceaux*), which accompany figural scenes in the first half of the 14th century. The last group consists of a limited number of fragments from decorated and yellow-stained quarries of the second half of the 14th century, and one or two fragments of costume detail which are probably 15th century. This evidence outlines the main glazing schemes at the priory which will be discussed in detail following this section (pp.445–64).

Grisaille

Two different date ranges of grisaille were found: 13th century (A) and late 13th/early 14th century (B) (see pp.541–2 for key to glass type codes). Within these two date ranges, four groups of grisaille motifs were identified. The forms and uses of grisaille are briefly described prior to the detailed discussion of the Fishergate material. The patterns employed on grisaille glass were often vegetal and floral motifs, and the glass was leaded into panels of interrelated geometric shapes, often lozenges, *vesicas* and circles.

From the late 12th century and during most of the 13th century grisaille glass painted with a trilobed motif, the trefoil, was widely used in England. The trefoil in glass may have been the equivalent of the sculptured stiff leaf in stone. As in architectural sculpture, stylised foliage began to be superseded by more naturalistic foliage forms in the third quarter of the 13th century (cf. the leaves in sculpture and glass in York Minster chapter house). Natural designs in grisaille glass were employed at least until the 1330s in the British Isles (Newton 1978, 129).

The first type of grisaille from St Andrew's featured the trefoil motif on a cross-hatched background. The second used a similar motif on a plain ground. The third used a repeated quatrefoil motif. The fourth type used oak leaf and acorn motifs. Within these types there

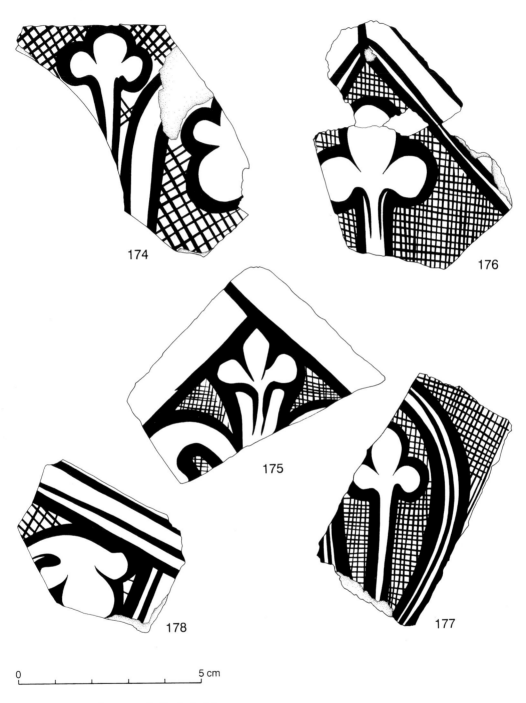

Fig.168   Thirteenth century grisaille. Scale 1:1

were variations in form. The discussion of each type ends by considering the quality of the glass and execution of the paintwork.

13th century grisaille: trefoil motifs on a cross-hatched ground
(Figs.168–72)

This was characterised by curling vegetal motifs with trefoil heads set on a ground of cross-hatching. There are two main diagnostic elements on a trefoil: the head, which is divided into three lobes by two pointed cusps, and the point where the head joins the stem where there are sometimes two pointed spurs. Several forms of trefoil could be distinguished and it is by no means certain that they all formed central panels; some of the designs could have been employed in borders. The first type had an upright central trefoil flanked by leaves curling outward to left and right (A1), such as on *174*, and probably sf424 and sf2082. A similar arrangement, but within *strapwork* and forming a *quarry*, was found on *175*. The motif parallels, almost exactly, that on some background quarries in West Horsley church, Surrey, on which a coloured roundel is set (J. Baker 1978, pl.20). The roundel itself has been dated to c.1210–25 (ibid., 6). Morgan considers this to be the earliest example in England of a coloured figure panel set in a grisaille system (Morgan 1983, 39, n.5). Two fragments from Rievaulx Abbey, North Yorkshire, also reflect this motif.

In concept, the design is close to the geometric grisaille at Lincoln Cathedral, described and illustrated in Morgan (ibid., 40, figs.C2 and 12). The Fishergate trefoils have short spurs where the stem joins the head which the Lincoln example does not. The Fishergate quarries are also defined by painted strapwork edges which do not occur on their closest parallel at Lincoln, but do appear on other Lincoln quarries contemporary with it, i.e. the first half of the 13th century (ibid.). Excavated quarries from Bayham Abbey, a Premonstratensian site in Kent, were very similar to this but Kerr has dated them to the second half of the 13th century (Kerr 1983, 61, 63, fig.17.41). Morgan considers the latticed geometrical grisailles to be a characteristically English phenomenon in the 13th century, only appearing in France in the following century, when in both countries they formed ornamental backgrounds to coloured figures. The Lincoln evidence suggests that here, however, the foliate grisailles were used as a complete ornamental system. These designs are closely related to the motifs of ornamental floor tiles, at least in the 13th century (ibid.; Norton 1983).

Variations on this type appear in Messingham and Norton Disney parish churches, both in Lincolnshire (I 5c and nIII A2 respectively). Similar quarries were used at Westwell church, Kent, but with the addition of a small trefoil at the base of the stem and berries hanging from the side-curling foliage (Winston 1867, II pl.1). These quarries, no longer extant, were dated by Winston to the end of the first quarter of the 13th century (ibid., 2). There was a small group of pieces which may have been fragments of this design, for example *176*, with an upright trefoil, central to the quarry axis, but with strapwork defined by double lines (A2). Alternatively, this may represent a discrete form of quarry with no subsidiary trefoils on either side (cf. sf2139, sf262). The lowermost painted curve of the

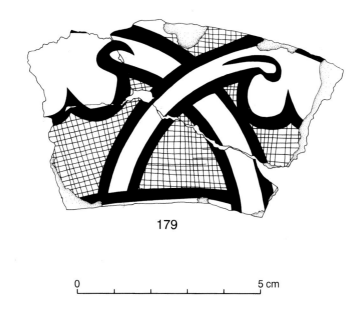

179

0   5 cm

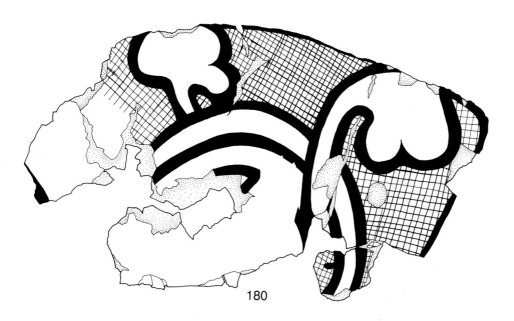

180

Fig. 169   Thirteenth century grisaille fragments. Scale 1:1

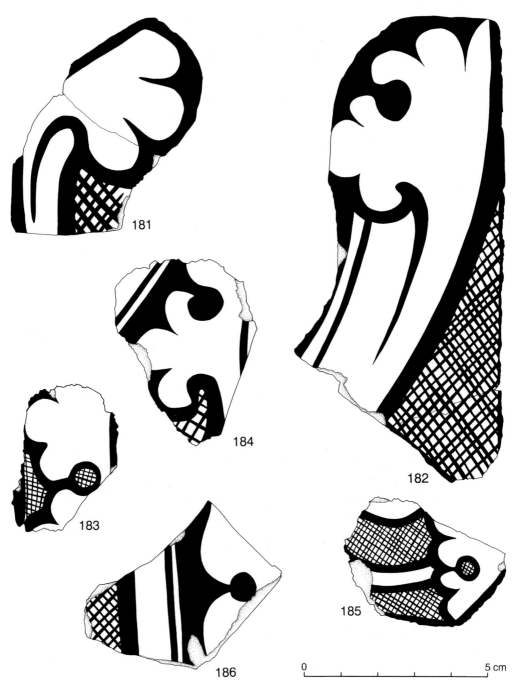

Fig.170   Thirteenth century grisaille fragments. Scale 1:1

design from sf2082 might suggest a second row of subsidiary foliage. In this it is perhaps closer to another design at Lincoln, found in the roundels of two windows either side of the central north transept lancet (NXXXI and NXXXIII), rather than the single quarry motif (illustrated in Morgan 1983, fig.C12). The glass in these windows is thought to be earlier than the grisailles at Salisbury, Southwell or Westminster (ibid., 40). Each roundel was originally made up of four pieces of glass whose shape matches that of A4 (see below). Another form of upright trefoil, with two rows of subsidiary side-curling foliage, can be seen amongst the fragments from the Gilbertine priory at Ellerton, outside York, and now releaded into panels in a window in the nave north aisle of Selby Abbey, East Riding of Yorkshire (see pp.486–95). In this instance the head is double, but the shape of the stem, with thick, uneven spurs, is close to the Fishergate designs.

The single upright trefoils of A2 (*177*) are similar to both the triangular and vesica-shaped panes found in the earliest grisaille in York Minster, in the south transept windows sXXXV and sXXVI. These grisailles form simpler patterns than those found in the north transept (nXVI), and pre-date them by between ten and twenty years as some of the windows may have been in place by 1230 (O'Connor and Haselock 1977, 325).

A third group of grisaille at Fishergate also uses strapwork (A3); *178*, sf2128, sf3354 and sf3609 contain a partial trefoil which is not central to the apex of the quarry, and the strapwork is defined by double lines, unlike sf9173. These may be a distinct form of quarry or they may be broken side-curling trefoils from the first type (A1). Sf2180 has a side-curling trefoil with single lines defining the quarry edge which makes it similar to sf9173.3. Consequently, all these fragments of A1–3 may be parts of a single grisaille quarry motif, with slight variations in size and with both single and double lines defining the strapwork of the quarry edge.

179 is a complete example of a curved shape containing two crossed, outward curling trefoils (A4). Further examples are found in *180*, sf456 and sf467. The curve of the bottom edge suggests that the pieces were originally arranged around a circular panel or vesica. This is a simple design; the nearest York equivalent is perhaps that contained within a diamond-shaped panel in window nIII of St Denys' parish church, York (Knowles 1936, 150, fig.65). A composition of four similarly shaped pieces has been noted above at Lincoln, dating to the first half of the 13th century (Morgan 1983, fig.C12). The radii of the Fishergate examples do not meet at 90°, but it is possible to conceive of a circle consisting of eight similarly shaped panes, with an internal radius of c.8cm. Alternatively, linear fillets of glazing may have separated each shaped pane, crossing at the centre of the circle as can be seen in Salisbury grisailles (Marks 1987, 142, fig.108). This kind of glazing was less usual in English grisailles. It may simply be that the curved Fishergate panes were shaped to fit the curve of a lancet window arch.

A fifth form of trefoil (A5) was painted on a curling stem, with the head to the inner side of the curve, such as *181* and sf3045.8. Such trefoils occur in the Five Sisters Window, York Minster (nXVI). Portions of double head are found amongst the Fishergate fragments, for example *182*, sf2180 and sf2172 (A6). In some of the double fragments, the

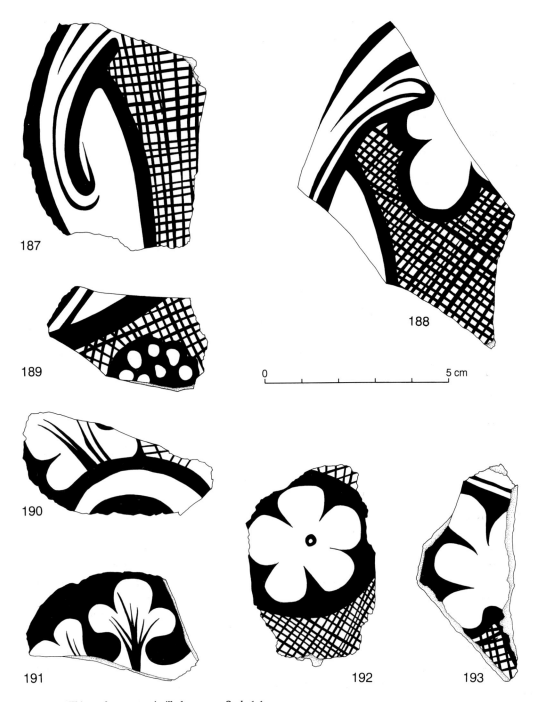

Fig.171   Thirteenth century grisaille fragments. Scale 1:1

round terminal to the cusp dividing the two trefoils is solid (*182*, possibly *186*); in others it is either open (sf2463) or cross-hatched (*183*). Similar features can be found on excavated grisaille from Rievaulx Abbey. The variation in Fishergate has a cross-hatched terminal and the trefoils lie across two curling lines or stems (*184–5*).

Some trefoils have split and twisting stems, with one part of the stem crossing over the other. This is illustrated in *187* (A7) and perhaps in *188*. Other examples of this are found on sf2180, sf2082 (at least three fragments) and sf3045. Only sf3045.8 has a partial trefoil attached to the twisting stem. Twisted stems occur in the grisaille lancets in York Minster (NXXXI, NXXXIII), in the Salisbury grisailles and in the Five Sisters Window, York Minster (nXVI, panels of a, c, d, e; Browne 1847). The grozing on sf3045.8 was complete and formed the same shape as another fragment from the same context.

There were only two examples of trefoils with berries: *189* and sf57 (A8). Many English grisailles featured fruiting foliage of this kind. In the grisaille panels at Salisbury, however, clusters of eight to twelve berries are most usual. Browne's drawings of the panels of the Five Sisters Window, York Minster, rarely show more than five berries, most often three, attached to each discrete leaf.

Trefoils with thin internal lines defining stamens or veins (A9) occurred on two fragments, *190* and sf3609. This detail appears within trefoils on a plain ground from Beverley Dominican Priory, East Riding of Yorkshire (Graves 1996, e.g. 128, fig.72, nos.116, 118). The only similar detail amongst the remaining Fishergate grisaille was perhaps in *191*. As the trefoil of sf2363 was drawn on a curving line it resembled a decorated circular fillet found in an excavated window panel from Bradwell Abbey, Buckinghamshire, c.1270, integrated into a complex geometric glazing scheme (Croft and Mynard 1986, 111). The Bradwell trefoils run in a continuous band and are painted in reserve on a plain ground, whereas the Fishergate example is isolated, on a cross-hatched ground; cf. sf3609. The Fishergate examples are similar to a fragment from Haverholme Gilbertine priory, which has two veined trefoils, side by side, on a cross-hatched ground (Fig.230, *Hav3*, p.496).

The Fishergate assemblage did not have a motif comparable to the simple background grisaille quarries in the north aisle of St Denys' parish church (nIII). These quarries have strapwork round the edges, with a floral motif in reserve on a large cross-hatched ground, dated to c.1225 (O'Connor 1989, XX). The closest Fishergate parallels are *192–6* and *198* (A10). There were many fragments whose cross-hatched background was defined by plain fillet borders. These could all be broken quarries of grisaille with strapwork edging. It is clear, however, that the existing grozing on some of these fragments cuts across the original design. This may be evidence of releading in the medieval period when the pieces were broken, mixed up with other glass or deliberately reshaped to fit into a convenient space in a reglazing operation.

The quality of the painted linework varies enormously in these pieces. There is a distinct category of boldly outlined trefoils on a ground of thickly defined cross-hatching in contrast to more delicate trefoil forms with single hair-breadth cross-hatching. This distinction of

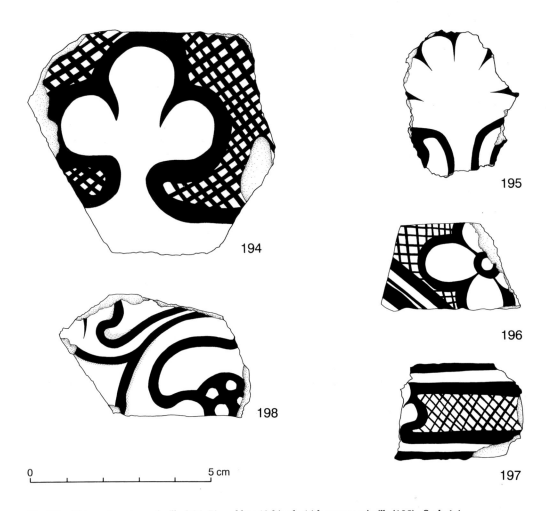

Fig. 172   Thirteenth century grisaille (194–7) and late 13th/early 14th century grisaille (198). Scale 1:1

draughtsmanship is concomitant with a difference in the quality of glass. The larger, cruder grisaille occurs on thick (3–6mm), dark green-tinted glass with an uneven surface texture. The finer painting occurs on glass of a more even surface, usually with a yellow/green tint, and more resistant to corrosion. The variation in quality of paintwork is not unusual; Knowles observed that 'windows such as the Five Sisters . . . do not surpass in skill many of those in the parish churches' (Knowles 1936, 42). The excavated 13th century grisaille from Kellington church, near Selby, for example, is of a better quality than that from Fishergate.

Late 13th/early 14th century grisaille: trefoil motifs on a plain ground (Fig.172)

The second type of grisaille is characterised by smaller curling trefoils with berries on a plain ground (B1). Although there is only one example, *198*, this represents a common form in the second half of the 13th century/early 14th century. Examples in situ can be seen at Chartham, Kent (Winston 1867, I, 99, Cut 12; II, pl.20), and Selling, Kent, c.1299/1307 (ibid., II, pl.18). Plain and cross-hatched grounds, though often indicators of date, are not always mutually exclusive. Although there are no examples in the Fishergate material, other assemblages from Yorkshire contain fragments where both cross-hatched and plain grounds occur together on the same piece of glass, including examples from Beverley Dominican Priory (e.g. Graves 1996, 133, fig.75, no.383).

Late 13th/early 14th century grisaille: quatrefoil motifs (Fig.173)

There are three forms of grisaille quatrefoil quarries. They all employ a strapwork edging which would create the effect of a trellis when leaded together. The first form has pointed lobes (B2; *200*), the second has rounded lobes (B3; *199, 201*) and the third has pointed lobes with serpentine edges (B4; *202*). The first two forms have a tear-shape in reserve in the painted space between the lobes, and crossed, tapered lines as formalised stamens. A piece of type B2 (sf2148) has one grozed edge with lead stain parallel to the outer edge of the design, and a second grozed edge across the middle of the design. There is too little left of the first grozed edge to be able to tell whether both edges have been executed in the same way, and are thus likely to be contemporary. The second line of grozing may represent a releading: the lead stain is of a different colour from that on the first edge. If the second grozed edge was original, however, it may have defined a triangular pane for the edge of a quarry lattice.

Some fragments of type B3 have an area of cross-hatching beyond the strapwork edges in the interstices between the lobe and strapwork (such as sf425) or at the base of the cusp (*201*). Cross-hatching is entirely absent from the other types. This, perhaps, represents an overlap with the earlier grisaille and could date this form to the late 13th century.

Quarries of this sort would be used as backgrounds to figured panels, cf. the Crucifixion panel in the east window at Wells Cathedral (Woodforde 1946, pl.VIII), or the figures of SS Thomas of Canterbury and Thomas of Hereford, St Mary's church, Credenhill, Herefordshire (sIV 2a, c.1300; O'Connor 1987, 212, cat.29). The Fishergate quarries were probably mass-produced.

Late 13th/early 14th century grisaille: oak leaf and acorn motifs (Fig.174)

The fourth type of grisaille (B6) depicts a pattern of oak leaves and acorns outlined on a plain ground. Some strapwork is evident, as on *203*, but with convex and concave edges, suggesting a leaded pattern like that in the chapter house windows of York Minster, c.1285 (O'Connor and Haselock 1977, 334–41 *passim*; pl.98). A serpentine line often ran up the

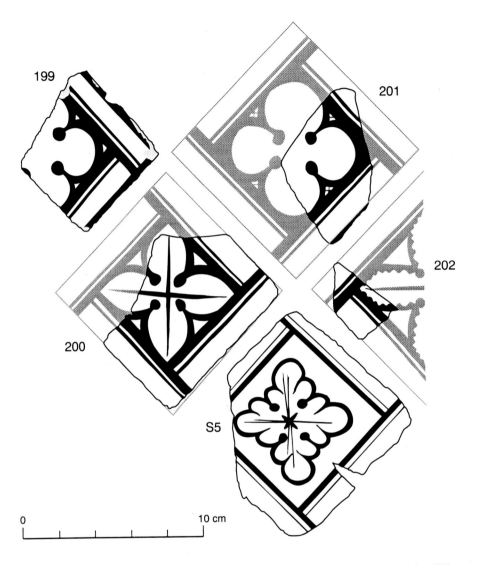

Fig.173   Late 13th/early 14th century grisaille: quatrefoil patterns on a plain ground. 199–202 from Fishergate, S5 from Sempringham Priory. Scale 1:2

centre of the foliage stem, such as *204*, sf2172 and sf2139, all from context 3163. This context also contained a stem of a small *rinceau* pattern of curling trefoils alternating with dots which may be from oak leaf grisaille, including *207* and sf2181.23 (see also *205*). The *rinceau* resembles that often found on 13th century wall painting and partially reflects a design found amongst the painted wall fragments from Fishergate itself (pp.304–5, *AY* 11/2). The oak leaves are all drawn in outline, similar in form, and only vary slightly in

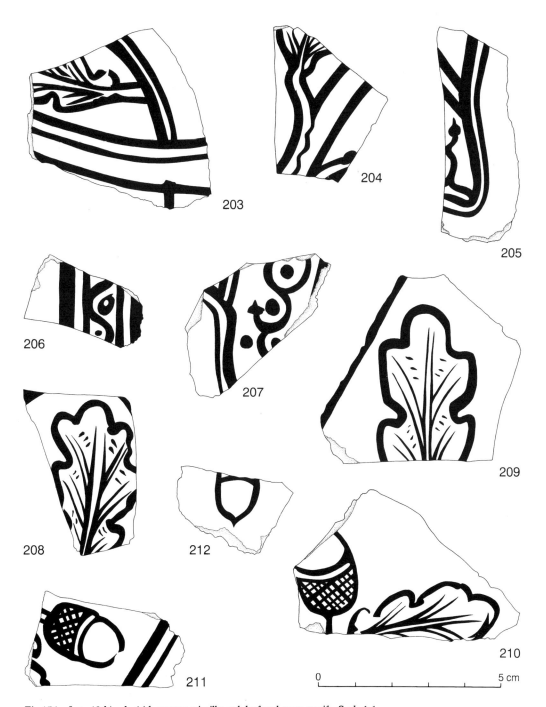

Fig. 174 Late 13th/early 14th century grisaille: oak leaf and acorn motifs. Scale 1:1

size. Most are articulated with a conventionalised double vein pattern, although some have short lines or dots beneath each indentation on the leaf edge, *208–9*. The accompanying acorns are crudely drawn in trace line and vary in shape from elliptical (*210*) to almost rectangular (e.g. *211*). One example has a more naturalistic shape, *212*. The internal detail is confined to the shell of the acorn, which is rendered by a double trace line and internal cross-hatching. The pattern of *206* is likley to be the central stem of naturalistic grisaille, such as can be seen in the chapter house windows, York Minster.

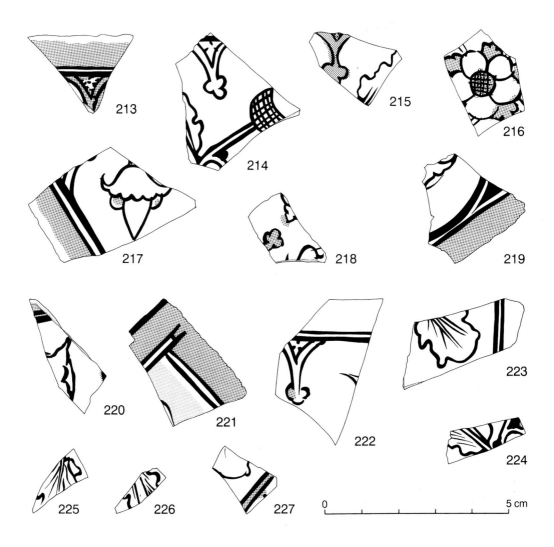

Fig.175   Patterned quarries. Scale 1:1

The stems of acorns and leaves appear to bend over the central stem in a way that is paralleled in the similar grisaille from Sempringham Priory and from Ellerton Priory, now in Selby Abbey (pp.470, 490).

Patterned quarries (Figs.175–7)

A number of fragments of white glass were painted as patterned quarries, with a yellow-stained strapwork edge or line frame (Fig.176). These would have been leaded into a diamond lattice and used to glaze large areas or separate bands of figures as a standard practice in the 14th century. This type of glass may also be called grisaille. The Fishergate glass is consistently transparent, thin (average 1–2mm) and contains few seeds. The edges are very finely grozed. The strapwork may be painted with a small trefoil projection (*214* and possibly *213*) and stained yellow (*214, 221*).

There are three designs: a rose, a sort of lily or rose bud and oak leaves with acorns. The rose, for example *216*, has small trefoil leaves in yellow stain in the interstices of the petals and the centre is cross-hatched. There are four sets of thin parallel lines which, by analogy with other rose quarry designs, could be reconstructed as shown in Fig.177. This is a conflation of the rose quarries found in Holy Trinity parish church, Goodramgate (sIII A2 and nII 1a).

Fig.176   Patterned quarries, including 213, 216, 217, 218 and 222. Fragment on right 4cm long

Variations on this rose were common in both French and English glazing in the 14th century, e.g. the quarry background in the De Moulins window in Evreux Cathedral illustrated in Westlake (1882, pl.XCI, a; without linear projections). The design can also be compared to releaded grisaille in the east window of Beverley Minster (e.g. I 1b). The rose quarries in two north aisle windows in St Denys' church, Walmgate (nIII 1a and nIV 1b), are similar, but, like the Beverley examples, mostly 19th century copies of mid 14th century forms. The roses in nIII 1a even have the cross-hatched centre. Rose grisaille can be found elsewhere in Yorkshire, for example, in the north transept of Dewsbury church, West Yorkshire.

The lily or rosebud seen on fragments *217–20* has been drawn with the same thin trace line, with a curling stem. The oak leaf variation is best illustrated by sf2670.37 and sf2670.38 and the slivers from *223–6*. The type of acorn which accompanies these leaves is shown in *214* and *227* (see also Fig.176), and has a cross-hatched cap, sometimes yellow stained. These are more crudely drawn than the fine line acorn quarries in Holy Trinity, Goodramgate (nII 1a). The complete quarries usually only have staining on two edges, to emphasise the lattice.

Diaper (Figs.178–9)

Diaper is the term applied to a regularly repeated pattern usually forming the background to a figural composition. Some diaper designs are called *rinceaux*: patterns of flowing or curling foliage. Five types of *rinceaux* have been identified by French and O'Connor (1987, 7, 19, pl.19) in the west windows of York Minster. Three of these patterns are found in the Fishergate assemblage: the frond, the thistle and a leaf pattern. Each example of these *rinceaux* has been painted in reserve or picked out of a dilute wash of red/brown enamel paint. Very fine details have been scratched out of the background, usually tiny circles or arcs, which add to an impression of delicacy.

The frond *rinceau*, with closely spaced lines making up the leaf, looks hurriedly and erratically scratched (*228–30*). For this reason, the Fishergate examples are best compared with the second class of frond *rinceaux* found in nXXX of the Minster, rather than the more carefully executed examples of the west window glazing (French and O'Connor 1987, 7, pl.vi). This *rinceau* occurs on pot-metal yellow and white, whereas in the Minster blue, ruby and green are used (ibid.). There is no hook-frond design comparable to that found in the west wall of the Minster (ibid., pl.19 ii).

The thistle consists of a number of circular terminals sprouting from a curling stem. The background is decorated with small scratched circles. The thistles are inaccurate, often sub-circular to ovoid, sometimes incomplete, with the tail of a scratch visible where the artisan has lifted the stick or needle away (*231*). This *rinceau* occurs on yellow pot-metal.

The third *rinceau* has a small leaf with indented edge and fine details scratched out of the thin wash background to decorate the line frame around it (*243–5*). This is similar to *rinceau* in window nXXX of the Minster (French and O'Connor 1987, 7 and pl.19.ix), but

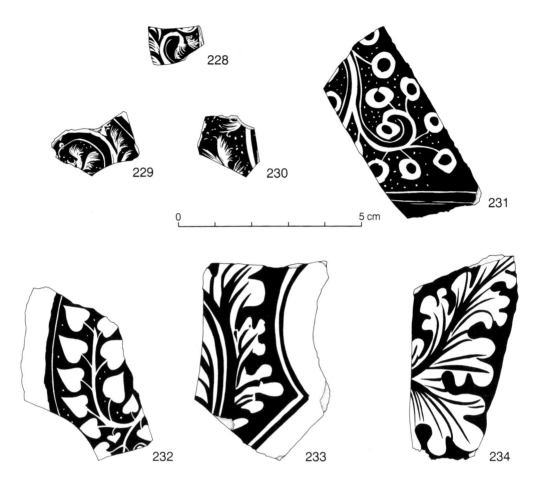

Fig.178   Diaper fragments. Scale 1:1

closer in execution to panels removed from north clerestory window NXXI, again from the early 14th century, probably the mid 1330s (ibid., 347, figs.104–5). The quality of all Fishergate examples is second rate, however, when compared to the Minster.

In addition to the above, Fishergate has produced a spade-like leaf in reserve on a mid-green pot-metal, such as *232*, sf3045. The paint in this case is much thicker than the dilute washes of the foregoing; the same design is found on a fragment of white glass, with a dilute wash, sf3609.43. This leaf shape is paralleled in the background to a panel depicting St John the Evangelist in the sacristy of Selby Abbey (Sacristy sII, 2b), and Christ from a coronation scene at Nether Poppleton, North Yorkshire (sII, A2) (French and O'Connor

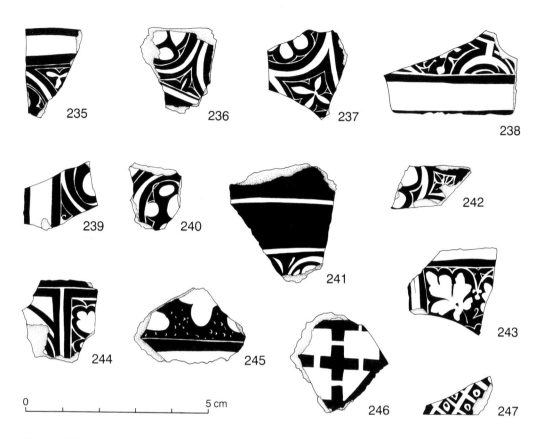

Fig.179   Diaper fragments. Scale 1:1

1987, pls 27b and 28b). There is also some evidence for trefoil and possibly quatrefoil variations.

A single fragment of a *rinceau* or diaper which may have had trefoil leaves, *245,* also had small curves scratched out of the background wash, making it more akin to the fern, spade-leaf and thistle *rinceaux*. Incomplete as the design is, it is still most likely to be contemporary with the other early to mid 14th century *rinceaux* as trefoil diapers are found as backgrounds to the canopy figures of the Heraldic window, York Minster nave north aisle (nXXIII), c.1310–20 (O'Connor and Haselock 1977, 351, fig.108), and elsewhere (cf. the background to the heraldic shield from Ellerton Priory, now 2c in Selby Abbey, first half of the 14th century; see p.486).

The greatest area of diaper was painted with a seaweed *rinceau*, with characteristic multi-lobate edges (*233–4*). All examples of this type have been painted in reserve with the normal, thick red/brown paint. This pattern occurs in the background to figures in the parish church of St Martin-cum-Gregory, Micklegate (nIV, c).

There are numerous fragments of a diaper design of quatrefoils within circles and concave-sided lozenges (*235–42*). This kind of pattern can be seen in the background to bells in the panels of grisaille in the Bell-Founder's window, York Minster (nXXIV, c.1325; O'Connor and Haselock 1977, 352, fig.109; Drake 1736, 18, 104, pl.LXXXVI), or the east window of Beverley Minster (I 3a).

Two examples of a chequer or cross diaper were found at Fishergate (*246–7*). On the first the pattern was made by painting a ground of consistently thick cross-hatching, through which a stick was drawn to produce a parallel pattern in reserve, *stickwork* (see Knowles 1936, 69, fig.16). Although a common pattern in the 14th century, Knowles believed that its use on canopy shaftings and pinnacles was a characteristic feature of York work, mainly restricted to white and yellow stained glass. The Fishergate examples are on white and flashed ruby. A fragment of ruby cross diaper occurs in the west window of All Saints, Pavement, originally from the east window of St Saviour's parish church, York, dated to c.1370/80. The second chequer diaper (*247*) was made by picking a cross-hatched design out of a painted ground, to create a series of small squares or lozenges. These in turn have had circles scratched out of them. Such a pattern can be seen behind the left shoulder of the knight in the east window of Tewkesbury Abbey, Gloucestershire, (J. Baker 1978, pl.31). An excavated example from medieval tenements in The Hamel, Oxford, had small scratched lozenges instead of circles, and was dated to the first half of the 14th century (Newton and Kerr 1980, 197, fig.37.19, fiche **EO1**).

Most of these patterns are repeated in near contemporary glazing elsewhere, such as the panels at the west of St Helen's parish church, in St Mary, Castlegate, St Martin-cum-Gregory and formerly St John, Ousebridge (now in the Minster). All these are consistent with a date in the first half of the 14th century; the Minster comparisons give a pivotal date based on the glazing contracts for the west window of 1338/9.

Other vegetal and floral decoration (Figs.180–1)

There were many fragments ($465 \cdot 5cm^2$) painted with foliate or floral motifs which could not be assigned to one of the other categories with certainty, e.g. grisaille or diaper. One of the most prevalent designs is divided into three lobes, upright in the apex of a quarry, such as *248, 249*, sf2172, sf2178. It is very like a fleur-de-lys, but there is some evidence from sf3609 for a pattern with four similar lobes. The design occurred on mid-green pot-metal. This is the sort of quarry which might have been a focal spot of colour in a geometric grisaille pattern (cf. panel of nXVI c, York Minster, illustrated in Browne 1847). Alternatively, these designs may have formed borders or a pattern of background quarries to figures. Similar foliate designs, but with more rounded lobes and internal veins, were probably background quarries (*250*). A third variant, with fringed leaves, came from sf2181. These are all probably late 13th/early 14th century and can be compared with examples from Eaton Bishop, Herefordshire (I, c.1317–21; J. Baker 1978, pl.42).

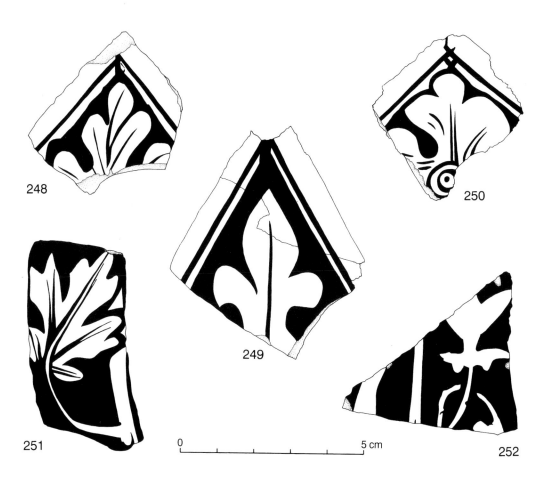

248

250

249

251

252

0 _____ 5 cm

Fig.180   Vegetal and floral decorated fragments. Scale 1:1

One fragment from *251* was the only example of a complete foliate border pattern. The leaf and stem are in reserve, and the glass is opaque. It is probably a hawthorn leaf from a border of similar leaves with some coloured feature like berries between. The borders of the north aisle window of All Saints, North Street, York (nII), reflect this common 14th century arrangement, although a different species of leaf is depicted. Other examples can be seen in St Martin-cum-Gregory, York, and from Rievaulx Abbey. By analogy, it is possible that the Fishergate leaf was originally yellow stained on the reverse. Although the conventional arrangement was for leaves to decorate the periphery of each light, the small scale of this piece might suggest that it bordered a roundel or small panel.

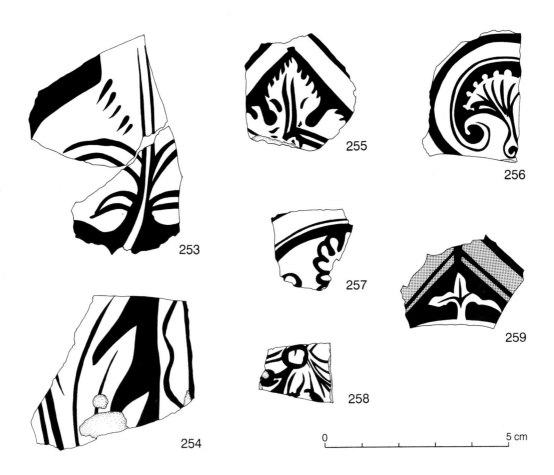

Fig.181   Vegetal and floral decorated fragments. Scale 1:1

A rough and improbable looking fragment, *252*, probably fulfilled the same function as a border and can be matched directly by foliage on a window from St John, Ousebridge, now in York Minster (nXXI 2a; detail in Centre for Medieval Studies, University of York, Photograph Collection, neg. no.761/7 21). These leaves are in reserve, with groups of three berries, and issue from a winding stem, alternating with birds.

Two fragments may have been part of a large vine or ivy leaf from another 14th century border or background quarry, *253*. A leaf (*254*) is similar to an example from the Gilbertine priory at Haverholme, Lincolnshire (26-27-A 13e DoE D627).

Four fragments with foliate designs also have edging patterns and cut-lines, but only one has discernible yellow staining (*259*); the others are miscellaneous examples, possibly from background patterns or occasional foliate decoration (*255–7*). One small fragment came from the centre of a floral design (*258*). These are all designs which may have been used in the first half of the 14th century and, with the exception of *259*, the late 13th century.

Figures

Heads (Figs.182–4)

There are at least five partial heads featuring eyes, two more which have been broken above the jaw line, and several pieces of hair. The first is a narrow piece of white glass depicting a left eye looking towards the right (*260*). Only a few strokes of hair remain at the top and some fine, wavy lines, perhaps depicting a beard at the bottom. The eye is large and rounded, defined by tapering brush strokes. The second fragment depicts eyes looking to the left, and a fringe of hair (*261*). The stylistic composition of the eyes is similar on the two fragments, having a high arched and tapered brow, and a thin line defining the crease of the upper lid. A third fragment has a left eye, looking to the left, with long hair defining the left side of the face (*263*). The fourth fragment shows a figure with curly hair and the right eye (*262*). Short curly hair was often, but not exclusively, used to portray angels and male saints in the first half of the 14th century. The final piece portraying the eyes of a figure, *264*, shows both eyes, looking to the right, the nose and mouth. The first three are all drawn to a similar scale, and the last two are slightly smaller. The sidelong glances of the eyes in each case are a convention of narrative panels, where the original subject figure was the focus of attention for the surrounding figures.

All these pieces are most likely to have dated from the first half of the 14th century. It is the detail of the eyes which is most diagnostic, particularly the thinner lines which indicate the upper lids. Nothing can be said about the particular iconography of any of these pieces.

Two pieces of finer white glass, from different contexts, are evidently from the same head, *265*. This had been drawn with a variety of techniques. The lower part of the face is shown, in three-quarter aspect, with thin, almost cursory lines defining the outline and the features of nose and mouth. Some random dots on the lower jaw and chin give an impression of stubble, but may serve as minimalist modelling. The hair has been formed out of several strokes of wash with thicker lines articulating depth and contour. These pieces appear to be later in date than most of the foregoing, probably the second quarter to the mid 14th century.

There are, besides these pieces, several fragments which probably show details of hair, variously long and wavy, such as sf3855, or with layered curls (*266*). This latter has yellow stain applied to the outer surface and compares with the arrangement of hair on a fragment from Wolvesey Palace, Winchester (Kerr and Biddle 1990, 401, fig.93, 861), dated to the mid–late 14th century.

The largest scale figural representation appears to be *267* (Figs.183–4). This shows most of the lower part of the face below the eyes. The outline of the head is a broad line,

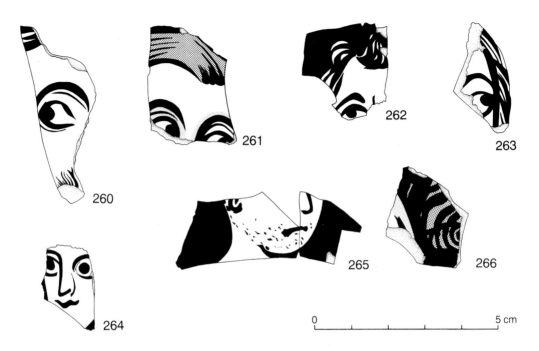

Fig.182   Figural fragments: heads. Scale 1:1

continuous with that defining the neck, which is contoured by swagging, tapered brush strokes and fine shading in a light wash on either side of these lines. There are light washes suggesting some modelling of the cheeks and chin. The thick, broad line at the top edge of the fragment indicates the mouth. The hair falls in cascades down both sides of the face, which has a full-frontal aspect. The general characteristics of this face, especially the mouth, chin and neck, can be compared with early–mid 13th century figures (the figure of a female holding a book in White Notley parish church, Essex, or the refectory wall-painting of St Faith at the Priory of Horsham St Faith, Norfolk, c.1260; J. Baker 1978, pl.16; Binski 1991, 61, pl.58).

A little more detail can be postulated in connection with a head, made up of two fragments, consisting of $14 \cdot 5 cm^2$ of $2 \cdot 5$–$3 \cdot 3mm$ thickness, semi-transparent white glass, grozed to a curved edge (*269–70*). The fragments are painted with a mass of curly flowing hair defining the face. A band with rings bound round it crosses the forehead. Only the left eye is wholly visible, with a thin line above the brow, an arched, tapering brow and an elongated eye. A possible brow above the right eye is just visible. On the reverse, the areas covering the hair above and below the band are shaded with a matt wash, and the face and eyes have been traced in outline. The arch of the upper lid of the right eye might be visible here, although the fracture of the glass towards the inner surface has broken the eye from

267

268

269

270

0   5 cm

Fig. 183   Figural fragments: heads. Scale 1:1

Fig.184   Figural fragments: head 267. Length 8cm

the front. The *back-painting* makes the hair appear golden brown when held to the light, although it has not been yellow stained. The face is full frontal and outward looking. The band round the head is almost certainly representative of the Crown of Thorns. The particular iconographical form of the crown is dated to after c.1300 (Woodforde 1946, 12; see pp.456–9). The style of hair and face suggests that this image is no later than the 1330s.

Full-figure detail (Fig.183)

The most recognisable of the figural pieces were three fragments of clear glass which fit together to show the figure of the Christ Child cradled in elegant hands, no doubt those of the Blessed Virgin Mary (*268*). The style of the depiction, especially the head and drapery of the Child, suggest a date in the 1320s/30s, contemporary with glass in the aisles of York Minster nave, though not of the same quality of execution.

The Christ Child's halo is defined by the outer circumference of the nimbus having been scratched out of a wash of paint. The tripartite division within it is a traditional distinction for a member of the Trinity. The scene depicts the transfer of a round object between Christ's left hand and the Virgin's right. Christ rests on the left side of His Mother, the side from which she traditionally gives suck in representations of Christ at His Mother's breast. This may be the scene to which the pieces relate, for many depictions merely portray the Virgin's breast as a round orb she profers with her hand towards the Child. This minimalist approach to representation is more likely on objects of small scale and difficult medium, for example seal matrices. In glass and manuscript illumination by the 14th century one would expect to see some distinction of the nipple, as, for example, the Virgin and Child scenes at Warndon and Fladbury, both Hereford and Worcester (Woodforde 1954, 12, pl.17). Based on the same cartoon of c.1330–40, these two scenes show the Virgin offering her breast and Christ holding a fruit (O'Connor 1987, 404–5, 472–3).

Hands and feet (Figs.185–7)

There are at least four recognisable fragments of hands, painted in reserve. The first is an outstretched palm, where the grozing reflects the subject and the fingers are very long and straight (*271*). As there is no wound represented in the hand, it is not likely to have come from a Crucifixion scene; open-handed gestures are common to many narrative scenes (cf. the figure of a bishop in the church of St Mary, Ponteland, Northumberland, sII, with that of the Virgin, Beverley Minster, I 6d, both second quarter 14th century; French and O'Connor 1987, pls.27c, 28c). The second hand has curling fingers probably holding something (*272*). The only detail is the thumbnail. A much finer quality of glass was used for a small hand, again painted in reserve, and of a later date than most of the other limbs, probably in the second half of the 14th century (*273*). Fragments (*274*) may represent curling fingers on a larger scale than any of the above. At least three short, paired lines indicate the joints and are a detail to be seen, for example in the west window of York Minster, wI, 6c (French and O'Connor 1987, pl.21). Another fragment may represent curling fingers, although the exaggerated proportions may be more indicative of a beast's paw (*275*).

A small, but very detailed piece of glass, *276*, shows a hand in a close-fitting buttoned sleeve, resting on a belt or other detail of dress, which has been partially highlighted with yellow stain. The fingers are long and bent, with nails painted in. The buttoned sleeve indicates a date in the first half of the 14th century, but also suggests a member of the laity. The figure of a kneeling civilian donor in St Denys' church (nIII, 1b), of mid 14th century date, has this sort of sleeve. The detail beneath the hand may be part of a purse or pouch (*gypcière*) and can be compared with that worn by a donor figure in St Denys (nIV 1c). It is quite common, as in the St Denys example, for the pouch to be made with an aperture at the top through which a dagger or knife (*anelace*) may be hung, and this can be seen in many manuscript illuminations (e.g. the mass miniature from the Walters manuscript, c.1340–50) or on monumental brasses (e.g. that of a civilian at Hampsthwaite, North Yorkshire, c.1350–60, see Fig.186a; Alexander and Binski 1987, 255, no.152). The St

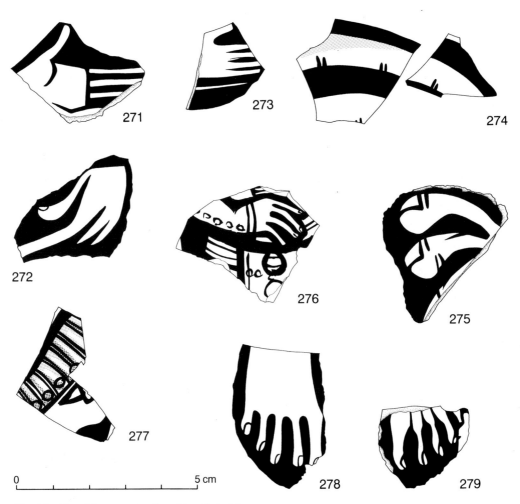

Fig.185   Figural fragments: hands and feet. Scale 1:1

Andrew's fragment would appear to show a purse of this type, but without the dagger; instead the figure's belt shows through the circular hole at the top. A leather purse of this form has been excavated from 16–22 Coppergate, York (YAT 1987.7; sf2650) (Fig.186c; *AY* 17/16 in prep.). The lower circle on the glass fragment probably defines an area of decoration on the purse as shown on the St Denys example. The Coppergate purse has holes in this position by which a piece of decorated metal or leather could be attached.

A superficially similar style of painting and staining of details has been employed on five small slivers of glass which fit together, *277* (Fig.187). It is most likely that this second detail is of the overlapping plates and rivets in armour covering a knight's foot, representing

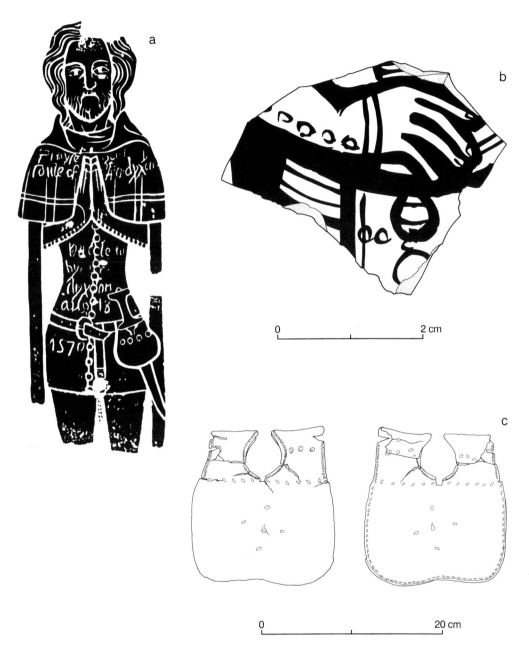

Fig.186   a) Brass rubbing from the church of St Thomas à Becket, Hampsthwaite, North Yorkshire, c.1350–60. Illustration from A Visual History of Costume: The 14th and 15th Centuries by Margaret Scott, reproduced by courtesy of B.T. Batsford Ltd, © Victoria and Albert Museum. Accessories include a knotted belt with a purse and a dagger thrust through the purse. b) Fragment of glass with purse (276). Scale 2:1. c) Leather purse (sf2650) from 16–22 Coppergate. Scale 1:4

Fig.187   Figural fragments: feet (277), hands (276) and drapery (280). 277 3cm high

*Fig.188   Detail of sabaton from Sir John de la Pole, brass rubbing from Church of the Holy Trinity, Chrishall, Essex
(© The Board of Trustees of the Victoria and Albert Museum)*

laminated *sabatons*. This type of armour typically dates from the mid 14th to the late 15th century, although the narrower the plates, generally, the later the armour; compare the sabotons of Hugh le Despenser the Younger, Tewkesbury Abbey, Gloucestershire, c.1340–4, with those of Sir Robert Wingfield, east window (I 1a) of the parish church of St Peter and St Paul, East Harling, Norfolk, c.1480, Crewe 1987, 36, pl.20; or on the memorial brass to Sir John de la Pole, Church of the Holy Trinity, Chrishall, Essex (Fig.188). Despite the similarity in execution between the buttoned sleeve and this sabaton, a date in the 15th century seems more probable for the latter.

Some fragments may represent feet. They are so crudely drawn as to be ambiguous; however, the individual digits appear to be too short for fingers (*278–9*). Each toe has been painted with a nail and the grozing reflects the shape of the foot. These pieces are so similar as to suggest a reversed cut-line from the same cartoon. The treatment of the feet can be compared with the right foot of an early 14th century St James the Great, originally from the north nave clerestory of the Minster (NXXI) (O'Connor and Haselock 1977, pl.105).

Drapery (Figs.187, 189–90)

Drapery is represented by 183cm^2 of glass, mostly flashed ruby, and pot-metal colours. There are only two fragments of this kind of dress detail in yellow stain (*280–1*, Fig.189) and no obvious diaper patterned drapery. *280* has vermicular folds, the edges of which have been highlighted by scraping away the shading in a curve following the hem of the gown. The small scale of the design implies that the fragment came from either a small figure in an historiated scene subordinate to the main image of the window, or perhaps a figure in the borders of the window. This piece shows more sophistication in the shading and the highlighting of the fold than is seen in the rest of the assemblage. Due to surface deterioration the glass gives the impression of having stipple shading, but on close inspection, there appears to be simply *smear shading* and varyingly dilute washes. Vermicular folds in drapery were used in the 1330s but stipple shading is only known towards the end of the century. In the thickness of the glass and in scale this piece matches *276*.

The largest example of drapery is from *282* and represents the lower chest area of a figure, with deeply troughed hook folds in a tunic pulled in at the waist by a belt or girdle. The drapery on the right side (figure's left side) hangs over the girdle, as it would have done on the other side as well, following common 13th century depictions on both male and female figures (cf. the Coronation of David in the Glazier Psalter, c.1230; Morgan 1988, cat.8, 199–200), mainly between the second and third quarters of the 13th century. The almost equal arrangement of folds would imply a figure whose torso was facing forward, and from the scale of the piece, a seated figure of c.30–40cm can be inferred, or a standing figure of c.35–50cm. The glass is a deep ruby and can be seen in section to be composed of numerous layers of red interspersed with white. This technique is known as multi-layering, although precisely how it was achieved is as yet in dispute (Spitzer-Aronson 1974, 1975, 1976, 1977). The technique is known to have been used in the 12th and 13th centuries. Multi-layered red glass is also known from the nave aisle windows of York Minster (nXXX 5a and sXXXVI 3a–5a), however, and the technique must have

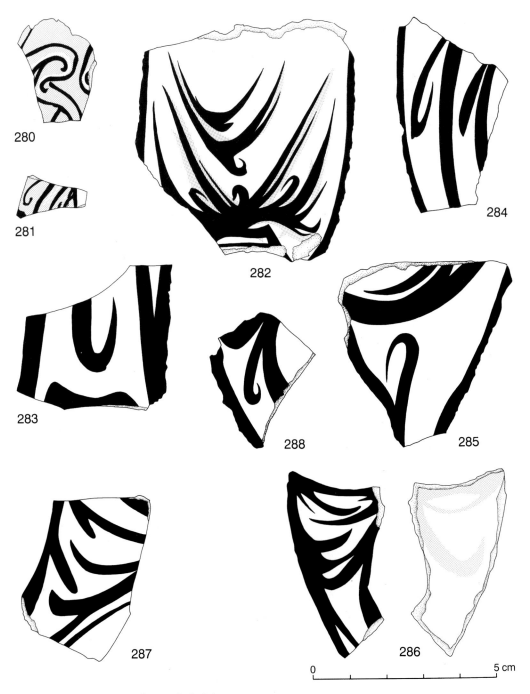

Fig. 189   Figural fragments: drapery. Scale 1:1

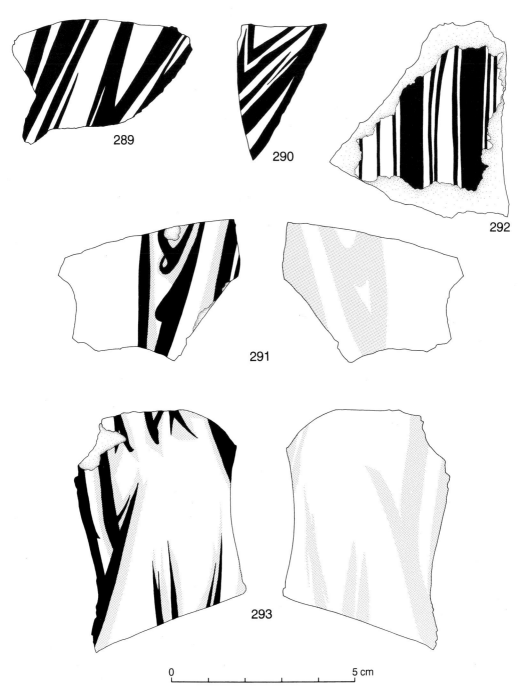

Fig. 190   Figural fragments: drapery. Scale 1:1

survived into the 1330s (French and O'Connor 1987, 13, n.4; Spitzen-Aronson 1979, 26–34).

One fragment of rich blue pot-metal no longer has any paintwork surviving on the surface (*292*). The place occupied by paint can still be discerned, however, as the paint had protected the surface of the glass immediately beneath. Thus, the spaces between the former paint lines have corroded at a faster rate than the rest, leaving the formerly painted surfaces standing proud. These lines are most likely to have been folds of drapery.

Quite a few of the drapery fragments show related stylistic details, with hook folds of differing scale occurring in *283–4*, *288–91*. The grozing round one fragment (*291*) suggests the modelling round the shoulder or upper arm. Similarly, *286*, on pot-metal yellow glass, has been grozed to the shape of an arm, and although the folds of the drapery are devoid of the distinctive hooks of the above pieces, it is likely to have come from roughly contemporary glazing. In scale, it would be compatible with the chest fragment, *282*.

Many fragments of drapery have some degree of back-painting which would add an impression of depth to the folds (*286* and *293*). The latter depicts a movement or angle of a limb beneath the drapery, and the combination of shading and back-painting emphasises this. Context 2114 produced some drapery on ruby flashed glass which had both back-painting and smear shading which merged with a lead stain defining the edge of the piece. Newton (1961) noted that in the first half of the 14th century 'Lead was used to emphasise the folds of drapery and there are clear attempts to hide some leads within heavily shaded areas'. He identifies this with concurrent attempts in other media to represent three dimensions in the modelling of figures and the spatial forms of architecture. He cites the best examples of this form of painting as the reset windows from the old choir of York Minster, c.1335 (ibid.).

Miscellaneous figural detail (Fig.191)

Amongst the miscellaneous fragments there is a possible representation of a strap/belt, dagger or sword chape, defined by grozing and decorated with a small circle with radiating wavy lines (*298*). This may be a simple design, like a star, or it may be a sketchy spider, although it compares unfavourably with that on a figure of St James, c.1340, in the south aisle of St Mary Castlegate, York (sIII 2c). The grozed shape of the glass echoes the simple U-shaped sword or dagger chapes common until the mid 14th century (cf. *LMMC* 1940, 280, pl.LXXX). Alternatively, it may represent one of the wounds of Christ from a Passion scene (D. O'Connor, pers. comm.). These can be compared with the wounds on Christ's hands and feet in the central light of the east window of Holy Trinity, Goodramgate, featuring the Corpus Christi (I 2c), c.1470 (RCHMY 5). It may relate to the same scene as the head of the crucified Christ described above (pp.388–90).

There is only one piece of a wing that may have come from the figure of an angel (*295*). The two tapered lines which appear on occasional feathers are particularly characteristic of angels' as opposed to birds' feathers. As such, *295* may be contrasted with *294* and *297*. These pieces are both more likely to depict birds' wings. Birds often appeared in window

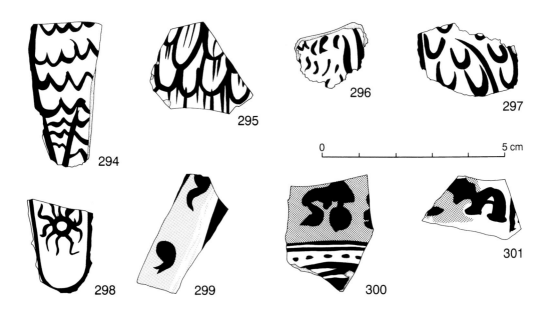

Fig.191   Miscellaneous figural fragments. Scale 1:1

borders such as that excavated at Bradwell Abbey, Buckinghamshire, and dated to c.1270 (Croft and Mynard 1986, fig.8). Birds, along with other zoomorphic motifs and hybrid mythological beasts, appeared in the marginalia of illuminated manuscripts from the late 13th century (Alexander and Binski 1987, 354–7). They appeared increasingly in the painted glass windows throughout the first half of the 14th century, usually amid foliage (e.g. York Minster nave south aisle, sXXXI and sXXXII, nXXI; nave north aisle, nXXXV; Holy Trinity, Goodramgate, window nII; St John's church, Ousebridge, nXXI, 4a illustrated in French and O'Connor 1987, pl.25d; for a fuller discussion see Marks 1993, 153–4). By analogy with contemporary examples, the Fishergate birds may have inhabited foliage borders (cf. the more complete examples from Sempringham Priory, Lincolnshire, p.468, Fig.218).

The small fragment, *296*, may depict a bird's breast. Alternative interpretations are the pelt of a beast or even a representation of chainmail. Chainmail is usually divided into horizontal bands by lines, which this piece omits. One of the 14th century beasts in the borders of nII in Holy Trinity, Goodramgate, has similar markings on its legs.

The next three fragments from this category relate to high-status human figures. These pieces depict fragments of crown (*300–1*), and an ermine trim (*299*). The crowns show small upright elements between taller shapes, probably fleurs-de-lys here rather than strawberry leaves. Fragment *300* appears to show a jewelled rim at the base of the crown.

Whilst these depictions may have come from window borders, they are quite small in scale and differ from the more stylised crowns shown in Fig.198 (*359–61*) discussed below under heraldry (pp.412–13). Although it is by no means certain, it can be suggested that the crowns discussed here were worn by figures rather than free-standing symbols in themselves. Indeed, *300* may show some hair beneath the rim. The tails of the ermine trim (*299*) can be compared with those of type 'n' identified by Gee in the glass of All Saints' church, North Street, and with those in window sIII 1b of St Denys' parish church (Gee 1969, pl.XVIII). This is one of the few pieces from Fishergate which suggest a 15th century date.

Architecture (Figs.192–4)

In both stained glass and manuscript illumination, depictions of architecture tend to reflect the current styles in building; thus the canopied niches within which saints stand use the type of capital, buttress, gable and *crocket* forms of the period. In the 15th century a canopy form appeared in stained glass which was more or less unique to that medium. Details within gables are often abstracted and sculpture or pattern is rendered by the use of stickwork and other techniques more appropriate to the medium of glass-painting. Consequently, some of the decoration which appears in this section is also found below (pp.405–8).

The majority of fragments of architectural detail are comparable with early 14th century depictions, although the quality and thickness of glass varies considerably. The most recognisable features are canopy gables with crockets and internal cusping. Two pieces fit together to show the side of a canopy or niche (*302*). The capital of the side shaft or respond is shown, with a cusped arch springing from it, all painted in reserve with red/brown paint. The cusp is pierced and it may have extended into a trefoil-headed arch, or, given the radius of the curve, it may have formed one of five cusps on a larger arch. Examples of both can be seen in the Bell Founder's Window of York Minster nave (nXXIV 3c), c.1325 (O'Connor and Haselock 1977, pl.110). The canopy gable is detailed, with stickwork in two registers, the first resembling the border pattern of circles interspersed with smaller circles, the second with two rows of gadrooning. The edge of the gable is decorated with small foliated crockets in reserve on yellow stain. A small fragment, *303*, is similar in scale and execution to this, with slightly more bulbous crockets.

Both the canopy described above (*302*) and another from the same context (*304*) have a scalloped or gadrooned pattern, the former picked out in stickwork, the latter painted over a pale wash. This sort of decoration can be seen within the topmost part of a canopy in panel 5a of the east window of Beverley Minster, dating to the second quarter of the 14th century (O'Connor 1989, 70). O'Connor has called attention to the other details of design and ornament in this canopy which make it typical of the windows in the west end of York Minster (ibid.). A large fragment, *305*, may be part of a canopy or other architectural feature, and has been painted with a more undulating line than the gadrooning referred to above. This kind of line appears on the battlemented shafting offsets of the mid 14th century window nIV 2a in St Denys' parish church, Walmgate. It can also be seen

Fig. 192   Architectural fragments. Scale 1:1

on the putative column capital, *320* (Fig.194, p.404). The shaped fragment *197* (Fig.172, p.374) may also have orginated as ornament within a gable.

The range of crocket forms is limited and shown in Figs.192–3. The largest (*312*) resembles those on canopies in the north aisle of the parish church of St Martin-cum-Gregory (Knowles 1936, 54, fig.7c). The only piece of canopy detail with this sort of crocket is from *303*. The majority of crockets are of a consistent size, c.1cm, and are similar to those in the former west window of St Martin-le-Grand, Coney Street, or the west window of St Helen, Stonegate, both in York, dating to the mid 14th century (Knowles 1936, fig.7d and g respectively). Whilst most of the crockets are painted in reserve on yellow stain, there are a few which have been left white. Fragment *307* is of the same design as the crockets on the canopy gable, *302*. The larger fragment *310* (Fig.192), however, appears to be a variation on the ornate cabbage leaf crockets which occur in the second quarter of the 14th century in, for example, St Martin-cum-Gregory window sII. This type of crocket could be as late as c.1360.

Although there are no whole finials from a canopy or gable, there are several fragments from the base rings of foliate finials, such as *317* (cf. York Minster nXXV 3b, c.1320) and probably *306*.

Various pieces of stickwork and reserve patterning resemble the kind of detail found within canopies, as well as the articulation of cusping beneath, for example *308–9*, *311*, *314–16*. Only one piece, *313*, can be identified as a possible representation of a window or traceried architectural construction within a canopy.

It is difficult to recognise whether there are examples of perspective drawing in some of these pieces as they are so fragmentary. A number of linear arrangements, especially those with shading, may be attempts at representing depth in architecture, particularly in the attenuated buttresses which would frame a figure under a canopy.

Two fragments are painted with architectural column capitals or bases, and a number of other fragments may belong in this category. The largest is *319* which shows the capital/base in reserve, with a rounded neck ring or astragal, possibly a scalloped capital form and a square abacus. The way in which the piece has been grozed in relation to the painting effectively halves the capital, suggesting that it represents the respond to an arcade or more probably a canopy support. The second example is smaller, but shows a short length of column, a rounded astragal and just a plain bell neck which has been broken off (*321*); the top of the capital could have taken any form. By analogy with these two examples, the grozed shape and the segmentation of the painted form of *320* probably also represents a capital. If painted glass capitals reflect contemporary architecture, the approximation of *319* to a scallop would give a date after c.1080–1160 in York. This seems unlikely as the glass itself is in every other way comparable to the 13th/early 14th century component of the assemblage. A more feasible comparison is with the scalloped base forms on early 14th century canopies such as that surrounding St Catherine from Wood Walton, Cambridge-shire (c.1310–30), or St Peter from Stanford, Northamptonshire (c.1315–26) (Marks

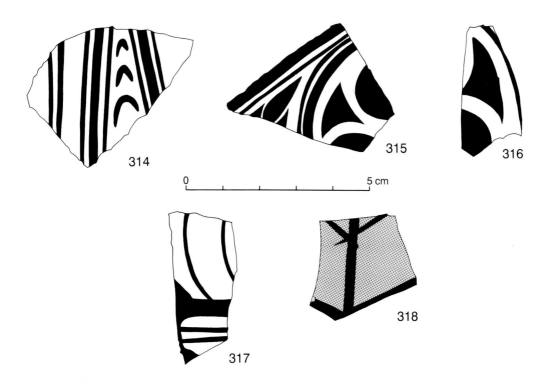

Fig.193   Architectural fragments. Scale 1:1

1987, 445–6, 559–60). Both these examples have additional painted decoration in the reserved space. The shape of *320* can perhaps be compared to the capitals and bases of the arcading on the Ulvik altar frontal of the mid 13th century, from Norway (Tudor-Craig 1987, 132, fig.101), or the half base on the left side of the Nativity panel in the mid 14th century east window of St Michael-le-Belfrey, York.

Fragment *306* may be identified as a capital when compared with that on sf6.64. The simple linear divisions resemble the moulded abaci and decorated capitals of the late 13th century. In the nave aisle and west end windows of York Minster the necks of these capitals are often decorated with foliage, but nothing of that nature survives at Fishergate. In the extant glass, the abaci and neck rings of these capitals are often picked out in yellow stain. The combination of linear division and yellow stain might suggest that numerous fragments, such as *317*, are also from architectural settings.

There are at least two fragments of crenellation (*322, 323*), each showing a *merlon* with a cross-slit, and the former possibly showing some indication of three dimensions. Similar

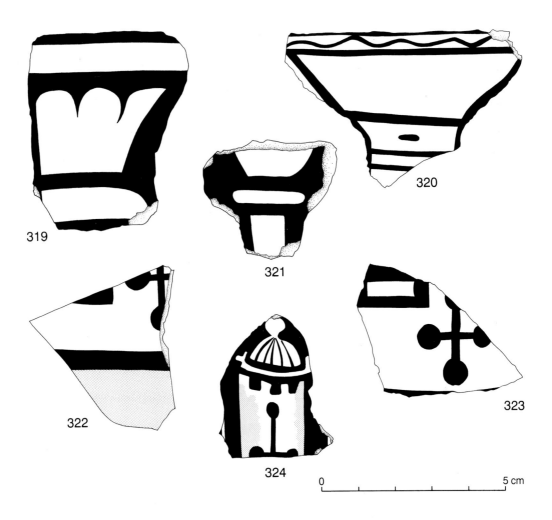

Fig. 194   Architectural fragments. Scale 1:1

cross-slits appear on the crenellations of the prison in which St Catherine is visited by an angel in the Heraldic Window (nXXIII) of York Minster nave north aisle, c.1310–20 (O'Connor and Haselock 1977, 348 pl.107). A similar attempt to convey three dimensions is seen in a fragment of angled corner (*318*). This may have been part of a canopy buttress or an architectural plinth. Again, this is a feature of glass-painting from the early 14th century onwards. Experiments with perspective were being made as early as the Heraldic Window in York Minster (ibid., 349).

There is one small depiction of a roofed turret (*324*). The turret has a cross-slit opening and crenellations. The roof is domed, surmounted by a round finial. In many glass and manuscript depictions of towers or turrets, the roofs are conical or slightly concave. It is more unusual to have a dome. Domed towers appear in the *Genealogical Roll* of kings of Britain, of the late 13th century, and with an ex-libris of c.1300 from St Mary's Abbey, York, and a psalter of c.1330, with a provenance in the diocese of Ely, illustrates domed turrets of exactly this sort (Sandler 1986, 121–2, *109*, pl.283; 1987, 200–1, *10*; Brescia, Biblioteca Queriniana MS AV17). Other similar depictions range between the late 13th century and 1340s. The quality of the glass, style of painting and shading are consistent with other glass datable to the 1330s in the Fishergate assemblage.

Linear stickwork patterns and geometric borders (Figs.195–6)

This section encompasses patterns usually painted in reserve or picked out from a matt wash of red/brown paint. Many of these patterns are linear or curvilinear and may have served either as narrow borders to panels or as fillet borders to smaller roundels and geometric shapes set in systems of grisaille, including figure roundels. The same stickwork patterns could be used to edge garments on figures, architecture and furniture in figural scenes. The patterns are executed on both white and coloured glass.

Twenty-two border designs were found at Fishergate (H1–22), most of which are 14th century in date. Some of these patterns were used recurrently, over long periods of time.

H1. Plain open beading (e.g. *325–6*): that is, a row of open circles of equal shape painted in reserve on a broad band of paint. This pattern occurs in strips of 10–15mm, 20mm, 25mm width (Table 6).

H2. Open beading with internal dots (e.g. *327*). There are two main sizes of beading. The larger occurs on strips 25mm wide, of which there are 21cm^2 on white glass and 8·5cm^2 on opaque glass; the smaller pattern occurs on strips 12–15mm wide, of which there are 4·5cm^2 on opaque glass.

H3. Open beading interspersed with pairs of smaller beads (e.g. *328*): 2·5cm^2 of opaque glass. This is a common border pattern with a broad date range, but consistent with use in the 14th century: cf. All Saints, North Street, York, south light II (Gee 1969) or an excavated example from Oxford (Newton and Kerr 1980, 197, fig.37, 14–16, fiche E01).

H4. Open beading interspersed with pairs of linked circles (e.g. *329*): this occurs once on 4cm^2 of white glass, on a strip of 12mm width.

H5. Open beading with internal dots interspersed with pairs of linked circles (e.g. *330*).

H6. Circles interspersed with pairs of smaller circles (e.g. *331*).

H7. Circles with internal beading interspersed with pairs of circles (e.g. *332–3*). All the examples of this pattern are on strips of c.20mm width: 9·5cm^2 on pink glass, 10cm^2 on opaque glass.

H8. Circles with internal beading interspersed with pairs of linked circles (e.g. *334*).

Table 6   Amount of plain open beading pattern (H1) found in cm^2

Colour of Glass	Pattern Width		
	10–15mm	20mm	25mm
On white	4.0	–	2.5
Light–mid-green	5.0	9.0	–
Deep green	–	6.0	–
Pot-metal yellow	2.0	6.5	–
Opaque glass	6.5	36.0	13.5

H9. Circles with internal beading and further internal dots interspersed with pairs of linked circles (e.g. *335*).

H10. Open beading with internal dots alternating with circles, with both internal beading and further internal dots, interspersed with pairs of linked circles (*336*). All the examples of this pattern are on strips c.20mm wide: 3cm^2 on ruby flashed glass, 7cm^2 on light–mid green (a curved border), and 8·5cm^2 on opaque glass (7cm^2 of which were curved).

H11. Circles alternating with crosses with circular terminals, with pairs of circles between (e.g. *337*). All the examples occur on strips of c.20mm width: 38cm^2 on deep green, 20cm^2 of which is curved.

H12. Quatrefoils (e.g. *338*). All complete examples occur on strips 20–25mm wide: 6cm^2 on possibly yellow stained glass, 11·5cm^2 on opaque glass.

H13. Quatrefoils interspersed with pairs of circles (e.g. *339*). All complete examples of this pattern occur on strips 25mm wide: 6cm^2 on pot-metal yellow, 8cm^2 in reserve on yellow stained glass, 2cm^2 on white and 6·5cm^2 on opaque glass (curved).

H14. Quatrefoils interspersed with pairs of triangles (e.g. *340*). On strips 25mm wide: 3cm^2 on possibly yellow-stained white glass, 2·5cm^2 on white, and 3cm^2 on opaque glass.

H15. Quatrefoils within circles alternating with open beading interspersed with pairs of circles (e.g. *341*). Examples of this pattern occur on strips c.20mm wide: 10cm^2 on ruby flashed glass (5cm^2 of which is streaky), and 1·5cm^2 on pot-metal yellow.

H16. Quatrefoils within circles alternating with crosses with circular terminals, interspersed with pairs of circles (e.g. *342–3*). Two examples occur on strips 20mm wide: 10·5cm^2 on white glass, 3cm^2 on red.

H17. Quatrefoils within circles interspersed with pairs of triangles (e.g. *344*). This pattern occurs on a strip 25mm wide: 8cm^2 on rose glass.

H18. Circles interspersed with pairs of vertical lines (e.g. *345*): 3cm^2 on opaque glass.

H19. Saltire crosses between cross-hatched panels (e.g. *346*). Complete examples are on strips c.25mm wide: 25cm^2 on pink glass, 5·5cm^2 on opaque glass. This pattern can be found, for example, in St Denys' parish church,

Fig.195   Linear stickwork, H1–19. Scale 1:1

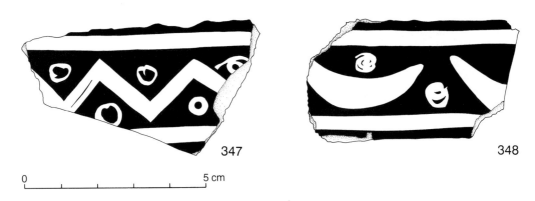

347

348

0   5 cm

Fig.196   Linear stickwork, H20–21. Scale 1:1

Walmgate (nV A2), and All Saints, North Street, York (N light II; Gee 1969, pl.xvi.l), and dates to the 14th century.

H20. Zig-zag line with circles (e.g. *347*). One example is on a curved strip 20mm wide: 3cm^2 on green pot-metal. Another is 35mm wide: 14cm^2 on opaque glass. The design can be seen amongst fragments of grisaille released as the background to a figured roundel from the Theophilus legend in the north choir aisle, and amongst grisaille in the south transept lancets (second from west), of Lincoln Cathedral, c.1230 (e.g. Crewe 1987, pl.11).

H21. Crescents with circles (e.g. *348*). A larger border than most of the preceding at 35mm wide. There are two examples: 21cm^2 on white glass.

H22. It is possible to reconstruct part of a geometric border design from slivers (8cm^2) of very thin, yellow-stained glass sf9175. Such borders with distinctive hoops at the corners can be seen in St Denys, Walmgate (nII), and in Roos church, East Riding of Yorkshire.

Stickwork patterns H6 and H13 occur on architectural canopy gables on *302* and *311* respectively (Fig.192, p.401).

Heraldry (Figs.197–8)

There are numerous fragments of a large fleur-de-lys of standardised form and size (a cartouche approximately 60 × 110mm). The design is in reserve, very plainly divided into three leaves, a central band and the stems beneath. It seems in at least two cases that the stems are not even differentiated (*349–50*). None of the examples retain enough uncorroded glass to verify whether they were originally white, with or without yellow stain, or coloured pot-metals. Fleurs-de-lys of similar proportions occur in the borders of the west windows of the vestibule to the chapter house of York Minster, dated to c.1285.

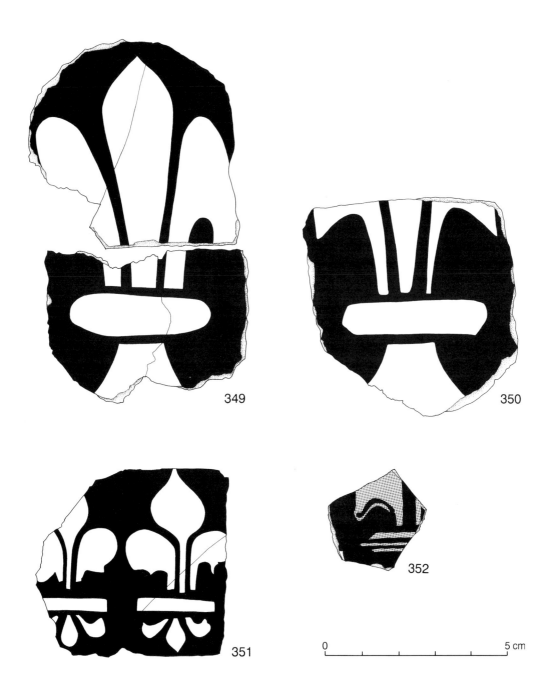

349

350

351

352

0   5 cm

Fig. 197   Heraldic decoration. Scale 1:1

A number of smaller fleurs-de-lys have been painted in reserve on yellow stain and some are paired (*351*). The pairing suggests specific heraldry rather than the more general border motif above. They may have come from a coat of arms and the most obvious would be those of England after c.1340, when Edward III 'adopted both the style and the arms of the kings of France, which he quartered with the lions of England' (Friar 1987, 358). Only five fragments, possibly six, of heraldic beasts have been identified: a semi-complete animal (*353*), a paw (*354*), three limb fragments (*356–8*) and part of a mouth (*355*). Three limbs and one paw are all probably from lions. These are all painted in reserve on various depths of yellow stain. The legs and paws could have come from lions rampant, passant or salient. Two have line frames, *354–5*, and all are drawn to a similar scale which would not be incompatible with the double fleur-de-lys described above. The mouth, however, cannot belong to a lion from the arms of England because the face is not frontal (for passant guardant). On the other hand, golden lions and fleurs-de-lys appear in borders of panels in York Minster from c.1320 and in the west wall glazing (e.g. wI 8e–11e), alternating with ruby squares patterned in reserve with elongated quatrefoils set in lozenges (O'Connor and Haselock 1977, pls.112, 116; French and O'Connor 1987, pl.4, see also detail in pl.20, v).

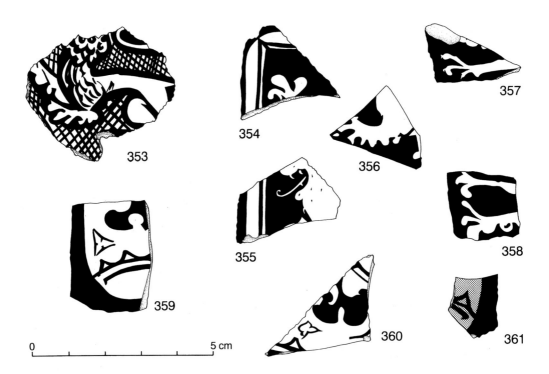

Fig.198   Heraldic decoration. Scale 1:1

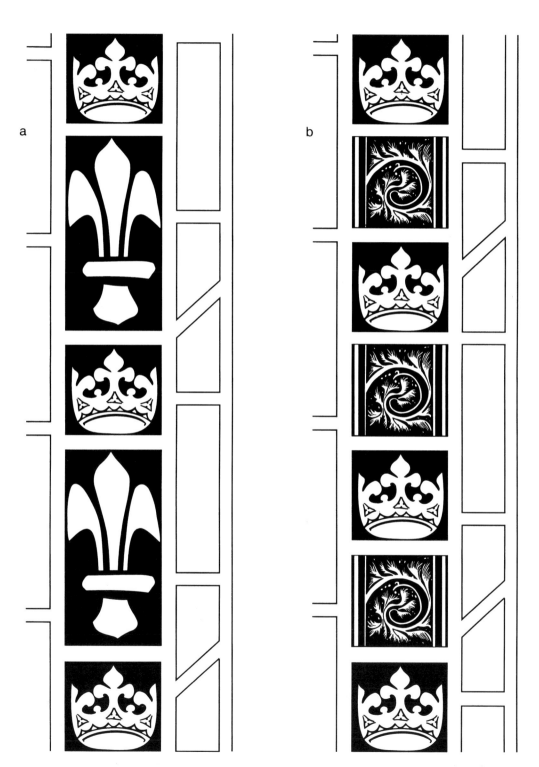

Fig.199   Reconstruction of window borders: a) crown and fleur-de-lys border; b) crown and rinceau *border*

Some fragments of a stylised crown motif may have come from border panes (*359–61*). The different fragments allow the general form and detail of the crown to be reconstructed but give no indication of the width (Fig.199). By analogy with other crown borders, for example, one from Rievaulx Abbey, these may originally have had three upright fleurs-de-

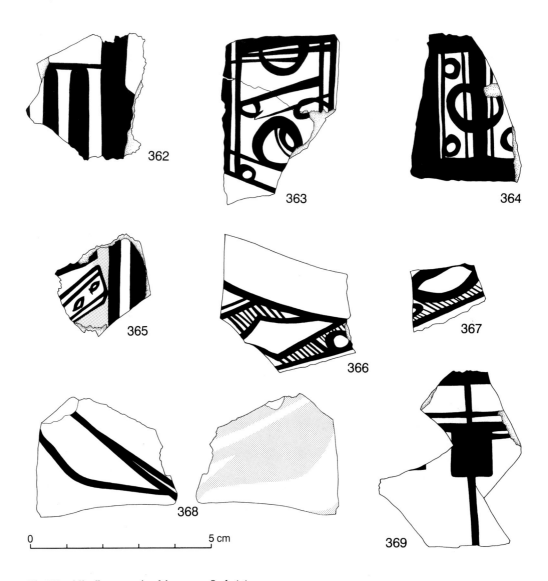

Fig.200   Miscellaneous painted fragments. Scale 1:1

lys. Tripartite crowns appear in the borders of windows in the Minster west wall, alternating with squares of patterned colour (e.g. wI, 8d–11d) (French and O'Connor 1987, pl.4, see also detail in pl.20.1v). The Minster crowns are larger than the Fishergate examples, and the detail of the fillet differs. The perspective effect of the slightly tilted crown has been attempted, by means of shading in a light wash, on the Fishergate examples.

Miscellaneous painted designs (Figs.200–1)

A number of fragments have painted designs which are not recognisable or diagnostic on first inspection. Since some doubt remains as to their ascription, they have been grouped together, but only the most interesting are illustrated and described here. The only fragment which appears to have any trace of an inscription on it is *362*. This probably shows black letter script, used from the 14th century onwards. The letters appear to be in reserve from a painted ground, but are too partial to be read. The second fragment is perhaps a jewelled book cover, showing some of the leaves of the book at the top, and perhaps the thumb of its holder (*363*). The third fragment (*364*) may well show a similarly decorated book binding. Saints were often depicted holding books with decorated covers, symbolic of religious texts. However the absence of an obvious strap and fastening casts some doubt on this identification.

It is likely that *373* and *374* are both variations on architectural canopy gable crockets from the first half of the 14th century; the crocket design is created mainly in reserve from

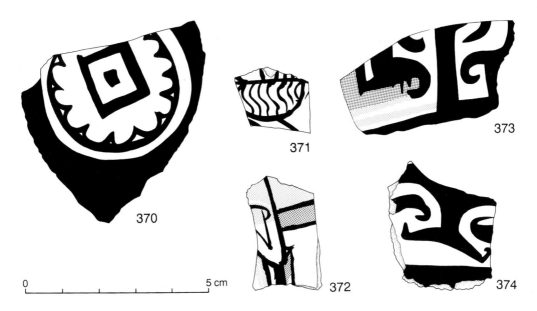

Fig.201   Miscellaneous painted fragments. Scale 1:1

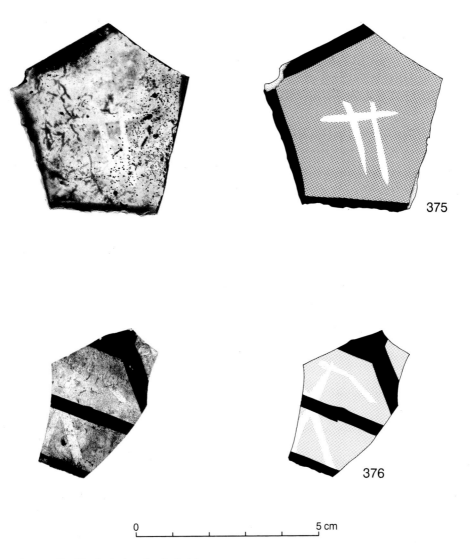

Fig.202   Possible glaziers' marks. Scale 1:1

a matt ground. The partial geometric arrangement of *369* may also be architectural, perhaps some form of crenellation. This is made of very thin glass and probably belongs, with the rest of the 1–2mm thick glass, in the second quarter of the 14th century. Fragment *370* may also originate from an architectural detail. However, it has been grozed carefully to form a shape with convex sides which might suggest a shoe. Figures were sometimes depicted in glass-painting with a decorated shoe peeking out from beneath the hem of their dress or vestment. Often, the saints and even Jesus were depicted with a bare foot appearing from beneath swathes of robe or gown lying in folds against the floor (cf. York Minster west window wI). Even when appearing crowned and in a Coronation of the Virgin scene, Christ might be bare-footed (Psalter of Robert de Lisle, BL Arundel MS 83 Pt.11 fo.134v illustrated in French and O'Connor 1987, pl.31b). In medieval society, people would have been acutely aware of both the social and symbolic distinctions of the shod and the unshod.

There are two fragments which are decorated with a ground of hatching in one direction (*366–7*). This kind of shading was used as a filler for space in the second half of the 14th century and in the 15th century.

Four separate fragments have painted detail which cannot be placed in a wider context: *365*, which may be related to the stem pattern found with naturalistic grisaille of the early 14th century; *371*, which has a semi-circular design filled with wavy lines; *372*, which attempts to show three dimensions and has tentatively been identified as a belt buckle, though this is by no means certain; and *368*, which has a design drawn in outline, with either shading or yellow stain on the reverse. The glass of the last three fragments is consistently thin and smooth. Yellow stain has been used to highlight certain areas of *372*. This piece is most likely to date from the mid 14th to 15th century.

Both *375* and *376* (Fig.202) are partially stipple-shaded, but each also has linear painted decoration. The larger fragment (*375*) has paint on the grozed edges, and a small amount of yellow stain. From each fragment a distinct linear design has been picked out of the stipple-shaded ground. Lines and cross-hatching were picked out of stipple-shaded areas to lighten or emphasise features. An example can be seen above the eyes on a 15th century head of St James the Great, Victoria and Albert Museum (Reyntiens 1977, 63, pl.55). The marks on the Fishergate examples, whilst they could have formed part of some larger design element in a window, seem to be isolated. The similarity between the mark on the second piece, in particular, and some masons' marks on stone, makes it possible that they are a form of glazier's mark.

Colour

Red

There were more fragments of red than any other colour (765cm^2), with a range of tones, the palest of which are discussed below under pink (p.418). The fragments varied in thickness between 1·8 and 4·5mm. There were no pot-metal reds; instead there was definite evidence of 'multi-layering', that is, a number of fine layers of alternating ruby and white glass folded back upon one another (at least 84·5cm^2). Fig.234 (p.535) shows a magnified section through one of these multi-layered reds. This technique was used in the 12th to early 14th centuries, although it is not yet known how the effect was achieved (Newton and Davison 1989, 95). Samples of multi-layered red have been found in nXXX 5a and sXXXVI 3a–5a in the west wall of the nave of York Minster, dating to the 1330s (French and O'Connor 1987, 13, n.4; Spitzer-Aronson 1979, 26–34). Some multi-layered

Fig.203   Range of colours found on glass: a) blue; b) ruby diaper; c) green, fragment with corroded paintwork; d) green with painted foliate (spade) decoration

glasses have the layers alternating throughout the thickness of the glass. The amount of copper present in a homogeneous ruby makes a glass which is too dense to transmit light, but if the colour is prepared in a very dilute form, in order to make a translucent glass, it is naturally non-homogeneous enough to result in a layered effect (ibid., 96). All the Fishergate examples are only multi-layered in half their thickness (between 1·1 and 3·0mm), the other half being white glass, usually with a strong green tint. There are some 12th century glasses like this, but the painting on the drapery of *282* (Fig.189, p.396) can be dated to the 13th century. It has been suggested that the green-tinted part is 'a copper-containing glass which failed to strike during the essential reheating process, or it may be an early attempt at producing a flashed glass' (Newton and Davison 1989, 95).

Flashed glass was developed in the 14th century. A glass which would strike a red colour when reheated would be used as the first gather. A second, colourless gather would be made over this and the normal procedure for cylinder or crown production followed. The flat glass would then be subjected to a second, controlled reheating process during which the glass of the first gather would 'strike' or turn red (ibid.). The thickness of the ruby layers on the flashed glass from Fishergate varies between 0·1 and 1·6mm, and is often congruent with the quality and thinness of the white glass upon which it is set (for example the seaweed *rinceau* from context 2001, 0·1–0·2mm thick).

The condition of the rubies varies from almost opaque (sf6) to translucent but seldom transparent. Some examples have partially corroded to a distinctive opaque, blue-green product, often laminated in section: 78·5cm^2 is known to be ruby, such as sf3609 and sf456. This is no doubt due to the presence of copper. A similar corrosion product can be seen on examples of green pot-metal, however, which will be discussed below (p.418). A glass containing copper will turn blue-green in oxidised conditions.

There were 356·5cm^2 of painted ruby glass. The designs included small foliate roundels, seaweed *rinceaux*, cross diaper, drapery and stickwork border patterns H3 and H16 (Fig.203b). Most of the borders were curved, and c.20mm wide.

Unpainted ruby glass constituted 408·5cm^2. A number of shapes occurred in this colour: rectangular and curved borders, for example sf547, sf425, and spacer shapes, sf456 and sf460.

Blue

There were 535cm^2 of pot-metal blue glass which varied from pale grey-blue to an intense tone (Fig.203a), with a range of thickness from 2·2–5·6mm. Fire-rounded edges from context 2114 proved that the grey-blues and mid-blues were produced by the cylinder method. Many of the deeper blues were free of corrosion, but one piece provided an example of differential corrosion between painted and plain surfaces (Fig.203a). The areas formerly painted have precipitated a greater rate of decay than the unpainted face. Similarly, a piece of drapery (sf2364) has decayed along the strokes of a very fine wash.

There were 213cm^2 of painted blue fragments. These included seaweed *rinceaux,* a circle and lozenge diaper, a semi-circular floral pane, possible architectural detail and drapery. Unpainted glass amounted to 322cm^2, some occurring as rectangular borders, c.20mm wide.

Green

There were 658·5cm^2 of green pot-metal fragments, between 1·3 and 4·7mm in thickness. Although there were some very deep and light tones, the majority were mid-green. Many examples had a powdery, opaque blue-green corrosion product similar to that found on some red glasses (197cm^2). In at least half the cases there could be no mistake that these were green pot-metals as the fragments remained partially translucent. On one fragment, sf9173, the pitting process which characterises potash glass began as concentric circles of this distinctive blue-green colour.

Approximately two-thirds of the green fragments were painted (451cm^2) (Fig.203c–d). The designs included some *rinceau* pattern (D5), but were mostly foliate, including a quarter roundel and some probable background quarries of the early 14th century. Some drapery and border patterns, H1, H4 and H21, occurred on green.

Pink

There was a smaller amount of pink pot-metal glass than any other colour (c.108cm^2). Although the range of thickness was c.1·7–4·3mm, more pieces fell into the thicker category than might have been expected based on the range occupied by other colours. The colour ranged from very pale, greyish-pink to a more robust rose. Some pieces of the greyish-pink verge towards violet in the spectrum, but they should not be confused with the *murrey* used in the 12th century. Few of the painted fragments of pink pot-metal were diagnostic, although there were some architectural pieces, drapery, border patterns and multi-lobate diaper. One piece of pink glass had smear shading in which brush strokes could still be seen (sf111). Only c.27cm^2 of this colour were unpainted.

Yellow (pot-metal)

Only c.388cm^2 of pot-metal yellow glass could be identified (1·4–5·6mm thick). These fragments varied from quite pale to amber, sometimes quite brown in depth (although the onset of corrosion made it difficult to be certain about the colour in some cases). Quite a few diaper patterns occurred on pot-metal yellow, especially the thistle *rinceau.* Some drapery and a cushion capital were amongst the most diagnostic designs painted on this colour. Up to c.56cm^2 were unpainted.

Yellow (stained)

A large proportion of the overall quantity of painted glass had traces of yellow staining (2,315cm^2). Staining appeared on glass with a thickness range between 1·2 and 5·5mm. Although there were one or two examples at the upper end of this range, by far the majority of staining occurred on very thin glass in the range of between 1·2mm and c.2·0mm. The yellow stain was usually used for highlighting rather than self-colour as it was a technique which allowed the glass-painter to put more than one colour on the same piece of glass. It therefore occurs on the details of architectural canopy gables, heraldry, figural painting and the set of fine quarry designs which featured oak leaf, rose and bud forms. Technically, it is often difficult to distinguish traces of yellow stain from thin washes of back-painting on the exterior faces of some fragments once the glass has corroded to an opaque appearance. This seldom had any dating implications, with the exception, perhaps, of designs like the head of Christ on *269–70* (Fig.183, p.389).

Shaped panes of plain glass (Figs.204–6)

There are a number of pieces which can be reconstructed to form recurring geometric shapes.

Variations on the rectangle or lozenge

One of the most frequently occurring shapes is a long rectangle, c.25–35mm in width, with edges at least 65–70mm in length (e.g. *377*). Some of these may have been leaded in unpainted abstract geometric patterns, where the lead lines formed the main compositional interest. Alternatively, they may have formed the unpainted border or glazier's strip which surrounds a window. The case for the former is strengthened by the repeated occurrence of pieces of the same general dimensions, with one or two short ends grozed to a triangular point (e.g. *378, 393–4*). These can be reconstructed in several ways. There are also a number of squares whose sides are the same length as the above (c.70mm; *395*). These can be arranged with the pointed panes as shown in Fig.207 (p.423). A glazing pattern of the latter type was excavated from remains of 18th century Williamsburg in the United States (Davies 1973, 88–90, fig.6), although similar patterns are known in the 16th and 17th centuries, for example, the glazing of the north range first storey window to the bishop's chamber, St William's College, York (Shaw 1848, pl.10). There is one panel of this pattern in the buttery of the Merchant Taylors' Hall in York. The lozenge motif has been found in undecorated ceramic floor tiles from the Cistercian Abbey of Fontenay in France; these were probably part of a geometric pavement (Norton 1983, 82, 84, fig.54). The rectangles with only one end grozed to a triangular point, fewer by comparison, can be reconstructed into slightly varied patterns.

The only apparent variation on the square came from *384*, which has five straight sides. This is a complete quarry. Four such pieces may have been leaded together to form a cross. Such a pattern is capable of being repeated, in at least two variations, to fill an entire window.

Quarries (Figs.204–5)

There are a few pieces of evidence for plain quarry glazing, including two partial triangular panes which may have fitted into the sides of a lattice panel, sf437 and sf4085.

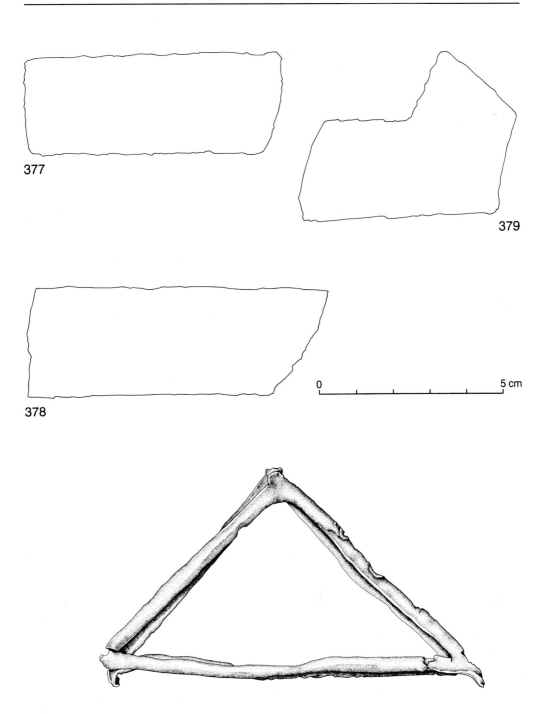

Fig.204   Shaped panes of plain glass and lead came (sf437). Scale 1:1

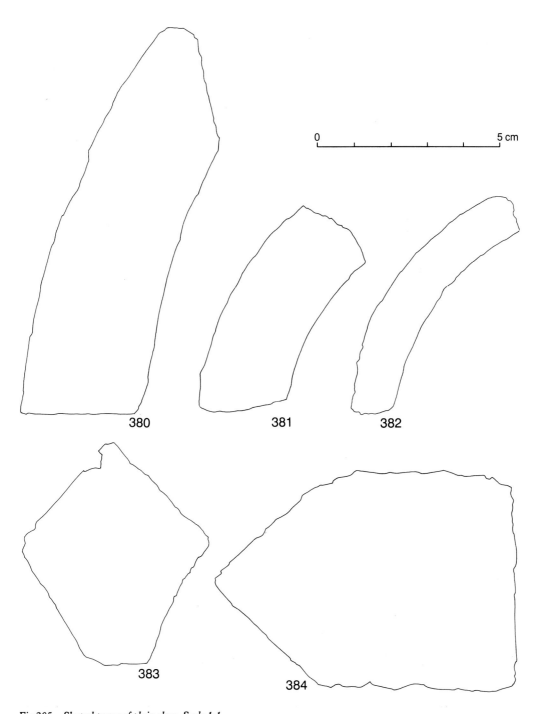

Fig.205   Shaped panes of plain glass. Scale 1:1

The former is still set into a frame of lead cames soldered into a triangle. It should be noted, however, that triangular panes of similar dimensions to the squares referred to above would be needed to fit into the edges of the geometric plain glazing schemes outlined above. The glass of sf437 is markedly finer and smoother than the other examples, with less corrosion and no pitting which would suggest that it is of late medieval date.

Curved shoulders

There are a number of curved panes, either those parts of a border which fit into the curved stonework of an arch-head or cusp, or plain fillets around curved geometrical panels (*380–2*). The former, in particular, may have formed the top or bottom of a vesica.

Angled shoulders

A few pieces of glass incorporate an obtuse angle which may have something to do with the shape of the stonework into which the panels fitted (*379*).

Quadrilaterals with two opposing concave sides

At least two complete panes form a shape with opposing concave sides. The grozing on a number of other fragments suggests a similar shape; two examples are of flashed ruby (*385–6*), the others are opqaue. This is the shape which is formed by the leading of *388* when untwisted, and these panes may have formed part of a border of alternating roundels and spacer shapes (Fig.212, p.428). Similarly, such shapes could have interspersed the

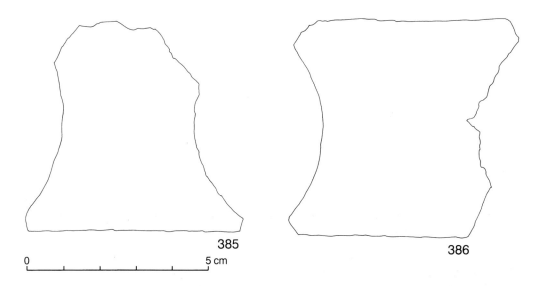

385

386

0   5 cm

Fig.206   Shaped panes of plain glass. Scale 1:1

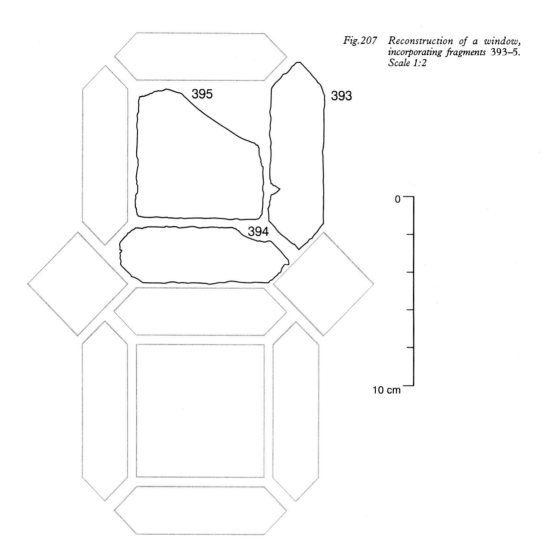

Fig.207   Reconstruction of a window, incorporating fragments 393–5. Scale 1:2

large fleur-de-lys designs painted on oval panes (Fig.199, p.411) as an heraldic border (cf. York Minster vestibule).

Perhaps related to these pieces and their function in spacing roundels are two shapes whose concave sides are not directly opposed but converging (for example, *383*). These echo the shapes found between roundels linked by diamond strapwork (cf. Marks 1987, 529–31, cat.734, dating between c.1220–60, and the central light of the south chancel

Fig.208 *Reconstruction of casement window remains from Nassau Street, Williamsburg, Virginia. Height 48cm.*
© *Colonial Williamsburg Foundation*

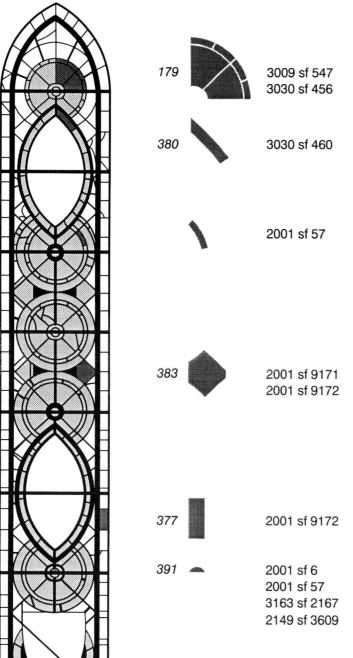

Fig. 209 Conjectural reconstruction of a lancet window, incorporating shaped grisaille and border pieces found at Fishergate. Glass fragments with similar shapes are indicated by catalogue numbers (in italics), and context and sf numbers

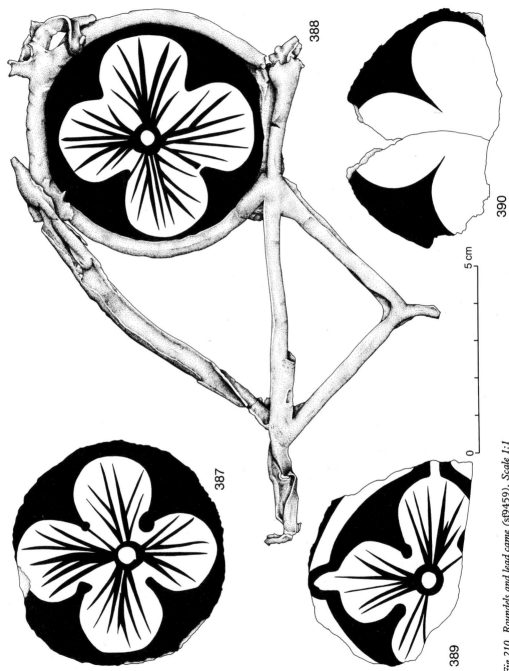

387

388

389

390

5 cm

0

Fig. 210 Roundels and lead came (sf9459). Scale 1:1

grisaille window (sII) of the former Augustinian Priory church at Chetwode, Buckingham-shire, probably c.1260–80). The geometry of the cut-lines for a panel such as Chetwode incorporates several other shapes found at Fishergate, and it is possible that they fitted into a design similar to this (cf. Fig.209).

Roundels (Figs.210–11)

There are two sizes of roundels. The first share the same diameter as that associated with the spacer panes above (*387–90*), c.60–65mm. They have all been painted with quatrefoil flowers restricted to two versions. The remaining roundels appear to be unpainted (sf555.116), but in neither category has colour been identifiable due to the extent of corrosion. This means it is not possible to say whether the roundels and spacers used alternate colours.

The second form of roundels is c.45mm in diameter, and the painting, which is in reserve, is more detailed. Rather than quatrefoil flowers, there are five or six petals, each with radiating stamens (*391–2*). All the examples are opaque due to corrosion.

Leadwork

Theophilus described how to make both iron and wooden bivalve moulds, with longitudinal grooves with which to cast H-sectioned cames (Dodwell 1961, 53–6). Chalk moulds and their cast products have both been found in 14th century contexts in the excavations at St Denis, Paris. When the came had been cast, the excess casting material, and the inevitable ridge where the two halves of the mould met, would be cut off manually with a knife. This means that the sides of lead cames are often irregular and one can sometimes identify the flat facets of the knife cuts. Conversely, a came found amongst destruction level deposits at Chelmsford Dominican Priory had tapered, triangular-shaped flanges, and, although it has been suggested that this is a distinct form of came, it is perhaps simply one whose casting ridge and flange have not been cut off (Drury 1974, 59, 62,

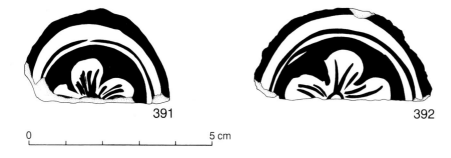

391   392

0 _____ 5 cm

Fig.211   Roundels. Scale 1:1

*Fig.212   Reconstruction of border of alternating
roundels and spacer shapes, based on
fragments 385–9 found at Fishergate*

fig.11.31). Cames with a convex profile are also known to have been used in the medieval period (Gibson 1989, 257). The long sides of the came are termed the *leaves*, whilst the cross-bar is called the *core*. It seems that no lead cames yet recovered from Dissolution deposits or medieval contexts have been milled.

N.S.H. Rogers contributes the following report on the lead came assemblage from 46–54 Fishergate.

A total of 154 fragments of lead alloy window cames were recovered from the site. Of these, only 29 fragments (17·9%) came from pre-Dissolution levels. The recovered cames undoubtedly represent a tiny fraction of the original amount used in the construction of the windows of the priory, as the vast majority would have been melted down during the priory's destruction.

The cames, which were cast in moulds, have the usual H-shaped section, although some are longitudinally split, either partially (e.g. sf1263) or completely (e.g. sf2494). Casting ridges along the sides of the cames were usually trimmed off, but are sometimes visible as on the twisted fragment sf4062. Although window glass of varying thicknesses was used in the windows of the priory, all the cames appear to have been cast with channel widths of 4–5mm; this apparent discrepancy was also recognised at Lurk Lane, Beverley (Foreman 1991, 158). The widths across the sides of leaves of the cames are variable, however, ranging from a minimum of 3·4mm up to a maximum of 5·8mm; it seems probable that the broader cames were designed to appear more prominently than the narrower examples in the design of the window. Several fragments retain traces of solder, used to attach them to linking cames, and occasionally the shape of a quarry is indicated by cames which are still joined (e.g. sf2076). The function of a small lead nail attached to came fragment sf2966 is uncertain.

Both lead strips and lengths of copper wire are known to have been used as ties to attach completed window panels to the iron window bars or saddle-bars which supported them (Archer 1985, 9; Brown and O'Connor 1991, 64; Gibson 1989, 264). It has been suggested that longitudinally split cames may have been used as lead ties (Axworthy Rutter 1990, 119), but the clear evidence of the dismantling of the windows of St Andrew's Priory indicates that the split cames recovered at 46–54 Fishergate most likely derive from this process of destruction. Small fragments of copper wire which were also found may have acted as ties.

As Table 7 shows, just over 50% of the cames derived from Period 7a contexts, all but four fragments being found in deposits of Phases 225 or 331. Phase 225 represents the robbing of the south range of the priory complex, which included the church, and 331 the demolition of the eastern range, which contained the chapter house and dorter. These concentrations of discarded cames may be compared to those of the window glass, which was also found in large quantities in Phase 225. These concentrations are most likely the result of the collection of the windows which had been taken down and removed to areas where the process of removing the lead from the glass was undertaken. A huge dump containing over 10,000 fragments of window glass but no window cames was found in Dissolution levels in the centre of the church (p.439), and is indicative of this process of separation.

There is no independent way of dating the cames, but their size, especially the narrow leaf and fine section, may indicate a degree of wear rather than the exact dimensions at the time of production. As the life of a lead came in a functioning window is somewhere in the

Table 7   Quantification of lead came fragments by period and phase. For list of phases see pp.559–60

Period	Phase	Number of Fragments
6a	319	1
6b	323	2
6c	216	1
	519	3
6d	327	1
6e	130	18
	131	
7a	137	1
	225	44
	329	1
	331	31
	442	1
	443	1
7b	444	1
7c	804	13
	806	5
8	226	1
	333	9
	527	8
10	335	1
11	021	1
	228	7
	336	1
	449	1
	609	1

region of 100–150 years, it would seem very unlikely that many cames from the original period of glazing (Period 6a) would have survived until the Dissolution. On the other hand, cames are found in deposits relating to all periods of activity except Period 6f. However, the 'notorious poverty' into which St Andrew's fell in the later medieval period may have prevented the chapter from contracting major releading operations. If this were the case, the earliest leads one might expect to have survived amongst the Period 7 demolition debris would be those of the 14th century (pp.432–5). Much of the glass which can be dated to before the 1320s/40s at Fishergate is thicker than 3mm; a great deal of the 14th century glass is quite thin, usually c.2mm or less. Lead stains can be observed on much of the material. On the thicker glass there can be an overlap of c.5–8mm, but on the thinner glass the lead stains are very close to the edge, as little as 2mm.

There is no way of establishing whether the thinner cames related to the thinner glass. Since the average size of the core of both types is 4–5mm a distinction between thick and thin leads for different thicknesses of glass seems unlikely. It is more probable that the thick cames were used for major lead lines, and that the thinner ones were for subsidiary leads which the glazier did not want to obtrude into the overall design of the glass panel. The difference in size would then be one of aesthetics rather than date or type of glass.

Distribution of the glass by period and phase

Window glass was recovered from occupation Periods 6a–d, 6z, and from demolition Periods 7a–c. All post-priory periods produced residual window glass. The distribution patterns may be used to determine whether there are concentrations of types in particular areas of the site, or in particular periods, or whether all deposits are equally varied. The type and condition of associated artefacts in each deposit are considered for any additional information they might reveal regarding the nature of the deposits, or circumstances of deposition. A list of all phases containing window glass appears on pp.559–60.

Period 6a: The original priory (1195–late 13th century)

Only 74cm^2 of glass came from layers associated with the building of the priory, and none of the contexts were within the area of the priory church. The only diagnostic designs were some grisaille (6cm^2) and a border design (6cm^2) which could have come from grisaille. Plain, unpainted glass (26cm^2) probably came from diamond quarries or triangular panes, although in some cases square panes are just as likely. These pieces all came from the fill of a circular post-hole (context 3283; Phase 319) for scaffolding connected with the construction of the northern corner of the eastern cloister alley (passage K, Fig.166, p.363). Some twisted lead came which shows signs of possible burning and several iron nails came from the same post-hole. Unpainted glass was found in a dump deposit in the north cloister alley (passage J), part of the dump of soil in both northern and eastern ranges to create a platform for the construction of the priory (context 4694; Phase 410). This dump also contained fragments of iron bar and lead alloy run-off. A tiny amount of unpainted glass was found outside the chapter house, in a grave fill deposit to the south of the eastern cloister alley (context 3236; Phase 321). The fill was associated with the first phase of use of the cloister, and included pottery dated between the 11th–12th centuries.

There was one fragment of unpainted glass from a building construction deposit of mortar and pebbles associated with the foundation for the east wall of the dormitory (context 4432; Phase 413). The dump included much iron slag, three lengths of square- and rectangular-sectioned iron bar, a collar with iron rod or peg, copper alloy and iron pins or strips, iron nails, clench bolts, an iron hook, some lead run-off and broken oyster shell. Some of this may have been waste from building operations, including the installation of window panels. The iron bar may be a window saddle-bar. We have no indication of how much of the window production process was carried out in a glazier's workshop off-site or how much would have to be done on the site in this particular instance. One might assume that there would be inevitable last minute alterations to be made during installation.

The assemblage from the cloister alley may have been trample or scraps from the general building operations; none the less, together with the dormitory find, they may suggest that there was some glazing in the surrounding cloister buildings (north and east ranges), rather than just the church and chapter house. No figural representations, drapery, animals or any architectural detail from which one might infer such imagery were found in Period 6a contexts.

Period 6b: First modifications to the priory (late 13th–early 14th century)

The first glass associated with the church came from the south side of the nave in Period 6b. A grave fill (context 2162, Burial 2163; Phase 215) produced one fragment ($3.5cm^2$) of a rectangular or diamond quarry, along with several nails, lumps of slag, flint, iron sheet and pottery dating up to the 12th/13th century. A second grave slightly to the west could have related to either Period 6b or 6c (context 2092, Burial 2090; Phase 220). The grave contained one tiny fragment of unpainted glass, with nails, a padlock and a fragment of floor tile which has been dated to 1350 or after and suggests either that the context is insecurely dated, or that some of the contents are intrusive (J. Stopford, p.299, *AY* 11/2). The pottery from this context dated from the 10th–13th/14th centuries. The condition of the glass in both contexts is compatible with the earliest painted material from the site.

Redeposited waste in the east cloister alley (context 3194; Phase 322) produced plain rectangular border fragments ($31cm^2$) and undiagnostic glass ($179cm^2$). The floor was associated with the phase of reconstruction of the west wall of the eastern cloister walk. Amongst the other finds from this context were a lead alloy point, dated to the 12th–15th century, and a short-cross penny of Henry II (1180–9), lead alloy run-off, copper alloy casting waste and slag. A levelling deposit in the north cloister alley (context 4053; Phase 417) contained unpainted glass ($1.5cm^2$) with iron nails and pottery from the 13th–14th centuries. The context may be associated with the rebuilding of the cloister alleys.

The total amount of glass recovered from this period was $216cm^2$.

Period 6c: Major reconstruction of the priory (early–mid 14th century) (Fig.213)

This period was characterised by major construction works affecting the east range and the church. It produced $540cm^2$ of window glass, the largest quantity of any period preceding the Dissolution of the priory. Three levelling deposits, possibly for a floor in the

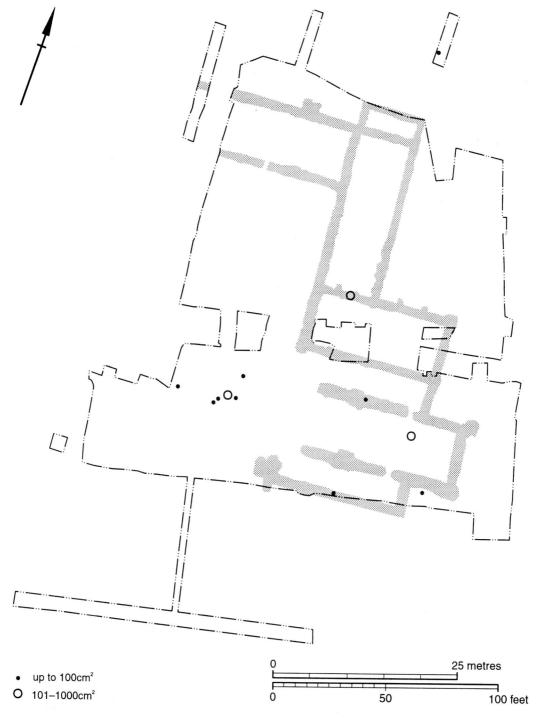

- • up to 100cm²
- O 101–1000cm²

0   25 metres

0   50   100 feet

Fig.213   Distribution of Period 6c glass by context plotted against the outline of the Period 6a priory. Scale 1:500

eastern-central part of the nave, relate to the phase in which the church was completely rebuilt (contexts 2155, 2158, 2166; Phase 216). They contained grisaille (20cm^2), plain rectangular border (10cm^2), small painted fragments (16cm^2) and unpainted glass (119cm^2), together with an iron feather or wedge, an iron bar of subrectangular section, window came, slag, floor tile, iron nails and ceramics dating up to the 11th/12th century. A charnel pit fill (context 2202 in pit 2203; Phase 216) which held one small fragment (1cm^2) also related to this episode.

Two grave fills in the nave (context 2015, Burial 2157; context 2113, Burial 2123; Phase 217) produced a fragment of grisaille (2cm^2), unpainted glass (10cm^2) and undiagnostic painted glass (4·5cm^2), slag, a large quantity of iron nails and fragments of floor tile and pottery dating up to the 11th/12th century.

Four contexts were associated with the robbed out foundations of the eastern arm of the Period 6a church which was demolished in Period 6c (Phase 519). A small amount of grisaille (2cm^2) was found in the sandy deposit from the robbed south transept chapel southern wall (context 5103), with some glassy waste and an iron drill bit. Further to the east, a deposit from the robbed presbytery wall trench (context 5113) contained grisaille (4cm^2), many nails, a fragment of lead alloy sheet and a short length of subrectangular-section iron bar. A demolition deposit within the east end (context 5131) contained a fragment painted with wavy lines which may represent hair or drapery (6cm^2), undiagnostic painted (93cm^2) and unpainted (118cm^2) fragments. This was the largest amount of glass yielded by a single Period 6c context (217cm^2). Most of the painted and unpainted glass is thin (c.2mm), with some finer fragments. Although all the pieces are small, some could be architectural, including some gadrooned detail such as is found on canopy gables (cf. *129*). The shading on most of these thin fragments compares with late 13th/early 14th century material. The same deposit produced medieval iron tongs, lead alloy sheet, some twisted lead came, split longitudinally, and pottery dating up to the 13th/14th century. The mortar and clay fill of a pit cut around the widened foundation raft for the north-eastern crossing pier/respond (context 5110) contained unpainted glass (3cm^2).

In the east range, the eastern and northern walls of the dormitory were rebuilt, and there were associated internal modifications. The mortar and loam fill of the robbed out south wall of the dormitory range, which formed the north wall of the chapter house vestibule (context 3174; Phase 325), contained grisaille (41·5cm^2), a border pattern of simple beading which could have come from the same grisaille (8cm^2), a single nail and some lumps of painted plaster. A piece of small-scale drapery with vermicular folds and highlighted with yellow stain came from this context, but may date to the late 1330s or after (*280*, Fig.189; see p.396). There was a further 76·5cm^2 of undiagnostic glass, although 5cm^2 was of the same transparent quality as some of the early 14th century glass found in context 5131, and elsewhere, and with similar paintwork.

At almost the northernmost extreme of the excavated area (Area 4e; Fig.213, p.433), close to the boundary wall, a dump deposit (context 4103; Phase 486) contained plain glass (2cm^2) and pottery dating from the 11th to the 14th century.

Period 6c produced at least 69.5cm^2 of identifiable grisaille, but it is probable that much of the remaining painted and unpainted material derived from grisaille, having similar thickness, corrosion patterns and grozing. By contrast, the thinner glass from context 3174 tends to be flatter, more transparent and with finer grozing. The only piece which stands out is a fragment depicting a drapery fold from context 3174.

Period 6d: Further modifications to the priory (late 14th–15th century)

Period 6d only produced 48.5cm^2 of window glass. A mortar and charcoal deposit in the rebuilt nave (context 2120; Phase 222) produced a 14th century border pattern (4.5cm^2) and unpainted glass (13cm^2). Some iron nails and an angle tie were the only finds from this floor which suggest debris from alterations to the fabric or furnishings, and the context was associated with the possible erection of screens within the church. A levelling deposit to the east of this (context 2304; Phase 222) contained painted glass (3cm^2), and a fragment from a glass vessel which had been grozed for re-use in glazing (sf5800, *AY* 17/15, in prep.). Nails, slag, a hone stone, an iron bar of subrectangular section with squared ends, a fragment of floor tile and pottery dating up to the 14th century were also found.

A plain rectangular border (10cm^2) and a small quantity of both painted and unpainted glass (6.5cm^2 and 6cm^2) were associated with the dry limestone wall which ran across the dormitory range (contexts 3181, 3200; Phase 327) and its foundation trench. This was possibly a low sleeper wall for a timber superstructure. A post-hole fill in the north range (context 4530; Phase 432) contained unpainted glass (5.5cm^2). The filling of the post-hole was associated with the dismantling of a scaffold platform and the removal of a possible laver. There was no grisaille recovered from this period.

All the glass could have been residual from the rebuilding or reglazing of the nave in Period 6c, although both contexts 2120 and 2304 were associated with minor construction works in Period 6d. Together, Periods 6c and 6d contain c.589cm^2 of window glass.

Period 6e: Continued use and modifications of the priory (15th–16th century)

The only window glass from this period (114cm^2 in total) came from a lined pit (1387) immediately to the east of the porch on the south of the church, possibly a cess pit (see also pp.203–5, *AY* 11/2). Part of the fill and abandonment deposits (contexts 1385, 1386; Phases 131, 130) were probably demolition dumps of silty rubbish, which contained 13th century grisaille (11cm^2), a piece of quarry design c.1300 (4cm^2), some early 14th century oak leaf grisaille (5cm^2), a piece of wing and figural glass (9cm^2), some border pattern (1.5cm^2), plain border pane (9cm^2) and painted and unpainted fragments (18·5 and 56cm^2). The same dump also contained soldered window came (sfs2175, 2237, 2327), wall plaster, an angle tie, a wedge or feather, lead and copper alloy sheet with off-cuts (sfs3785, 9332), mortar, lead run-off, a fired clay crucible and a fragment of glazed floor tile (*AY* 17/15, in prep.). The grouping of nails, hinge and hinge-pivot, hasp, latch rest, iron lock bolt and staple, and decorated 15th century key, must represent almost the entire fittings of a door (ibid.; p.203, *AY* 11/2). The soil of this deposit included mortar and charcoal. Glass from context 1385 has been heat distorted and the surface is matted, black and granular as if left in ash or embers. The lead run-off and fired clay crucible may also be evidence of destructive burning. As the pit was so close to the south porch, one can envisage the south door of the church having been taken down and stripped or burnt in the nearest open space outside the porch. When the fire died out, the charcoal residue together with the iron fittings would have been scraped up and dumped. From this implied proximity of source and dump one might reasonably infer that the window glass and other building materials also came from the nave.

Period 6f: Final modifications in the north range (16th century)

Two fragments of unpainted glass (7cm^2) were found in the fill of a post-hole near the east wall of the north range (context 4402). This related to the repartitioning of the eastern chamber of the refectory (Phase 439).

Period 6z: Period 6 traces not linked with 6a–f (13th–16th century)

An edge piece from either some early 14th century oak leaf grisaille or a thick 14th/15th century border design was found in the fill of a grave to the east of the east range (30cm^2, context 10007; Phase 022), with pottery dating up to the 14th century. A charnel pit to the south of the church contained a plain curved pane (18cm^2, context 1468; Phase 132). This period accounts for only 21cm^2 of glass altogether.

Period 7a: Demolition of the priory (c.1538) (Fig.214)

Period 7a represents demolition activity associated with the Dissolution of the Gilbertine priory in 1538 and after. Contexts yielding glass were, with one exception, found closely associated with the church and east range. The total amount of glass from Period 7a was 45,350cm^2. Since the total from all other periods excluding 7a was only 5,568cm^2 this is a striking figure. The point is even more significant when it is realised that the combined periods preceding Period 7a only produced c.1,022cm^2 and that the remaining c.4,546cm^2 must be in part attributable to the dispersal of glass after the main episode of destruction in Period 7a.

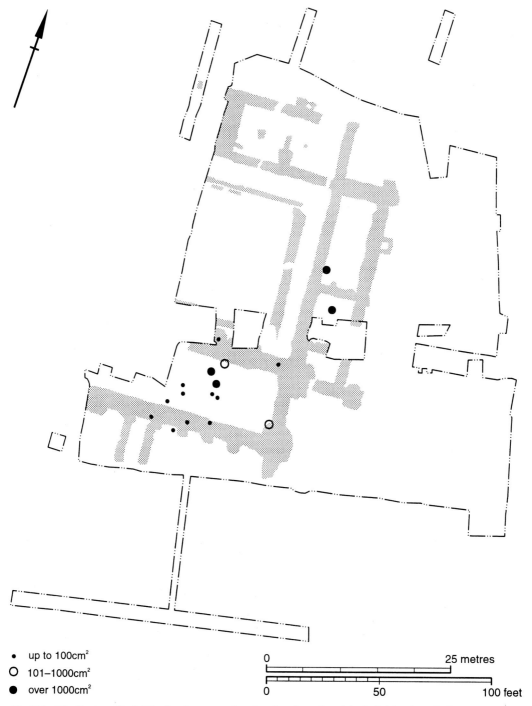

- •   up to 100cm²
- ○   101–1000cm²
- ●   over 1000cm²

0   25 metres

0   50   100 feet

Fig.214   Distribution of Period 7a glass by context plotted against the outline of the Period 6c priory. Scale 1:500

The church

Most of the contexts in and around the church which contained glass were large spreads of demolition material and very few discrete dumps of glass were found which might be related to specific windows.

Contexts 2005, 2029, 2050, 2061–63 (Phase 225) were all part of a spread of material from the mortary rubble backfill of robber trenches in the church (Fig.214). In the eastern-central part of the church grisaille ($18.5cm^2$), a plain rectangular border pane ($13cm^2$) and unpainted glass ($12cm^2$) were found with fragments of floor and ridge tile (context 2005). Unpainted glass ($13cm^2$), probably from a rectangular border pane, was found to the south of the church, together with slag and floor tile (context 2050). Grisaille ($34cm^2$) was found slightly to the east of this (context 2061), and iron bars of both rectangular and sub-circular section, nails, a wedge, a quantity of floor tile, wall plaster painted with red masonry pattern and a twisted lead alloy offcut were found throughout the same deposit. In the south-east of the church $216.5cm^2$ of glass was found (context 2062). Over half of this is homogeneous thin glass (average thickness c.2mm or less), transparent with smear shading and fine grozing. There is a merlon with cross arrow-slit and some attempt at three-dimensional representation, and three fragments of probable column capital or base. Many of the painted fragments, although not identifiable in themselves, are similar enough to these details to be from architectural designs. This glass is of the same quality and thickness as some fragments of oak leaf and acorn quarries, painted in fine outline. A fleur-de-lys decorated apex of a thin quarry, some foliage (sf3433) and the possible glazier's mark with yellow stain are all probably contemporary with this material in the mid 14th century. The same deposit, however, produced a small amount of grisaille ($15.5cm^2$), although only one fragment had a characteristic trefoil head ($4cm^2$). Lead window came, floor tile, wall plaster, an angle tie, iron slag, nails and a fragment of post-medieval glass vessel accompanied the window glass.

To the north, $274.5cm^2$ of glass lay in mortary rubble, with floor tile, window came, nails and lead run-off (context 2063). The glass included 13th century grisaille and an edge from a grisaille quarry of c.1300; the remainder was mainly plain or unpainted, of similar thickness and quality to the grisaille. There were two fragments comparable to the thin early–mid 14th century glass.

Contexts 2071, 2075, 2078–80 and 2082–3 (Phase 225) constituted a robbing-derived trample of silt and sand, with mortar and charcoal inclusions which covered a wide area in the centre of the church. Only $60cm^2$ of window glass came from these contexts, mostly unpainted ($25m^2$; contexts 2079, 2082), grisaille ($15cm^2$; contexts 2075, 2082), a fragment of plain curved shoulder ($5cm^2$, context 2083), some green pot-metal ($1.5cm^2$, context 2083) and painted white glass ($5.5cm^2$, context 2078). The trample also included iron slag, a large amount of floor tile, an offcut from lead alloy sheet and lead window came.

One of the largest glass assemblages (17,049·5cm^2) was a demolition deposit spread across the eastern-central part of the church (context 2001; Phase 225). Unlike most of the other Dissolution debris, glass made up the bulk of the dump, mixed with window cames, lead alloy run-off and sheet offcuts, floor tile and nails. It was associated with a sandy silt deposit with mortar and charcoal inclusions (context 2114; Phase 225). There were 691cm^2 of 13th century grisaille from context 2001. Amongst the pieces of thin 14th century glass was a small-scale canopy which joins a fragment from context 2114 slightly to the west (*302*). Out of the white, unpainted glass, 2,960cm^2 at least was translucent blue-green in tint. Thin glass made up 1,049cm^2 of the total from this context.

Only one fragment of plain rectangular border pane was found in the demolition deposit of limestone and mortar in the western interior of the church (context 6060; Phase 225).

There were four instances where glass may have been located close to the actual window from which it came, but none of these proved informative as to the nature of those windows. Such is the case of 20cm^2 which was found against the south wall of the church, between the third and fourth buttresses from the east (context 1448; Phase 137). Unfortunately, this glass is completely undiagnostic of date or type of decoration. Other deposits in this category included a fragment (1·5cm^2) of unpainted glass which was found at the east end of the north wall of the church, in robbing trample (context 2084). Unpainted glass was found in a demolition deposit of sandy silt and a robbing deposit of mortar with limestone and cobbles, both in the fill of the robbed out second buttress from the east on the north wall (contexts 3532, 3538). To the south of the church, some pot-metal green painted with a foliate design was found in a backfill deposit between the first and second buttresses from the east (context 1395; Phase 137).

Three fragments of unpainted glass were found in the robbed deposit associated with a southern porch (context 6051; Phase 137; see pp.435–6, Period 6e). Another backfill deposit to the west of the south porch produced a small quantity of plain glass, together with a chisel, lead alloy strip and nails (context 1384; Plase 137). Although such robbing deposits and backfills cannot be associated directly with the porch, it may be that the porch had small windows to the east and west which were glazed with plain, unpainted glass.

East range

Two of the largest dumps of glass in this period occurred between the room which replaced (and was partially built out of) the north transept/aisle of the church, and Room E, which had been the chapter house in the original priory (contexts 3163 and 3180, in particular; Phase 331). These dumps contained a large proportion of 13th century grisaille, as well as a large proportion of the figural glass of the early 14th century and designs which must, by analogy, have accompanied this figural glass. Indeed, some of the most diagnostic figural glass of the early 14th century came from these deposits in the south end of the east range, such as the head of Christ which possibly came from a Passion scene (*269–70*), the figure of the Christ Child in the

Virgin's arms (*268*) and at least two other human heads (*260, 265*) (Figs.182–3, pp.388–9). Context 3163 included at least four human heads (*261, 263–5*). One of these heads (*265*) joins a fragment from context 3180. Deposits of glass in the southern end of the east range make up 12,315cm^2 of the total from this period (45,350cm^2). This is slightly over a quarter (27%) of the total from this period. By contrast, the glass associated with the north end of the east range was sparse and either 13th century grisaille (c.52cm^2) or undiagnostic (6·5cm^2).

The glass deposits in the southern end of the east range included copper alloy mounts and a chisel, nails, slag and floor tile (3050); an awl, nails and painted wall plaster (3118); nails and floor tile from 3143; a late medieval strap-end, painted plaster and a bone comb (3161); window came, painted plaster, various pieces of copper alloy, nails, a padlock key and floor tile (3163); more floor tile from 3180; and lengths of copper wire as well as further nails and floor tile from 3182. The occurrence of the floor tile and painted plaster is consistent with the destruction of the suggested Period 6c replacement for the chapter house. The copper wire may well have been used to tie the leaded glass panels to the iron saddle-bars which supported it, although longitudinally split lead cames or thin lead strip may have been used instead (Archer 1985, 9; Axworthy Rutter 1990, 119; Brown and O'Connor 1991, 64; Gibson 1989, 264).

Period 7b: Demolition of north range (c.1540)

The fill of the eastern end of the robbing cut for the south wall (context 4019; Phase 444), and a demolition deposit at the south-east corner of that range (context 4048; Phase 444), produced one piece of 13th century grisaille (6cm^2 from context 4019), some heavily pitted, painted green pot-metal (Fig.203, p.416), unpainted glass and a plain curved shoulder (*189*, 19·5 and 10cm^2 from context 4048). The eastern end of the robbing cut for the northern wall (context 4448) contained grisaille with a double-headed trefoil (19cm^2) and unpainted glass (4cm^2), and copper alloy wire, although this could be associated with pin making. One small fragment came from a mortar and charcoal backfill deposit in the former garderobe on the northern wall (context 4666; Phase 444), together with slag and nails, some with wood still attached.

Only two demolition deposits within the north range produced glass: context 4016, with foliate or grisaille glass (1cm^2) and a residual jetton of Edward I (1272–1307), and 4023 (Phase 444), with unpainted glass (2cm^2) and a number of objects including window came, bone offcut, copper alloy manufacturing debris and sheet. Although the quantity of glass in these cases is minimal, the presence of lead came signifies former glazing (1·2% of all lead from Periods 6a–7c or 1·5% of all lead from Period 7a–c demolition deposits).

To the east of the north range, the fill of a robbing cut (context 4429; Phase 446) produced 15cm^2 of unpainted glass, floor tile and an iron object with mineralised textile.

Period 7c: Demolition period occupation (second half of the 16th century)

Three backfill deposits (context 8003, Phase 806; contexts 8016, 8023, Phase 804) and a pit cut deposit (context 8024, Phase 804) contained 13th century grisaille (4cm^2), a late 13th/early 14th century leaf design from a border (13cm^2), plain rectangular border panes (8cm^2), thin, unpainted glass (7cm^2) and undiagnostic thick glass (35cm^2). The glass was mixed with a large quantity of iron nails, glass and iron slag, lead alloy run-off, iron, lead and copper alloy sheet and offcuts, several fragments of rectangular- and square-sectioned iron bars, a drill bit, much lead came, angle ties, a staple, a silver cross penny and, in the case of context 8016, much charcoal (*AY* 17/15 in prep.). The pit fill (context 8024) contained similar objects, including iron tools, lead came and lead alloy run-off and thin glass similar to that thought to be of the early–mid 14th century, painted with what may be part of an architectural detail (10cm^2).

The main significance of these groups of material is the quantity of lead came and lead alloy run-off, especially some which appears to have run between stones or wooden boards (sf9298, context 8023). This may indicate that the lead cames were being gathered together and melted down after windows had been dismantled. The amount of lead found in this period was 12·8% of the total lead from Periods 6a–7c, or 15·9% from Periods 7a–c demolition deposits.

Period 8: Post-priory orchards (c.17th–19th centuries)

It must be supposed that the spatial distribution of post-priory window glass finds bears little relation to the origins of the glass. However, there was a distinct cluster of contexts in the area previously occupied by the southernmost room of the east range, in Periods 8 and 10. This accounts for c.2,771·5cm^2 and 127cm^2 respectively. Period 8 may be of interest since the site was given over to use as an orchard, and the glass may have lain in soil relatively undisturbed. The glass present in the Period 8 deposits represented mainly grisaille, other background motifs, border designs, plain shaped glass or undiagnostic fragments; there was only one small fragment from a figure (context 5060, 4cm^2).

Discussion of the Gilbertine glass

The vast majority of the glass was derived, archaeologically, from dumps which must represent the systematic breakage and stripping of priory windows at the time of the Dissolution (Periods 7a–c). The dumps are unlikely to have been created far from the point of installation of the glass, and the relatively limited distribution of deposits therefore suggests, as might be expected, that the painted glass came from the church and the chapter house. The frequent mixture of glass with twisted and torn lead came, as well as lead run-off, implies that the lead was being ripped out in order to recover as much as possible. Indeed, 66% of all the lead from Periods 6a–7c came from the Period 7a deposits, chiefly from the area of the church and south-east cloister structures. The lead was almost certainly being melted down into ingots on site, for ease of transportation off site (cf. ingots found at Rievaulx Abbey; Dunning 1952). This leaves us in rather a curious position *vis à vis* the window glass, for the deposits which remain constitute the archaeology of lead stripping, rather than an immediate reflection of the way in which the windows were dismantled in the first place.

This conclusion has an important implication for the interpretation of the appearance of the priory windows at different points in the institution's history. Had some glass been taken out at the time of the Dissolution as intact panels to be sold for private use, as happened at Rievaulx Abbey (Coppack 1986; cf. p.186, *AY* 11/2)? If so, how representative is what remains of the full programme of glazing in the priory in 1538? Had there been a deliberate theologically Protestant-inspired iconoclastic targeting of the most obvious (and therefore offensive) figural glass? Does the nature of the remaining glass suggest that such a selection process occurred? These are questions to which the general archaeological discussion will return below.

Dissolution deposits are relatively easy to identify; it is less easy to distinguish the pattern of breakage and loss which might result from window installation, or from the perhaps random disintegration or breakage of a leaded window in the course of the use of the building. Perhaps it is because painted window glass has been for so long the preserve of glass art-historians that we do not understand the nature and possible manifestations of such practices and processes. One consideration may be the degree to which monastic inner courts and claustral buildings were kept clean of debris. In dealing with monastic window glass assemblages, one often has to apply retrospective interpretation. As Biddle and Hunter have observed, 'When eventually a window is altered or a building demolished, glass of any previous date, even centuries old, may be incorporated in the demolition deposits' (Biddle and Hunter 1990, 351–2). At Fishergate, for example, the glazing of the original Period 6a priory church has to be inferred from deposits linked to its destruction (Period 6c) and the glazing of the successor church has to be inferred from the deposits linked to its destruction (Periods 7a–c).

The previous points coincide in the consideration of the Period 6a glass assemblage. The glass found in layers associated with the building of the late 12th/early 13th century priory may have come from breakage in the course of installation. Alternatively, and especially since they are not particularly diagnostic in terms of decoration, these may be fragments which relate in some way to another church on or near this site. The existence of a previous church dedicated to St Andrew and documented in Domesday Book has been discussed elsewhere (pp.49–50, *AY* 11/2). The archaeology suggested that there may have been a stone church built in the later 11th/early 12th century (Period 4c; ibid., 89–90). It is thought that this church was probably demolished in the early 14th century (Period 6c) thus releasing a stone of a distinct geology (Millstone Grit) for re-use in the building of the Period 6c Gilbertine priory church (ibid., 122, 180). The possibility that the window glass fragments in Period 6a deposits may have come from late 12th/early 13th century alterations to the late 11th/early 12th century stone church should not be ruled out. On the other hand, some of the lead alloy run-off and fragments of iron bar found in Period 6a may relate to fenestration of the new priory church.

The greatest concentration of glass was found in layers attributed to Periods 7a and thereafter. This means that the next greatest concentration of broken window glass occurred in Period 6c — the period when major changes are detectable in the layout and use of the priory. These included the destruction of the east end of the original church and the chapter house. On the site of the nave of the old church a brand new church was built, on a buttressed rectangular plan, with possible north and south turrets at the east end. These changes have been dated to the early to mid 14th century (pp.161–97, *AY* 11/2). Such a plan and its projected superstructure can be linked to contemporary trends in the architecture of royal, magnate and collegiate chapels following on the example of St Stephen's, Westminster, 1292–1340s (ibid.,181–3). It has been argued that the changes may be attributable, at least in part, to the intervention of Henry Burghersh, bishop of Lincoln, sometime treasurer and chancellor of England who attended Parliament in York in the early 1330s (see p.355; pp.55–6, 190, *AY* 11/2). The majority of the diagnostic fragments of glass from this period can be dated to the early to mid 13th century, and are decorated with trefoil grisaille (c.70cm^2). These fragments, therefore, tell us more about the glazing of the original Period 6a cruciform church than the rebuilt Period 6c church. There are no unequivocally contemporary fragments of figural glass at all from the Period 6c deposits. The only fragment which jars with this picture is a small portion of obviously 14th century drapery, which in its sophistication post-dates most of the early 14th century drapery which has been identified. With this exception, then, the archaeological glass deposits accord with the destruction of the east end of an early to mid 13th century church.

The few pieces of glass recovered from Period 6b seem to have been plain. There are no standards for understanding the likelihood of breakage and loss during small-scale building modifications such as occurred during the late 13th/early 14th centuries at Fishergate. It is noticeable, however, that the greatest quantity from this period came from the east cloister alley, but may have been redeposited waste from the initial glazing of the chapter house.

It is obvious from the contents of the Periods 7a–c destruction deposits that a great deal of 13th century grisaille was deliberately re-used in the early 14th century Period 6c church and south-eastern claustral buildings. The pattern of recovery from the north range and northern corner of the east range may suggest that 13th century grisaille was used here as well; indeed, there is little convincing evidence for later glass here at all. It would not be unusual for old glass to be re-used, especially if it was required to supplement panels of more up-to-date 14th century grisaille in so-called band windows, or to provide a cheap background glass against which later glass could be set. It has been suggested that funds for the ambitious new building programme ran out following the fall from power of the priory's temporary patron Bishop Burghersh of Lincoln (p.193, *AY* 11/2). In straightened circumstances the ready availability of older glazing might have been eagerly seized upon.

The fact that little debris remains from Period 6c relative to the Dissolution deposits may be a reflection of the careful removal of most of the original glazing. It is known from sites like the Dominican Priory at Beverley that older glazing was retained for use in a new cloister (Graves 1996). At Beverley the new cloister was secondary in importance to the original cloister and served buildings like the infirmary. By analogy, the older, 13th century grisaille at Fishergate may have been intended for use in the ranges and buildings furthest from the church, and of lesser importance. Until that point these buildings may only have had plain glazing. One small detail which may support the idea that there were varying qualities of glass across the site, and at different periods in time, is the piece of vessel glass which has been grozed around its edges and which was found in Period 6d (context 2304 sf5800). There seems little reason why such a fragment should be worked on in this way unless it was intended for re-use in a window.

A deliberate iconographical re-use of the older glass may also be considered, however, as the early 14th century re-use of 12th century geometric glazing patterns and original 12th century figural glass in the nave clerestory of York Minster set a contemporary example (cf. Caviness 1973).

The fragments of glass associated with the south porch in the Dissolution period may indicate that this small structure had one or two small glazed windows as may be seen in the 15th century porches of some parish churches. The archaeology suggests that the south porch was built sometime between the late 14th and 15th century.

Finally, from a technical point of view, the occasional occurrence of square-sectioned iron bars amongst the Dissolution debris may be evidence of the saddle-bars which supported leaded glass panels within their stone embrasures. Reference has been made above to the short, twisted lengths of copper wire which may have been used to tie the leaded panels to the cross-bars. Strips of lead, often lead cames which had been split along the length of the central bar of the H-section, may have been used as ties and will be less obvious to detect now amongst the many short, torn and twisted strips of lead.

The implications of the distribution of the glass deposits will be discussed further in relation to the dating and glazing schemes at St Andrew's priory (pp.445–64).

Dating and Glazing Schemes at St Andrew's Priory, York

Introduction

The repertoire of design amongst any collection of excavated glass is an artefact of the recovery patterns rather than wholly representative of the original scheme. By stylistic comparison and analogy with existing medieval glazing schemes, the bulk of the excavated glass from Fishergate can be divided into two major groups and two smaller groups, representing distinct periods and types of glazing. The first of these types (Group 1) represents early to mid 13th century grisaille which featured trefoil designs on a cross-hatched ground. The second of these types is a far smaller group of glass which dates to the second half of the 13th century and includes the first figural glass, probably set on grisaille grounds and possibly under architectural canopies (Group 2). The third type represents glazing from the first half of the 14th century (Group 3) which featured both narrative panels and rows of single figures which were depicted standing beneath architectural canopies. Both forms of this second type of glazing might be set on a ground of grisaille which featured more naturalistic depictions of foliage than the trefoils which characterise the first and earlier type. There is no clear indication of the start of the glazing programme associated with this group; indeed, limited reglazing may have begun around the turn of the century. Smaller amounts of glass represent glazing in the mid 14th/early 15th century (Group 4).

When considering the glazing schemes which may have existed in the Gilbertine priory at different periods in its history any discernible or possible biases in the archaeological distribution of deposits and recovery have to be taken into consideration. At Fishergate, the virtual absence of designs which represent figures, or the narrative scenes associated with figures, of the early to mid 13th century may be significant in the overall interpretation of not only the glazing but the institutional aspirations of the Gilbertines in York at this time. The greater part of the 14th century material from the Period 7a and 7b deposits, however, represents either border patterns or background motifs which would have occupied the space around figures which stood beneath architectural canopies.

In this section the possible glazing schemes will be considered in turn. These are followed by a discussion of the bias of material represented, how that bias may have been created, and what the implications are for the general schemes of glazing which can be suggested for this site.

Early–mid 13th century: glazing of the original priory church and associated buildings (Group 1)

The archaeology of the site revealed that the original Gilbertine church which was built sometime after c.1195 was cruciform in shape, with an aisleless nave and either transepts with eastern chapels, or long aisles on either side of the choir. The presbytery projected beyond the side chapels and would probably have had an arrangement of tall, narrow lancets, probably stepped, as an east window. The priory buildings were arranged around a north cloister. A room interpreted as the chapter house, by analogy with other contemporary monastic arrangements, shared a wall with the north transept/aisle (see Fig.166, p.363). This arrangement may have restricted the amount of glazing possible on the north side of the church. The south side of the church, by contrast, may have been comparatively well lit. There is no evidence to suggest whether the nave was lit by a succession of single lancets, or had a gallery level. It is possible that the nave of Nun Monkton Priory church, North Yorkshire, with lancets running below roof height, gives a useful comparison in scale and architectural embellishment.

The chapter house was a buttressed rectangle, possibly incorporating an ante-chamber, and possibly vaulted. The spacing of the buttresses indicates where the windows may have been in this instance. There is little doubt that the eastern walls of both church and chapter house would have been used to make maximum use of the play of light on the interior spaces: the high altar and presbytery area in the church; the prior's seat and possible lectern in the chapter house. The sparse recovery of glass from the rest of the east and north ranges may indicate little and relatively plain glazing for these claustral buildings. The combined evidence of stonework, floor tile and painted plaster (pp.239–70, 302–7, *AY* 11/2) from across the site, however, suggests that this was a very simply decorated church and priory. The window glass confirms this impression.

General impressions of the glazing of the original priory can be gained from two types of glass within this group (1a and 1b). The first type (Group 1a), and most certainly identifiable, consists of the large body of fragments painted with early to mid 13th century grisaille designs (Figs.168–72). The second type (Group 1b), less certainly identifiable, consists of a number of shaped quarries of unpainted glass (Figs.204–6). It seems most likely that this second group would have been combined with the painted grisaille to create the illusion of overlapping 'planes' of geometric shapes in lancet windows. It is less likely, but nevertheless worth considering, that some elements of Group 1b may have been used in windows where the decoration was made up entirely from a combination of leadwork and shaped, unpainted quarries.

On the basis of stylistic comparison, the trefoil painted grisaille from St Andrew's (Group 1a) can be dated to between c.1225 and 1260, and would have filled lancet windows. Within this group represented by foliage on a cross-hatched ground, the pieces are so fragmented that no definitive interpretation of the original glazing schemes can be given. However, it is perhaps feasible to speculate on a distinction between those which have the remains of quarry or strapwork edging painted on them, and those which do not. The former seem to represent the most often repeated motifs, whereas the latter are more varied. One grisaille pattern from St Andrew's (Fig.168, *174–5*, p.367) may be paralleled in grisaille lancets in Westwell parish church, Kent (Marks 1993, 132, fig.104a), and Lincoln Cathedral (Morgan 1983, 40, figs.C2 and 12). From this we may posit a lattice of diamond or square quarries. Two other shapes (Fig.168, *176–7*, p.367) are similar to panes found in York Minster grisaille (south transept windows sXXXV and sXXVI), dating to between c.1220 and 1241 (Marks 1993, 133, fig.105 left). The York Minster lancets also indicate, however, that quarries both with and without strapwork edging may occur within the same overall composition. The repeated shapes (Fig.169, *179–80*, p.369) must have been leaded into some sort of circular arrangement, again, perhaps like the geometric planes represented in Lincoln grisaille (Marks 1993, 131, fig.102a). On the basis of this comparison, it is possible that the diamond or square quarries already referred to (A1; see p.368) may have formed the border pattern for such a window. A number of circular and semi-circular roundels which are painted with quatrefoil flowers, such as are shown in Figs.210–11 (pp.426–7, particularly *391–2*) may have acted as bosses around which circular arrangements of grisaille were focused. Similarly, edging patterns such as *183* (Fig.170, p.370) and *196* (Fig.172, p.374) may have been located within similar, early 13th century compositions (cf. Marks 1993, 131, fig.102: a, Lincoln Cathedral; b, Salisbury Cathedral; and c, Westminster Abbey).

Those elements of Group 1a grisaille foliage on cross-hatched grounds which do not seem to be confined within strapwork edging may be slightly later in date than the first, although still largely within the first half to mid 13th century. The principal characteristics of these motifs are double heads and crossing stems, such as *182* (Fig.170, p.370), *187* and *188* (Fig.172, p.374). Double heads on thick, curling stems may be seen in the Salisbury Cathedral grisailles recorded by Winston in 1856 (BL Add.35211 AA; Marks 1993, 131. fig.102b). The crossing or twisting stems occur not only in the Salisbury Cathedral designs but in the Five Sisters Window in the north transept of York Minster. The Five Sisters has been dated to c.1250, although intimations of a more naturalistic representation of foliage have been identified within the patterns (Marks 1993, 133). The recurrence of the shape represented by *188* (Fig.171, p.372) is a reminder that this grisaille would have been leaded into formal geometric patterns, although the overall design is now lost to us.

The second collection of glass, which the author considers to have formed part of the original glazing of St Andrew's priory, consists of unpainted fragments grozed into a number of geometric shapes which recur in the assemblage (Fig.204, p.420). These may have been used in the geometric arrangements of circles, vesicas and lozenges which create an illusion of overlapping 'planes' featuring in English grisaille of both the early and late 13th century. Although the fragments of this second group are unpainted, such plain shapes may have formed the boundaries of geometrical panels of quatrefoil-painted grisaille (see Fig.212, p.428).

An alternative use for these repeated and unpainted geometric shapes may have been in windows whose ornamental pattern was formed by the leading. Before considering this possibility, however, it is necessary to consider some of the more utilitarian functions which plain geometric panes might have served. Plain strips of between 20mm and 30mm wide, such as that shown in Fig.204 (e.g. *377*), recur in all periods of glazing as side strips. These were often sacrificial panes which enabled the glazier to remove the painted panels for releading or repairs. Curved versions, such as that shown in Fig.205 (such as *381*), may have been simply the side strips which separated the top of a lancet, cusp or tracery light from the surrounding stonework at the head of a window. The quantity of panes with at least one short edge deliberately grozed at an angle, both straight and curved (Figs.204–5, *378, 380*, pp.420–1), together with a number of recurring, irregular shapes such as *379* and *383* (Figs.204–5), suggest that there may have been a more elaborate use for these panes (Fig.212, p.428).

Few examples of geometric plain glazing remain in England, and Marks (1993, 128–30) has described those which do. Of particular interest here are the patterns which were recorded by Winston at Salisbury Cathedral in 1849 (BL MS Add.35211 AA), which have been dated to between 1220 and 1258, and the similar patterns which survive in York Minster, dating to the late 12th or early 13th century (Marks 1993, 130, fig.101). Indeed, the whole suite of shapes represented in the York Minster designs depicted by Marks can be found amongst the assemblage of unpainted panes from St Andrew's. These geometric forms of glazing have been found in, and on the sites of, monasteries which belonged to the Cistercian religious order, particularly on the Continent and from before c.1200. As Marks has stated, however:

> *There is insufficient evidence to resolve the question as to whether the white monks adopted window designs which were already in current usage or if they were the inventor of these patterns which were subsequently copied in non-Cistercian churches* (Marks 1993, 128).

A variety of vegetal and floral designs are known from Pontigny (Lillich 1984, 219, fig.9.6) and Obazine (Frodl-Kraft 1965, 23, fig.11), both variations on the fleur-de-lys, that is another form of stylised lily, and palmette motifs. Both these designs are formed purely by the shape of the glass panes and the leadwork. Some continental Cistercian window glass designs are composed of interlace, e.g. Eberbach (Germany) (Lillich 1984, 220, fig.9.7; Frodl-Kraft 1965, 21, fig.2); Obazine (France), Heiligenkreuz (Austria), La Bénisson-Dieu (France), Pontigny (France), Marienstatt (Germany), Mussy-sur-Seine (France), Chalons-sur-Marne (France), Newkloster and Haina (both Germany) (Frodl-Kraft 1965, 21–6 *passim*; Zakin 1979 *passim*).

Other more abstract geometric patterns seem to have existed, for example, a box-like arrangement at La Bénisson-Dieu (Lillich 1984, 221, fig.9.8). All three general variations in unpainted window glass design were echoed in floor tile both on the Continent and in England, dating to the period c.1190–1220 (Norton 1983, 1986a; Marks 1986, 213). There are a limited number of individual elements of such designs which are echoed in the shapes of the plain quarries at Fishergate. In the context of the British Isles, geometric glazing designs have been found in very few instances. A late 12th century example exists in the parish church at Brabourne, Kent (Marks 1978, 141). This has affinities with the Cistercian glass at Obazine, dating to c.1176–90 (Marks 1986, 214; Zakin 1979, pl.8). Until the mid 1970s two rows of a repeated fish-scale-like pattern survived at the Cistercian Abbey Dore (sVII; Marks 1986, 214). This can be compared to floor tile patterns found at La Bénisson-Dieu. Similar designs occurred as a painted masonry pattern at Fountains

Abbey, probably 1170s–80s, and in a non-Cistercian clerestory window at Notre Dame de Valere bei Sitton, Switzerland (ibid.). A variation on the box-like pattern was recorded at Salisbury Cathedral by Winston in 1841 (Marks 1987, 141, fig.107). Interlace patterning is even less frequent from the 12th century in England. It was observed in sculptural detail on pier bases and capitals, corbels, imposts and, most significantly for our present concern, on window tracery at the Cistercian abbey church at Kirkstall, near Leeds, West Yorkshire (Irvine 1892).

A series of geometric window designs were created in the nave clerestory of York Minster in the early 14th century. These designs have been discussed in relation to Cistercian precedents of the 12th century (Knowles 1936, 137–57). It is unknown whether the Minster designs were based on patterns which were visible in Yorkshire abbeys in the 14th century but which have been lost to us since the Dissolution, or whether the patterns were influenced by continental designs.

A variation on the circular interlace design to be seen in York Minster occurs within a lancet window at Hastingleigh parish church in Kent (Marks 1993, 138, fig.108 left). An unprovenanced panel of plain interlace glazing is held in a private collection and has been dated to c.1220–60 (Marks 1987, 529, fig.734). A panel of geometrical patterned glazing of unknown provenance has also been reset in Selby Abbey.

The above provide comparanda and analogies for the range of grisailles which may have been used at St Andrew's Gilbertine Priory, York. The evidence for the second form, that is, grisaille where the pattern was made up by the lead lines around selected shapes of glass, is the more limited of the two. What part may such grisailles have played in the glazing of the priory?

The dating of the glass is consistent with the building of the priory in the early part of the 13th century. It has been argued that grisaille may have become a ubiquitous form of glazing from the late 12th century and into the first half of the 13th century in not only the great churches, such as the cathedrals at Salisbury, Lincoln and York, and Westminster Abbey, but in buildings of lesser status as well, as in the parish churches of Hastingleigh, Stockbury and Westwell, Kent, and Stowbardolph, Norfolk (Marks 1993, 132, fig.104, after Winston 1843, 1853 and 1852, BL MS Add.35211 AA, O, K). Excavation on numerous monastic sites has revealed that early 13th century grisaille was used extensively, and that portions were often retained until the Dissolution, such as at Battle Abbey (Kerr 1985), Bayham Abbey (Kerr 1983), Jedburgh Abbey (Graves 1995), Rievaulx Abbey and Newminster Abbey (Northumberand). One reason for this popularity which has been put forward is that the grisaille was cheaper to produce than full coloured windows. Another reason is that the greater use of white glass allowed more light to fall into the interior of the churches, in turn allowing the increasingly complex mouldings and foliage of contemporary architecture to be seen to full effect. The dense colours of earlier glazing schemes would have obscured these effects. Such architectural fragments as were recovered from the original priory at St Andrew's, York, indicate that the church may have had very simple decoration, with little or no use of complex mouldings (pp.226–82, *AY* 11/2). Indeed, the only indication of stiff-leaf embellishment seems to have come from the cloister arcade (ibid., *36*, 134–7). Similarly, the painted wall plaster was restricted and simple in design. So far as we can tell, therefore, the first Gilbertine priory at York was not built to display the new concerns with depth and the play of light in architectural decoration. Indeed, when the simple ornament is considered in conjunction with the excavated plan of the priory church, there is reason to believe that the Gilbertine house at York was the result of deliberately conservative planning (ibid., 125–31). It is possible that the choice of predominantly grisaille glazing in this institution was equally deliberate, serving not only the limited economy of the house, but also a particular aesthetic option. Before considering this further, however, we must consider the alternative interpretation.

There is some evidence from Westminster Abbey, and from lesser churches such as Westwell, Kent, that grisaille windows may have been alternated with historiated, coloured windows. In parish churches and those of modestly and poorly endowed institutions, it is likely that full coloured windows of this period were exceptional (Marks 1993, 137). Instead, on the basis of analogy with extant and recorded glazing, for example at St Denys (RCHMY 5, pl.55 6), and West Horsley, Surrey (Marks 1993, 139, fig.109), it seems most likely that any historiated or figural glass at St Andrew's would have been confined to panels, often simple geometric shapes such as roundels, vesicas, squares or lozenges, and set on backgrounds of grisaille decoration.

The evidence for figural decoration contemporary with the earliest grisaille at St Andrew's is extremely limited and inconclusive in terms of its dating. None of the architectural details (Figs.192–4) need be earlier than the late 13th century. All the drapery fragments which could possibly be early are very fragmented (Figs.189–90, *283–5, 287, 289–90, 292,* pp.396–7). The torso represented by *282* (Fig.189) shows a tunic draped over a belt or girdle. The hooked folds suggest that it is contemporary with many of the fragments shown in Fig.189. Both the depiction of the tunic and the hooked folds can be found in glass and manuscript illumination throughout most of the 13th century, particularly the middle decades. This convention can be seen in the windows of the Trinity Chapel, Canterbury, 1213–20, for instance. It is seldom seen in the last decade of the 13th century, and had disappeared as a convention by c.1320. As discussed above (p.395), the symmetrical arrangement of the drapery suggests a full frontal depiction of the figure from which it came. This might be a standing figure, male or female (but probably not a cleric, since the chasuble would be shown rather than a tunic). The St Andrew's tunic has been painted on multi-layered red or ruby glass (pp.534–5) — a technique which seems to have been used in the 12th and 13th centuries, but which had been superseded by single layer flashing by the 14th century (Spitzer-Aronson 1974, 1976; Newton and Davison 1989, 96). The evidence combines to suggest that there were figures depicted in the priory glass in the 13th century, but the stylistic details cannot be attributed definitively to the first half of the 13th century. It is possible, therefore, that the initial glazing programme for the priory church and chapter house employed little or no figural or historiated glass, but that this was introduced in the mid to second half of the 13th century, at about the time the first alterations to the priory were made in Period 6b (pp.139–49, *AY* 11/2).

The original priory, therefore, undoubtedly had a glazed church and chapter house. The extent of glazing elsewhere is more limited, although one would have expected the refectory to be glazed. The windows would probably have been narrow lancets, with deep splays opening out into the interior of the buildings they lit. The windows would seem to have contained arrangements of predominantly white glass, either painted with trefoil grisaille and leaded into geometric shapes, or with the glass unpainted and the pattern created by the combination of shapes alone. The windows would probably have introduced a uniform tone of light into the interior of the buildings. This glazing would complement a simple architectural form and simple wall and floor surface decoration. In plan, architectural and decorative simplicity, the priory at Fishergate conforms to the ascetic requirements of the Gilbertine Rule (discussed further on pp.503–8).

Mid–late 13th century: modifications to the priory buildings (Group 2)

Minor modifications took place within the church during this period. More substantial work was carried out on the cloisters, including the reconstruction of the walls between the alleys and the cloister garth which had probably been affected by subsidence. Buttresses were erected to support the northern cloister arcade. It can only be conjectured, therefore, that such glazing evidence as there is for this period may simply represent the updating of the glazing of already extant windows, or the modification of single windows.

Stylised grisaille of the second half of the 13th century is only represented by one fragment of glass: (Fig.172, *198*, p.374). The tight-headed trefoil appears on a plain ground, with a cluster of berries. Glass of this sort can be seen as a background to heraldic glass at Stanton St John, Oxfordshire, dating to c.1285–1300, and was recorded at Chartham, Kent, dating to between c.1293–4 and c.1300 (Marks 1993, 148, fig.119, 150, fig.121 after BL MS Add. 35211 K). The heraldic fragments from St Andrew's date from the early 14th century, and would, therefore, seem to be too late to have been used in conjuction with this type of trefoil grisaille. However, there are a number of other fragments which suggest border patterns of naturalistic foliage, perhaps inhabited by birds. Such border patterns may well have accompanied this grisaille.

At least three fragments of glass depict the wing, breast and possible shoulder of birds which may have been located in the borders of grisaille panels of the second half of the 13th century (Fig.191, *294*, *296–7*, p.399). These can be compared with an excavated window from Bradwell Abbey, Buckinghamshire, dated to c.1270 (Kerr 1986). Birds appeared amongst the marginalia of illuminated manuscripts from the late 13th century, and probably influenced the increasing occurrence of birds and other zoomorphic motifs in the borders of windows throughout the first half of the 14th century (see Marks 1993, 153–5). The grisaille which accompanies the Bradwell Abbey border birds is a variation of the type represented by *198* (Fig.172, p.374). See also *S3–4* from Sempringham, p.468, Fig.218.

The leaf pane shown in Fig.180 (*251*, p.385) is not only of the right shape for such a border, but almost exactly parallels borders which were used in the chapter house of York Minster, c.1285–90, in conjunction with oak leaf grisaille (Marks 1993, 147, fig.117, from an etching by John Browne). Oak leaf grisaille, painted within frames of overlapping strapwork, is well represented at St Andrew's (Fig.174, p.377). The combination of border pattern and grisaille seen in the chapter house at York Minster gives one of the best comparisons for date at St Andrew's. Despite this, the quantity of glass which may be dated with confidence to around the same time is limited. Instead, the stylistic traits represent a range of dates from the last decades of the 13th century to c.1300 and into the 1330s (that is, Group 2 or Group 3).

A number of diamond- or square-shaped quarries have plain grounds and feature a single quatrefoil shape in the centre. The edges are painted with strapwork which, when leaded together, would give the impression of an overlapping trellis (Fig.173, p.376). These seem to fall into a stylistic category between the grisaille quarries seen in St Denys, Walmgate, and the quarries which appear behind a Crucifixion in the choir south aisle of Wells Cathedral, c.1310–20 (Marks 1993, 12, fig.8). However, only one variation displays any vestige of a cross-hatched ground to these motifs. This may place them in the mid to second half of the 13th century.

The figural details which might be assigned to this period of glazing in the second half of the 13th century have been referred to already (*282–7*, Fig.189, p.396). To these may be added some of the details from architecture, that is, the column capitals and bases which supported two-dimensional representations of architectural canopies and niches (*319–21*, Fig.194, p.404). These, however, could equally well belong to Group 3.

The extent of reglazing in this period cannot be estimated on current evidence. Where new glazing was installed, it featured a form of grisaille without background cross-hatching, and possibly with the figures of birds in foliage in the margins of the panels. There is no indication as to whether any larger windows were installed to replace earlier lancets. The most significant changes would have been the introduction of figures to the glazing of the church and chapter house. Whereas the amount of light admitted to these buildings may not have changed, the tone would have been affected by the introduction of colour. The ascetic principle of simplicity would have been eroded by these innovations.

Early–mid 14th century: the rebuilt priory church and buildings (Group 3)

The archaeology of the site shows that more or less the entire original early 13th century church was demolished. In its place, and directly on top of the former nave, a new buttressed rectangular chapel was erected. The former chapter house was radically foreshortened and the function of the chapter house may even have been removed to the smaller room created on the footprint of the western half of the former transept/aisle. The east range was re-ordered and possibly given a new façade. The north range, including the presumed refectory, was also re-ordered. The new buttressed rectangle belongs to a class of building whose lineage of form can be traced back to the church of St Etheldreda, Holborn, in London, and the Lady Chapel at Ely, for example. The most significant of models at this time was the Chapel of St Stephen, at Westminster. The plan implies an architectural form associated with court circles and ecclesiastical magnates.

The buttressed church at Fishergate would have provided ample space for a new type of window. Indeed, the tendency in contemporary architecture was to give more and more space over to windows. These would probably have had decorated tracery in the heads, and there would have been space for a large east window. The form of the new church complements the date and type of glass found.

The accumulated evidence for glass of the first half of the 14th century (Group 3) includes architectural canopies and architectural settings (Figs.192–4, pp.401, 403–4), figural detail in the form of heads and facial details, hands and feet, and drapery (Figs.185–9, pp.392–4, 396; *281* on Fig.189 definitely belongs in Group 3, whereas *282–7* could equally well belong in Group 2), background *rinceaux* and diaper patterns (Figs.178–9, pp.382–3), repeated border and edging patterns (Figs.195–7), and oak leaf and acorn grisaille (Fig.174, p.377; Group 2 or Group 3). We cannot know exactly what individual windows looked like, but we can suggest a number of possible combinations. For example, the oak leaf grisaille probably filled panels which were interspersed by coloured, figured or narrative panels — the combination known as 'band' windows. The figural details suggest at least two scenes whose iconography we can reasonably presume. The first is a scene from Christ's Passion (*269–70*, Fig.183, p.389) or possibly a related Last Judgement, and the second is a Virgin and Child (*268*, Fig.183).

What would have been the components of such windows? Firstly, the coloured components will be described, then the architectural settings for figures, the figures themselves, the background patterns which filled the space between the figures and their micro-architectural settings, and finally the borders to these windows. Secondly, the grisaille which provided the bands of light which separated these bands of colour will be described. The discussion will then turn to a fuller iconographic discussion of the windows.

There is evidence for architectural canopies with traceried gables and crockets on the external slopes of the gables. The gables were supported by columns with decorated bases and capitals, and sometimes by buttresses. There are a few fragments depicting crenellations and turrets which may have been combined with the canopies in ascending arrangements, or which may have come from smaller, narrative scenes.

The canopy gables make good use of yellow stain to highlight the detail which has been drawn in stickwork or scratched out of them (Fig.193, p.403). The canopies emulate contemporary architecture in miniature. The architectural column capitals probably only occurred at the sides of a scene, supporting a canopy (*319–21*, Fig.194, p.404; Group 2 or Group 3). The crenellations (*322–3*, Fig.194), which are more likely to belong to Group 3 than Group 2, may have been used to symbolise a town or city, or simply as a device to divide historiated scenes. Stylised crenellations might also be used to set the scene for the sleeping soldiers in a Resurrection narrative (cf. York Minster, west window wI, 8e and 8f; French and O'Connor 1987, pl.11 a and b). Perhaps the scale and form of the St Andrew's merlons are closest to the series of marginal architectural niches which are occupied by busts of, alternately, kings and prophets which made up the jambs and archivolt of a niche surrounding the Virgin and Child in the north aisle west window (nXXX, 2b–3b) of York Minster (French and O'Connor 1987, 72, pls.15b, 22a and c). Such jamb scenes might also account for the small-scale canopy represented by *302* (Fig.192, p.401).

The majority of the figural details can be dated to the first half of the 14th century, notably a collection of eyes, facial details and hair (Fig.182, p.388). Most facial details depict small-scale figures, with their eyes averted to one side or other. This appears to be a convention which drew the eye of the observer to the main figure or significant action of the scene depicted. The attention to detail shown in the buttoned sleeve of *276* (Figs.185–6, pp.392–3) indicates that civilian or secular figures were depicted in contemporary dress. There is very little variation in scale of the figures. The numerous portions of drapery do indicate a greater variation in scale of figures. The only attributes by which saints might have been recognised are two possible books (*363–4*, Fig.200, p.412).

These figures would have been set against backgrounds of richly coloured *rinceaux* and diaper, similar to many examples seen in the nave aisles and west wall of York Minster and in the parish churches of the city. The term 'diaper' is used to describe a woven pattern on fabric consisting of a small repeating design, and the word is used to refer to any similar repeating pattern. Whilst 'diaper' in glass painting has been used to denote repeating patterns, it might be suggested that the patterns themselves may have been intended to imitate contemporary textiles (cf., for example, the late 14th century Italian silk lampas woven cloth illustrated in Crowfoot, Pritchard and Staniland 1992, 118, fig.89). Designs which appeared on silks and imported cloths may have been emulated in glass and their use as backgrounds to figures may have been a way of imputing status and reverence to the subject. By approximating patterns of imported textile, which would normally have been used for dress, in a context comparable to wall hangings, the composition evoked an impossibly rich setting, beyond the resources of earthly rulers, but fitting in a contemporary conception of heavenly mansions.

A number of designs may have been combined in a series of border arrangements at the periphery of windows at St Andrew's priory. The large fleurs-de-lys seem almost certainly to have been border designs, by their size and shape. Heraldic border designs became popular in glass from the late 13th century (e.g. Merton College chapel, York Minster chapter house). Heraldic borders appear in several of the windows of York Minster nave aisles in the first half of the 14th century, most notably in the Heraldic Window (nXXIII), dated to 1307–12 (Marks 1993, 154). The heraldic lions passant guardant represented by fragments at St Andrew's (*353* and probably *356–8*, Fig.198, p.410) may have formed part of heraldic shields, but more probably featured in border arrangements.

Heraldic lions appear in borders in the west wall glazing of York Minster (wI, 56e surrounding the figure of St Paul; see French and O'Connor 1987, pls.8b, 20v) and around the mid 14th century east window Resurrection panel of St Michael-le-Belfrey. The fragments of crown found at St Andrew's can be reconstructed as shown in Fig.199, p.411. The border pattern in Fig.199b has been reconstructed as alternating with samples of the frond *rinceau* found at St Andrew's (cf. *228–30*, Fig.178, p.382). The alternating border arrangement can be compared with that found in the west window of York Minster (wI, 7–9d; French and O'Connor 1987, pls.5b, 20 iv). The fragment which is painted with a shape which may be identified as an architectural column capital or a bell may equally be identified as one half of a covered cup (*320*, Fig.194, p.404). A form of this last design was used in borders, alternating with castles for Eleanor of Castile, in the east window of York Minster nave south aisle (sXXIX), and can also be seen in the borders of the west windows of the nave north and south aisles (nXXX and sXXXVI). The fragments of lion passant guardant alternatively may have been combined with the smaller of the fleurs-de-lys (*351–2*, Fig.197, p.409), in a shield representing the arms of England and France, quartered.

There are fragments which probably came from lions rampant as well (*354–6*, Fig.198, p.410). This combination of heraldic beasts suggests that there may have been panels of armorial shields, and not simply generalised heraldic motifs or badges used in the borders of the windows. Heraldic shields often occurred on grisaille backgrounds in band windows of this period (cf. nave aisles, York Minster). Fishergate lacks, however, the comparatively substantial heraldic evidence of Ellerton Priory (see p.484–95).

We can gain a fairly accurate impression of the grisaille which was used in the early 14th century at St Andrew's. It consisted of oak leaves and acorns on twisting stems, painted with strapwork at the edges of quarries. When leaded together, these would have produced the impression of leaves winding in and out of a form of trellis although not rigidly defined as a diamond quarry trellis. Again, parallels can be drawn with the glazing of the nave aisles of York Minster and the chapter house glass in terms of overall design. It must be stressed, however, that the quality of the Fishergate glass-painting is not as fine as that displayed in the Minster.

The integration of the glass evidence and the rest of the archaeology for this period is intriguing. Firstly, there is the contrast with the original priory. The shape of the new church and the provision of more windows would produce a far lighter interior than that known in the former church with its transepts/aisles and recesses. Here and in the new chapter house the light would have been brightly dappled due to the inclusion of figural panels, with reds, blues and yellow stain being the most prominent colours. There is evidence for a different type of wall painting, again incorporating polychrome (pp.306–7, *AY* 11/2). The find of a gilded lead star (ibid., 307–8, fig.147) in the Dissolution debris of the chapter house implies that the roof there, and possibly in the church, may have been painted blue in imitation of the heavens and powdered with such stars. The glass itself attests figures standing beneath architectural canopies. There may have been a series of these, perhaps echoing in the glass the sort of nichework or panelling produced in stone to decorate the walls between the windows which characterise prestigious late 13th and early 14th century rectangular chapels like St Etheldreda's, Holborn, London (ibid., 181–6). Heraldic emblems may have punctuated the glass, reflecting secular status and feudal hierarchy. This was all quite a different aesthetic from that which the archaeology suggests prevailed in the original priory.

Secondly, there is the seeming contradiction between the ambitious architecture and glazing of the church on the one hand, and the reduced size of the priory overall. Thirdly, there is the quantity of coloured, early 14th century, glazing which occupies the same Dissolution deposits as substantial amounts of early to mid 13th century grisaille. As discussed above, there can be no doubt that the new Period 6c priory buildings re-used a quantity of the older glazing which must have been saved from the first church and chapter house. It has been argued that the answer lies in the fluctuating fortunes of the canons of St Andrew's in the 14th century, and the timely intervention of a powerful patron. Janet Burton has described how the priory was never a rich institution (pp.61–3, *AY* 11/2). At the time that parliament was held in York during the Anglo-Scottish Wars of the 1330s, Henry Burghersh, bishop of Lincoln, donated large sums of money to the canons for the construction of new houses and the repair of others in the close and around the cloisters (see p.355). Burghersh held the offices of treasurer and chancellor of England until his dismissal in 1330; he was re-appointed treasurer in 1334 and remained in that office until his death in 1340. The canons conveyed three plots of land to Burghersh within their close, that he might stay there whenever parliament was held in the city. It has been argued that the form of the new church may have been influenced by the architecture of courtly patronage with which Burghersh would have been familiar. The cost of rebuilding may have been supported, initially, by Burghersh. The mixed glazing types — 13th and 14th century — may reflect the necessity to complete the building after the canons had lost their generous patron.

If this historical documentation provides a plausible context for the 14th century rebuilding at the priory of St Andrew, the archaeology provides some detail with which to consider the everyday environment created within these buildings, and in which the canons worshipped and worked. Only two images from the window glass assemblages can be identified through their iconography. The first is the head of Christ wearing the Crown of Thorns (*269–70*, Fig.183, p.389), the second is the figure of the Christ Child held in the Virgin's arms (*268*, Fig.183). The spatial location of the Dissolution deposits from which these images came suggests that they both originated from the new chapter house. The Fishergate Crown of Thorns is represented by rings (rushes) bound together with ties. The genesis of the Crown of Thorns is the belief that, prior to the Crucifixion, Pilate's soldiers took Christ to the palace, vested Him in purple, placed a twisted wreath of thorns on His head in imitation of Coronation, and made mock obeisance to Him. Medieval depictions of this episode are based on a conflation of accounts in three Gospels (Mark 15: 16–20; Matthew 27: 27–31; John 19: 2–3).

The iconography of the Crucifixion and the instruments of the Passion followed popular devotion. According to Woodforde (1946, 196) depictions of the crucified Christ showed nothing round his head until 1240. In that year the *Corona* or relic of the Crown of Thorns was brought to Paris and housed in the Sainte Chapelle, built by Saint Louis as a reliquary chapel. Horne argued that prior to this a royal diadem might be shown to signify Christ reigning from the Cross (Horne 1935, 49). Until about 1300, however, the Crown of Thorns was represented in art as a fillet or band around Christ's head, probably because the Sainte Chapelle Crown is a band of rushes (Woodforde 1946, 12). Horne notes that the rushes themselves were often depicted, as well as 'the cross or spiral ties, with which the original is bound' (Horne 1935, 49). The loops on the Fishergate glass may represent these binding ties. Woodforde recognised that iconographical changes 'were apt to appear later in painted glass than in some other branches of medieval art', but did not substantiate the claim (Woodforde 1946, n.1). Indeed, Newton has advised against strict adherence to Horne's typology of the Crown, especially his chronology, pointing out early uses of the fillet, and the variations used in the 13th and 14th centuries (Newton 1979, 24). Generally, however, he accepted that the more detailed representations, such as that found at Fishergate, probably do follow the model of the Sainte Chapelle relic, and that 'after 1300 the complete Crown of Thorns with long protruding points is more usual' (ibid.). The figure of Christ in the Crucifixion panel in the east choir window at Wells Cathedral, Somerset, for example, wears a fillet, and can be dated to c.1330 (cf. the fragment illustrated in Winston 1867, 2, pl.28). An excavated 14th century example probably came from Osney or Rewley Abbey, Oxford (Newton and Kerr 1980, 197, fig.37, no.33, EO1). For a Yorkshire parallel, there is a small excavated fragment from Rievaulx Abbey of comparable scale, showing the left side of a head with flowing hair and a very similar crown down to the detail of the binding loops in *269–70* (Fig.141b, p.287, *AY* 11/2).

Matthew Paris' description of the relic, which accompanies his drawings in his *Historia Maior*, clearly indicates thorns projecting from the bound rushes:

Talis est corona domini sicut de tricis cepar(um) et nodus in parte posteriori et est de iunccis marinis habentibus eminentissimos aculeos. ex iiii plectis contorta, coloris subalbi qual(es) solent esse cirpi marcidi. vnde plectentes de plecto vnde dicitur plecta hart (James 1926, 14, pl.XV 72; Corpus Christi, Cambridge MS 16f.139b; Newton 1979).

Of such a kind is the crown of the Lord, as it were of plaits of onions and a knot in the rear part, and it is of marine rushes which have most prominent points, twisted out from four plaits, of a slightly pale colour as marsh rushes are accustomed to be, when they are plaited from a plait whereby it is called a woven withy.

All these features are combined in the Crucifixion panel in the chapter house vestibule of York Minster (C/H nVI 2c). The vestibule was probably glazed shortly after the chapter house glazing was completed, suggesting a date in the late 1280s/early 1290s (O'Connor and Haselock 1977, 341). The Minster depiction is clearly of a better quality than the Fishergate example, but provides a link between the Fishergate or Rievaulx type of crown and the more accurate description of the relic.

The main difference, however, between orthodox Crucifixion iconography and the Fishergate fragment is the position and aspect of the head. The eyes are closed in the more conventional iconography, and the head tilts to one side, often with a three-quarters aspect (see Fig.141c, p.287, *AY* 11/2). This is true not only of the chapter house vestibule Crucifixion, but that in the central tracery light of window nIV, St Denys, Walmgate. The Fishergate depiction, therefore, may indicate some other iconographical reference. It could have come from an isolated devotional image, such as that at Cassington, or a Christ in Majesty, as at Sandford, both Oxfordshire parish churches (Newton 1979). Single roundels featuring heads fill the top tracery lights of St Denys and date to the mid-14th century. Of the known images of Christ in Majesty in York, four appear in the nave windows of York Minster, three dating to c.1320 and one to c.1339. That surmounting window nXXV (D1; c.1320) shows Christ fully robed and bareheaded although the angel to His right carries the Crown of Thorns among other instruments of the Passion (C1) (Davidson and O'Connor 1978, 112). This is drawn like a circlet of leaves rather than strips bound with

Fig.215   Last Judgement, with Christ wearing the Crown of Thorns, from the Huth Psalter (British Library Add. 38116, fo.13v), reproduced by permission of The British Library

ties. A gold and enamel English triptych of c.1350–70 shows a front-facing Christ being crowned with the thorns, although the hands of those placing the wreath on His head are clearly seen (Campbell 1987, 460–1, cat. no.585). Only one image of this Mocking of Christ is known from York, but that dates to the early 15th century (Davidson and O'Connor 1978, 75).

Last Judgement scenes are similar to those of Christ in Majesty in having Christ seated and facing forward. A Last Judgement panel in stained glass from York Minster chapter house c.1285, which has been lost since 1844, is also recorded as having had two smaller angels to each side holding Passion emblems, and may have served as a precedent for the nave Majesty described above (ibid., 114). A second lost scene of this type, with an angel holding the Crown of Thorns, was recorded by Torre in the 17th century in Bedern Chapel (nV), dating to c.1350 (ibid., 114). Although these images depict Christ facing forward, and the presence of the Passion instruments form a related subject matter with the Fishergate pieces, in none does he wear the Crown of Thorns himself. However, a Last Judgement scene in the Huth Psalter (after 1280) provides a northern precedent for this particular arrangement, with Christ displaying His wounds and wearing the Crown of Thorns (Fig.215). The inclusion of local saints days and the painting style both suggest either a Lincoln or York origin for the psalter (Morgan 1988, cat.167, 167–9, pl.339; London BL MS Add. 38116 fo.13v). Much later, c.1420, a similar combination of images formed the Last Judgement page of the Bolton Hours, another York manuscript (Davidson and O'Connor 1978, 115–16, fig.33). It might be suggested, therefore, that the Fishergate head of Christ came from a Last Judgement scene.

A Last Judgement would be particularly appropriate as an image in a chapter house. Here the discipline of the community was meted out, and the prior dispensed punishment for sins.

The second image which repays consideration is the Christ Child (*268*, Fig.183, p.389). It was suggested on p.391 that the most obvious interpretation of the Fishergate depiction is that of the child at his mother's breast. However, several iconographic scenes can be posited in the stead of the Child at breast. The first would be the Miracle of the Palm Tree. The occasion for the miracle was the flight of the Holy Family to Egypt. It is accounted in the *Gospel of the Pseudo-Matthew* that while the Virgin rested under a palm tree she found the dates too high up in the branches for her to reach. Christ commanded the palm to yield its fruit to His Mother. The tree bent in compliance allowing the Virgin to gather its harvest. Meanwhile, Joseph had been alarmed by the shortage in their supply of water. When Christ commanded the tree to rise again a spring appeared at its roots. On leaving the scene the following day Christ told the tree that angels would carry its branches up to heaven and plant them in His Father's Garden from which time it would be known as the palm of victory. The scene is shown on a chasuble orphrey of English origin, dated to between 1390 and 1420, originally part of the Whalley Abbey vestments, now kept in Towneley Hall, Burnley. This scene shows the Virgin handing a date to her son (or vice versa). The modified story is found in English vernacular tradition in a Christmas carol in which, variously, a cherry or an apple tree bends for the Virgin at the unborn Christ's command (Hone n.d., 90–3; Horton 1975, 118). This was more popular in the west than any other of the events in the Flight to Egypt.

It was a convention of some depictions of the Adoration of the Magi that Caspar should be shown offering Christ his gold in the form of a cup containing gold coins. The gold was a symbol of purity, divinity and kingship and attests the King's tribute to Christ's majesty (Metford 1983, 112, 154). Sometimes reception of the gift appears to be implied in Christ or His Mother handling a round object, usually a coin, as in the Adoration scene from an altar frontal panel in the Musée de Cluny, Paris, of East Anglian origin, probably from Thetford Dominican Priory, c.1335 (Norton et al. 1987; Park 1987, 448–9). There are various ambiguities involved when the Adoration is conventionalised as showing the Virgin and Child enthroned with the kings making obeisance before them. In a scene of Enthronement, either or both the Virgin and Child might be depicted holding an orb symbolising majesty over heaven and earth. Such ambiguity is evident in, for example, the Adoration in the illuminated Psalter Hart 21117, fo.8 (9), Borough of Blackburn (Alexander and Crossley 1976, pl. 2). The Psalter is of French workmanship, dating to between c.1220 and 1240, and shows the Virgin holding a large orb in Her right hand whilst Christ holds a small orb in His left hand. The Adoration of the Magi in iconography derived from the tribute paid by foreign potentates to the Roman Emperor (Warner 1985, 104–5) and hence the double Majesty of Christ and His Mother, as Queen of Heaven, is indicated. In York there was a roof boss of the Virgin and Child with an orb in the Guildhall, c.1446–59 (Davidson and O'Connor 1978, 52).

A third convention which might be reflected in the Fishergate glass is the subject of Mary as the Second Eve. To convey this allusion, the Virgin is pictured holding an apple. Through bearing Christ, the world's Saviour, the Virgin made possible remission of Adam and Eve's original sin of disobedience; for this reason She is known as the gateway to Redemption. St Jerome wrote that 'Death came through Eve, but life has come through Mary' (Warner 1985, 54). The association with Eve through the attribute of the apple may be seen in an early 14th century depiction of the Virgin and Child in Dorchester Abbey, Oxfordshire (I 4c), or, with hand positions very similar to the Fishergate representation, a 14th century French Madonna and Child in the Burrell Collection, Glasgow (Newton 1979, 81, pl.30g; Wells 1975, cat.6, 9–10). This convention was common on seals and has particular relevance for the Fishergate priory. Related to this is a fourth convention, where a gourd is a symbol of the redemption of humanity in contrast to the apple which occasioned the Fall. The gourd may also symbolise the Resurrection, possibly referring to the gourd tree which God created for Jonah, to 'deliver him from his grief' (Jonah 4: 6).

Whilst the Virgin and Child was a very popular subject, there may be some significance in the shared iconography of Gilbertine monastic seals. Of the fifteen seals of which we have impressions, nine represent the Virgin and Child Enthroned (Ellis 1986 for the following). Amongst the seals from double houses, the 13th century matrix of the seal *ad causas,* that is, the seal for everyday business, from Alvingham, Lincolnshire, depicts the

Virgin holding Her breast with Her right hand, the Child seated on Her left knee, and is known to have been used in 1304 and 1538. Bullington, Lincolnshire, had both a 14th century seal matrix and its counterseal showing the Virgin and Child in a similar arrangement. The same iconography appears on the seal of Catley, two seals from North Ormsby and Sixhills (Ellis 1986, 20, 66, 82). The latter has the legend '. . . *lactans virgo deum protege . . .*' (milk-giving Virgin protect God) in Lombardic script. The seal of the Yorkshire house of Watton Priory bore a similar scene. Of the single houses of Gilbertine canons, only that of St Andrew's, York, chose to depict the Virgin and Child on its seal *ad causas*. The seal has only a partial inscription '. . . *ate*(?)' in Lombardic script. It is possibly part of a petition to the Virgin and Child to pray for the brothers of the house. The impression is found on a document of 1538, the year of the priory's Dissolution, showing a vesica on red wax, attached by a tag.

Although *268–70* are only three of the many fragments found on the site of St Andrew's priory, the investigation of the iconography represented is of great interest for this particular house. The pieces came from the destruction debris of the chapter house. It has been shown that the choice and positioning of iconography depicted in the chapter house windows in York Minster were carefully thought out and that they reflect 'significant figures in the devotional life' of that institution (O'Connor and Haselock 1977, 340). Without wishing to erect too great an edifice of supposition on the chance survival of three tiny pieces of glass, the spiritual and the institutional do seem to come together in this instance, through two entirely distinct pieces of material culture, to present an intriguing insight into the life of the Gilbertine foundation in York.

Mid 14th/early 15th century: minor modifications to the priory (Group 4)

After the major reconstruction and remodelling of the early 14th century, occasional minor modifications were made to the priory. These included alterations to the internal layout of the church, possibly related to the installation of liturgical furniture, the addition of a south porch, and some re-organisation of the internal arrangements of the east and north ranges. The types of glass in this group do not so much imply the installation of new windows to replace earlier 14th century versions, but, rather, the continuation of a glazing programme from the early 14th century into the second half of that century, possibly as late as the 15th century. As these additions do not seem to have been extensive, they would have not have changed the internal impression of the buildings except, perhaps, to increase the ratio of white and yellow-stained glass to other pot-metal and flashed colours.

The last group of glass consists of a number of decorated quarry patterns (Figs.175–7, pp.378–80), almost all from demolition deposits within the church, some figural details like the laminated saboton (*277*, Fig.185, p.392), one human hand (*273*, Fig.185), an ermine trim (*299*, Fig.191, p.399), a piece of vermicular drapery (*280*, Fig.189, p.396) and two painted pieces of uncertain description (*371–2*, Fig.201, p.413). The parallels for the patterned quarries are cited above (pp.379–81). They, like all the pieces described here, have been painted on a consistently thin glass. Much of the architectural detail and many of the *rinceaux* fragments, along with some other figural details, also occurs on consistently fine glass. It is less easy to see a distinct break between some of the earlier 14th century glass and these pieces. The quarry patterns, in particular, could have fulfilled the function of the earlier 14th century grisaille in band windows. The saboton and the piece of drapery display a sophistication in drawing and shading which is absent from the earlier glass. It seems most likely that this last group represents a long drawn out attempt to complete an intended glazing programme started when funds were more plentiful. By 1360 the canons were again protesting their poverty (p.60, *AY* 11/2). It is worth repeating the seeming contradiction between the quality of some of this glass and the fact that Period 6d also produced a piece of vessel glass which had been grozed as if for use in a window.

The pattern of destruction

One of the most striking observations of the architectural detail painted on the fragments of this assemblage is the small scale of the drawing. Small canopy gables (such as *302*), crockets (*303, 307*) and cusp detail (*311*) imply that the figures which stood beneath were also small in scale (Fig.192, p.401). Although the figural details which survive are of varied size, there are very few which could represent a large-scale figure (except, perhaps, the fingers, *274*, Fig.185, p.392, and the possible shoe, *370*, Fig.201, p.413). Two conclusions may be drawn from this observation. The first is that the scenes which have remained in the debris of the Dissolution destruction deposits represent the peripheral zones and secondary subjects of the mainly 14th century glazing schemes. These would be borders with architecture, perhaps with small figures, and also the faces of background figures such as might appear in crowd scenes. The alternative is that the windows only ever contained small-scale panels, probably set on grisaille backgrounds.

Each of the above hypotheses has a different implication for the nature of the rebuilt priory church and chapter house. If what remained in the Dissolution debris represented predominantly the borders and marginal zones of the windows, it would seem reasonable to suggest that the windows were probably of the band variety popular in the early 14th century, and that a moderate investment had been made in the glazing of the priory. If, on the other hand, the glass is truly representative of the principal features of the windows then this might lead us to believe that the priory could not afford to use colour to the same extent. A large quantity of earlier, 13th century grisaille was evidently retained until the time of the Dissolution. The archaeology clearly demonstrated that the chapel and chapter house had been rebuilt, so the earlier glass must have been re-used to some extent in these new buildings. There are several reasons to suppose that the rebuilding was ambitious in intent, but several anomalies in the fittings, for example the floor tiles, suggest that funds may have dwindled towards the completion of the furnishing. The re-use of earlier glass in the new church tends to support this interpretation.

There are two further possibilities to be considered if the idea that the greater part of the 14th century glass represents marginal areas, that is, borders and backgrounds, is pursued. The first is that the glass may have been graded according to quality at the time of the Dissolution destruction. The best glass may have been protected as panels and sold for use elsewhere. Only the poorest quality may have been abandoned on site. This is the scenario implied by the survey taken at the Dissolution at Rievaulx Abbey, in 1538–9. Here the west window was to have been taken down carefully for private re-use in the castle at Helmsley. The rest was to be sorted into three grades: 'One the fayrest to be sortyd, The second sort to be sold. The iii sort to be taken out of the lede and the lede molten' (quoted in Coppack 1986, 108, 121). Further, in order to extract the best panels, some peripheral glass may have been sacrificed and broken.

The second related possibility presented by the particular patterning of Dissolution debris at St Andrew's, is that the marginal and background glass is all that survives from the deliberate and targeted destruction of Roman Catholic iconography, that is from iconoclasm. The supposition, based on contemporary glass image composition, is that the offending images would have occupied the more central positions in the panels. Once broken, the debris from the larger images may have been swept away. Only then would the remaining glass clinging to a mutilated network of lead cames be ripped out in order to salvage the lead. This scenario might be thought less plausible insofar as zealous iconoclasm is more normally associated with the reign of Henry VIII's son Edward VI. Aston has shown, however, that some aspects of iconoclasm were put in train from the very first (Aston 1988; 1989). In England this was officially sanctioned and organised, but sporadic and clandestine acts should not be discounted.

The public iconoclastic spectacle became part of the repertoire of government propaganda almost as soon as Henry VIII decided, under Thomas Cromwell's guiding hand, to sponsor the process of reform (Aston 1989, 49).

Individuals were ready to take their cue, and there were various occasions on which government iconoclasm was imitated or followed by illegal acts of destruction. The motives were doubtless mixed, ranging from conscience-stricken new belief to revenge on failed intercessors, youthful pranks or drunken demonstrations, and conscious efforts to challenge authority (ibid., 50).

This does raise the question of the continued occupation of the site from Period 7a to Period 7c in the second half of the 16th century. It is clear from the considerable assemblage of animal bone and other artefacts, as well as features in the ground, that a group occupied the priory for some time after the official Dissolution. The animal bone assemblage, in particular, was a kind 'not commonly encountered in medieval assemblages in York, and markedly different from all other animal bone assemblages from this site' (p.220, *AY* 11/2). The food taxa were diverse, and represented a 'rich and varied diet' (ibid.). Moreover, the meat was supplied as dressed carcasses suggesting an organised supply. This seemingly high-status group may well have been an official group commissioned both to remove items of idolaltry and strip remaining material assets. We should not take for granted the necessity to have official parties stationed on former monastic premises in order to undertake the business of Dissolution. The Rievaulx survey shows not only the thoroughness of the task, but the complexities in decision making and sorting of the component materials (Coppack 1986). This would have required time, organisation and liaison with carriers. The destruction of institutions and objects of veneration which had been defended in Crown legislation a few years, sometimes only months, before, presented a reversal of huge proportions to the ordinary people (Aston 1989, 64–5 and *passim*). For many the turnabout would have appeared sudden, incomprehensible and possibly even threatening. It would have served official interests, therefore, to have the parties charged with putting the changes into practice (that is to say, the workmen who had to dismantle abbeys and priories) billeted within the precinct walls, thus affording them immunity from popular grievance and curiosity.

Typology and Discussion of the Glass from Sempringham Priory, Lincolnshire

Sempringham was the mother house of the Gilbertine Order. Gilbert established a community of religious women attached to the parish church of St Andrew in c.1131. The success and popularity of this community in providing a pious and ascetic vocation for religious women at a time when the Cistercians did not receive women into their Order led to the establishment of a community for nuns, lay brethren and sisters. It is now thought that the formal institution of a priory was not made until the introduction of canons, following Gilbert's return from Citeaux in 1147 (Golding 1995, 198). Consequently, the buildings which housed and served the double community and which were constructed on the south side of the church probably date to after 1147 (Fig.216). Since the lordship of Sempringham was divided, the patronage of all the demesne lords was sought. The endowments are discussed by Golding (ibid., 198–202). It is recorded that, despite the Order's restrictions on numbers, there were 200 women in 1247 and again in 1319 (Graham 1940, 84, citing *Cal. Papal Letters*, **1**, 232, **2**, 273).

Sempringham Priory was excavated during the summers of 1938 and 1939 by the Lincolnshire Architectural Society and the findings were reported by Rose Graham (1940). These excavations revealed a church with a double nave — one to serve the nuns, the other to serve the canons — separated by a medial wall. It became clear that this building retained portions of wall from a 12th century church. A smaller single-cell rectangular building, which was assigned to the Norman period, was found to be attached to the north-west of the double church (Fig.216). A column from a 13th century crypt was located. There was evidence throughout of considerable rebuilding in the 14th century including vaulting. Breaks in the 14th century fabric of the medial wall between the nuns' and canons' choirs framed a short length of earlier walling which seemed to have been preserved. The foundations for this section had been subsequently widened and there was evidence for 14th century vaulting. Statuary was also found here. The excavators interpreted this as the original position of St Gilbert's tomb since it is recorded that he was buried 'between the altars of St Mary and St Andrew' (Graham 1940, 80).

A costly rebuilding was begun in 1301 by Prior John de Hamilton, and documentation shows the rebuilding to have been still incomplete 100 years later (ibid., 85). The pre-war excavations revealed that the whole of the canons' church had been rebuilt, saving the western and southern walls (Fig.217). This church was both wider and longer than its predecessor. A very large north transept of three bays, each with an eastern chapel was built at this time. Both churches and transept were vaulted throughout. A strange vaulted 14th century aisle was also located at the west end. The proportions of the church excavated in 1938–9 have been compared with those of the smaller cathedral churches (ibid., 90).

The rebuilding of Sempringham Priory was ambitious in scale and detail, but the historical evidence reveals that the prior and convent fell into debt very quickly in the first

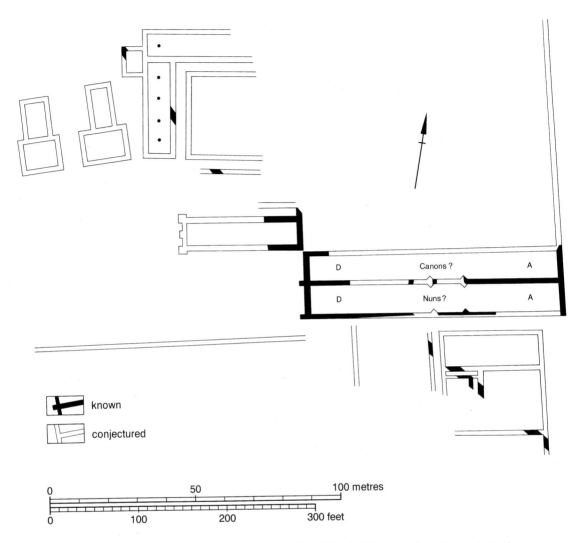

known

conjectured

| 0 | 50 | 100 metres |
| 0 | 100 | 200 | 300 feet |

*Fig.216   Plan of Sempringham Priory (after Graham 1940), late 12th/early 13th century phase: A = crossing/presbytery;
B= north transept chapel; D = nave. Scale 1:1250*

30 years of the 14th century. From 1320 the prior was borrowing very large sums from money-lenders (ibid., 88–9). The community sought indulgences from church magnates. Henry Burghersh, bishop of Lincoln, granted indulgences in 1334 and 1336 (p.55, *AY* 11/2; LAO Reg.5, fo.473; fo.537v.), and his successor, Bishop Thomas Bek, granted another (Graham 1940, 89, n.3). In 1334 and 1335, Burghersh expended 'many amounts and sums' on the Gilbertine priory of St Andrew in York (p.56, *AY* 11/2; PRO C66/185, 19–20; *Cal. Pat.* 1334–8, 102–3).

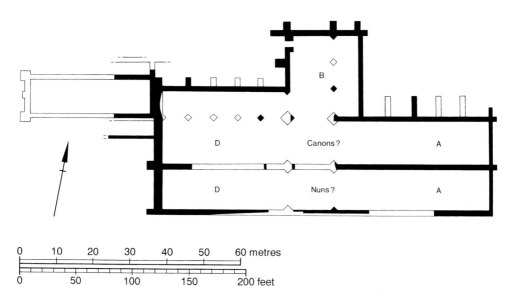

Fig.217   Plan of Sempringham Priory (after Graham 1940), 14th century phase. For room notation see Fig.216. Scale 1:1000

Quantities of fine architectural stonework were uncovered. Hugh Braun, who had dug the site in 1938, noted 'a considerable amount of fourteenth century glass and cames, the grooved leads which held it in place' (Graham 1940, 83). This passing reference is all that appears to be recorded of the glass.

Six trenches were cut across the site of Sempringham Priory in 1987 by English Heritage's Central Excavation Unit in order to assess the effects of cultivation on the monument (McAvoy 1989). Floor and roof tiles were uncovered, but no glass was found.

The glass

The Sempringham glass was inspected twice by the author. The first study took place in 1991. At that time three boxes of window glass from Sempringham were located in the Tithe Barn store of the Lincoln City and County Museum. The boxes were marked 83, 84, 85, Rev. Hearn 26.67 XII 'from excavations'. Museum staff could supply no explanation for the labelling and had no documentation to elucidate the references. There is considerable confusion over the provenance of most of the glass. A few handwritten notes had been packed with the glass, some pertaining to glass which had been found in specific areas of the church, for example 'the Shrine'. However, the glass inside the boxes was intermingled at the time of inspection, and has since been relocated and reboxed in the principal store of the same museum authority. When the second study took place in 1995–6 it became clear that, although Box 84 had been relocated, the majority of painted glass which was inspected in 1991 had become separated from this box, and has not been found. As a consequence, it is now unlikely that reliable distinctions can be made between assemblages which may have derived from different areas of the excavation. Moreover, the glass is untreated and much of it has deteriorated to such an extent that neither the surface painted decoration nor the original colour of the glass can be discerned. Consequently, the following account of the Sempringham glass is derived from a combination of the analysis made in 1995–6 and the notes made in 1991.

Grisaille (Figs.218–19)

There was very little grisaille of the early to mid 13th century (c.100cm^2) but it was all of a consistent quality, with very controlled cross-hatching. There were two fragments of

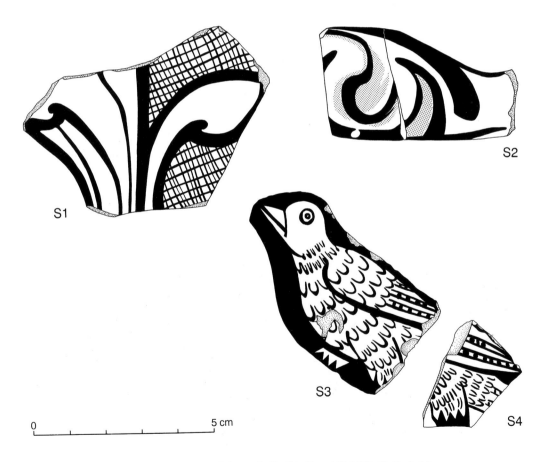

Fig.218   Glass fragments from Sempringham Priory: grisaille (S1–2) and bird (S3–4). Scale 1:1

0   5 cm

S5

S6

S7

S8

Fig.219   Decorated quarries from Sempringham Priory. Scale 1:1

side-curling trefoil: one slightly asymmetrical version springing from an upright stem (*S1*) and one trefoil on its own (*S2*).

Fragments from at least four birds (c.100cm^2) were recognised amongst the Sempringham assemblage of window glass. These were all painted in the same style and at the same scale, carefully grozed around the shape, e.g. *S3*, *S4*. They probably inhabited foliage in a border such as that excavated at Bradwell Abbey, Buckinghamshire, and dated to c.1270 (Croft and Mynard 1986, fig.8). They appear in the first half of the 14th century in York Minster south aisle, sXXXI and sXXXII, north aisle nXXV (see Marks 1993, 153–4). The Bradwell border accompanies a grisaille panel consisting of tight trefoils on a plain ground, but the Sempringham birds may have bounded grisaille on a cross-hatched ground, or perhaps the later oak leaf and acorn grisaille which is described below.

An almost complete quarry design featured a central quatrefoil leaf design in outline on a plain ground, with tapered and crossed internal lines, and edged with a strapwork design (*S5*). The glass was thick, bevelled and uneven. This was probably a common design, produced in quantity, and similar to those seen in the background to the figures of SS Thomas Becket and Thomas Cantilupe, at Credenhill, Herefordshire, c.1300, and in the background to the figure of Christ on the Cross in the south aisle of the choir of Wells Cathedral, Somerset, dating to c.1310–20 (Marks 1993, 77, figs.8, 12, 58). The Sempringham quarry can be compared with the crude quarries from Fishergate in Fig.173 (p.376).

Early to mid 14th century oak leaf grisaille was more numerous, although only two types are evident. The first (c.570cm^2) was comparable to the Fishergate oak leaf, with strapwork at the edges of variously shaped panes, and similar in quality (*S6*). One piece had a stem decorated with a serpentine line and dots, as are the bases of the grisaille panels in York Minster chapter house (e.g. C/H nIII, c.1285, illustrated in O'Connor and Haselock 1977, pl.98). The second type had very distinctive acorns, with finer cross-hatched cups, associated with a beaded border (c.200cm^2; *S7*). As has been discussed in relation to the Fishergate grisaille, sometime between the third and final quarters of the 13th century more naturalistic foliage started to be introduced into grisaille painting. Naturalistic leaves appear in grisaille in the chapter house of York Minster, c.1285–90, the chapter house vestibule of Wells Cathedral, Somerset, c.1286, the parish church of Stanton St John, Oxfordshire (nIV), c.1285–1300, Chartham, Kent (sIV, sV, nIV, nV), c.1293/4–1300, Merton College Chapel, Oxford, c.1294 (O'Connor and Haselock 1977, 334–41, pl.9; Marks 1993, 147, fig.118, 148, fig.119, 152, fig.123; Newton 1979, 188–9; Winston 1867, 99, pl.18). Naturalistic grisaille continued to be used into the mid 14th century.

The same beading pattern, or a variation with alternating lozenges and open beading interspersed with circles, can be found on both the Sempringham acorn grisaille and on grisaille painted with a simple rose or eglantine design on curling stems (total c.325cm^2; e.g. *S8*), similar to the Fishergate quarries except that only one example from Sempringham was highlighted in yellow stain. There was a further 350cm^2 of this border pattern on its own, but it also occurred on pieces of pot-metal yellow glass grozed to a consistent flared shape (45cm^2). These may have come from either some architectural detail, such as a canopy cusp, or from a geometric shape surrounding a figured panel. The beadwork is identical which implies that these details stood on a ground of grisaille, perhaps alternating lights of oak leaf and rose design. The rose design also occurred with a border of small open quatrefoils, with a further 15cm^2 of this border.

Diaper (Figs.220–1)

One fragment of *rinceau* pattern consists of a repeated trefoil, with finely fringed lobes and tendrils all in stickwork (10cm^2; *S9*). This appears on blue pot-metal and can be

Fig.220   *Diaper fragments from Sempringham Priory. Scale 1:1*

compared with a *rinceau* pattern seen in the west window (wI) of York Minster, which also occurs only on blue (French and O'Connor 1987, 7, pls.16c, 19iv). The west window dates to 1338/9. A second form of trilobed *rinceau* occurred on blue (219cm^2), on ruby flashed glass (75cm^2), on pot-metal yellow (225cm^2) and on white glass (100cm^2). A very finely executed reversed colour *rinceau* border also occurred on blue pot-metal (10cm^2; *S10*). Two fine borders each employed a variation on the trefoil terminal, executed in stickwork, on blue and green (e.g. *S11*).

Another diaper pattern is very similar to the circle and concave lozenge form found at Fishergate, although the scale of the motifs at Sempringham is larger (*S12*). This only occurs on two colours in this assemblage: on ruby flashed glass (145cm^2) and white (81cm^2). This is a common background diaper to figures in the middle of the 14th century, c.1330–50.

There is one fragment (6cm^2) of conventional cross-diaper on white glass (*S13*) comparable to the Fishergate example (Fig.179, *246*, p.383). A variation on the cross pattern on ruby flashed glass has a lattice of thin double lines, with the spaces divided into quatrefoils (5cm^2; *S14*) (cf. the pattern in the canopy column capital of the St Catherine in prison panel of the Heraldic Window in York Minster nave north aisle (nXXIII), c.1310–20, illustrated in O'Connor and Haselock 1977, pl.107).

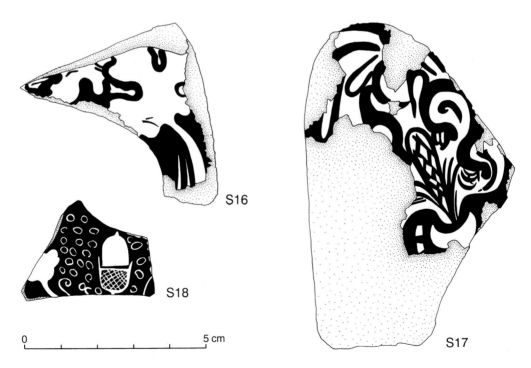

S16

S18

S17

0   5 cm

Fig.221   Diaper fragments from Sempringham Priory. Scale 1:100

There is a small amount of larger-scale diaper (*S15*) with a repeated leaf form. There is also a diaper pattern in a seaweed form (*S16, S17*). This occurred on blue pot-metal ($210cm^2$), ruby flashed glass ($75cm^2$), pot-metal yellow ($225cm^2$) and white ($100cm^2$). Seaweed diaper became a common 15th century background, having been used extensively in the influential Winchester College chapel glass of the late 1390s. Some of these pieces may have been used as a textile design (such as *S17*). A small fragment of finely scratched oak leaf and acorn detail (*S18*) may have come from a background, but it is uncertain. The execution links it to 14th century diapers.

Figures (Figs.222–3)

Heads

There were two small heads ($10cm^2$), with the eyes looking to the right, and framed by hair, each $5cm^2$ and dating to the late 13th/early 14th century (including *S19*). There are a further $12cm^2$ of a separate halo. The later period is represented by the hair of a saint with part of the halo, dating to the second half of the 14th century ($25cm^2$), and the eye and nose of a late 14th/early 15th century figure ($10\cdot5cm^2$). This last piece was very finely

a   b

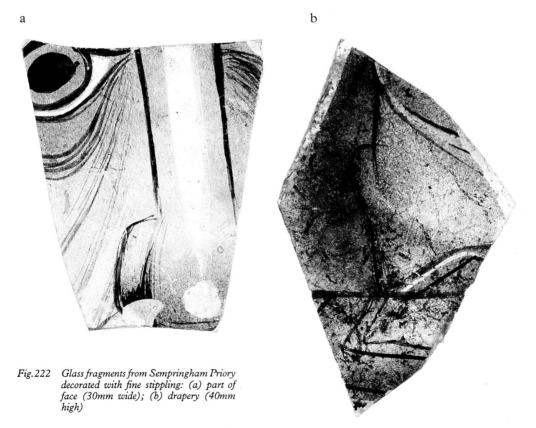

Fig.222   Glass fragments from Sempringham Priory decorated with fine stippling: (a) part of face (30mm wide); (b) drapery (40mm high)

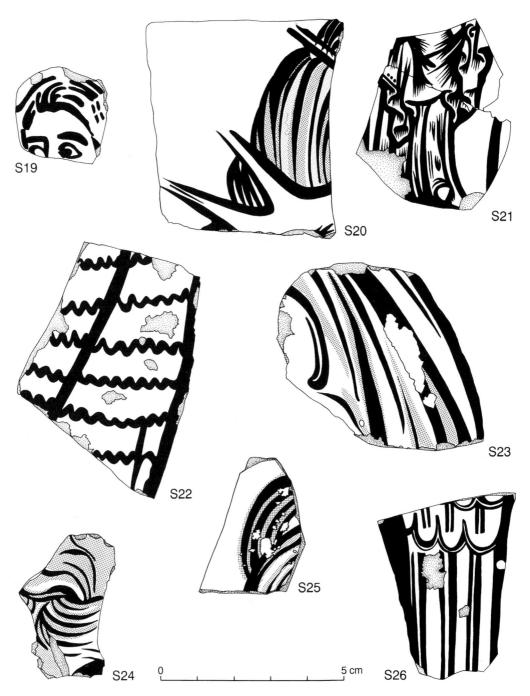

Fig. 223   Figural detail from Sempingham Priory. Scale 1:1

painted, with stipple shading used to model the face, and back-painting used to give depth to that modelling (Fig.222a, p.473). Part of a head of Christ, encircled by the Crown of Thorns, dates to the first half of the 15th century (*S20*).

Full-figure detail

The most detailed figural pieces (31·5cm^2) are very finely painted (Fig.222b, p.473). The small-scale drapery had tight, vermicular folds, and included a detail which may have been a censer bowl or an ointment jar (*S21*). If it is the latter, then this is almost certainly the figure of St Mary Magdalene. These three pieces date to between c.1330 and c.1350.

Miscellaneous figural detail

Amongst the figural fragments are a number of pieces with stylised chainmail (60cm^2; *S22*), which may have come from an historiated Biblical or hagiographical scene, or from a donor figure. There are at least three styles of drapery (e.g. *S23*): from the late 13th/early 14th century (c.40cm^2); from around the middle of the 14th century; and small details of dress and trimmings from the late 14th and 15th century. The latter includes fur trim, a possible buckle, a textile detail (10cm^2) and a decorated garment hem from a large-scale figure (12cm^2). There are many small portions of hair (*S24*, *S25*), feather and wing, some executed with great attention to shading giving the impression of layered feathers (*S26*).

Architecture (Figs.224–5)

There were a variety of architectural forms of a style and date compatible with the oak leaf grisaille. A number of pieces had stickwork detail indicating canopy gables, cusps, crockets and finials (c.403cm^2). Amongst these were three possible representations of rose windows (33cm^2), one set within a stickwork gable, with pointed trefoils in the spandrels (21cm^2) (*S27*). The edges of this and many similar details were decorated with a beading pattern of either large circles or open beading, each interspersed with two smaller circles; they can be compared with the 14th century canopies which appear in the tracery lights at Gedney, Lincolnshire. There was only one example of an architectural cross-slit with trefoil terminals (10cm^2; *S28*), such as would appear in the crenellated tops of walls, probably as part of a large canopy design. A distinct group of regularly repeated rectangles painted with a central stock in reserve in yellow stain and subsidiary forms probably represent buttresses or sideshafts, of the sort that framed figures and historiated scenes (c.450cm^2); these are likely to date from both the mid 14th century and the late 14th/early 15th century. Traceried windows and panelling, executed in stickwork, would also feature in these side shafts and buttresses (*S29*). There were 33cm^2 of this type of design, on both pot-metal yellow and blue. There is one very well preserved ring and lower portion of a foliate finial from the top of an architectural canopy gable dating to c.1350 (20cm^2; *S30*), and a fragment from a canopy finial which has the same stickwork detail noted above (*S31*).

Amongst the background diapers in this collection from Sempringham was a quantity of masonry pattern, some of which was painted on the same piece of glass as architectural

Fig.224   Architectural detail from Sempringham Priory. Scale 1:1

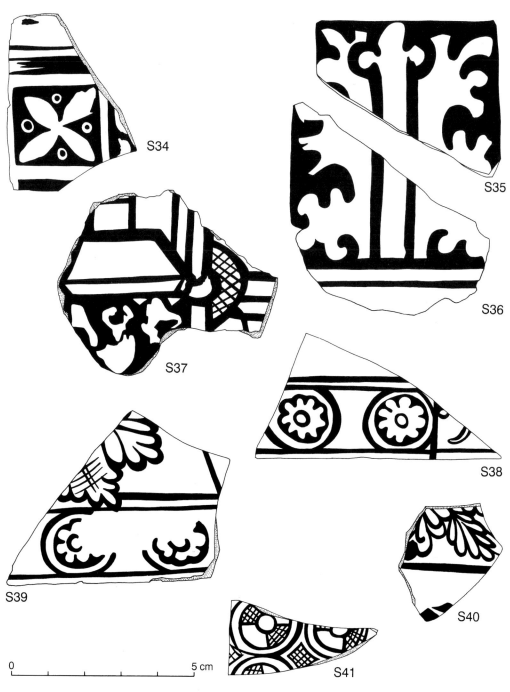

Fig.225   Architectural fragments from Sempringham Priory. Scale 1:1

Fig.226   Reconstruction of quatrefoil border design, based on S44.
Scale 1:1

0 _____ 5 cm

arches and gables (*S32, S33*). Both masonry pattern and architecture were painted alongside the same beading pattern which was found on both oak leaf and rose grisailles. The masonry pattern was created out of a thin wash of paint, with masonry lines either left in reserve or drawn out by stickwork. Each 'block' represented is decorated with a scratched quatrefoil. The pattern occurs on pot-metal yellow (420cm^2) or on white (130cm^2). A similar pattern, on a slightly larger scale, uses a quatrefoil with pointed lobes set saltire-wise on each block, with scratched circles between the lobes (*S34*). The majority of this is, again, on pot-metal yellow (c.50cm^2), with some on flashed ruby (12cm^2) and a very little on white glass (6cm^2). The masonry pattern dates to c.1340–c.1390.

At least one example of a canopy finial in reserve from a matt ground and highlighted with yellow stain may have been a repeated border pattern (*S35, S36*). It is clear from some fragments that an attempt was made to depict the architecture as three-dimensional by using both trace-lines and shading to convey angle and depth (*S37*). Concerns with the depiction of more than one plane grew from c.1390 and continued throughout the 15th century. At least c.50cm^2 of three-dimensional architecture were found, together with c.15cm^2 of characteristic 15th century pinnacles with simple rounded crockets. An assortment of 15th century foliage designs may have originated from architecture or background fill (*S38–41*).

Linear stickwork patterns and geometric borders (Figs.226–7)

There were fewer border patterns amongst this selection from Sempringham Priory than were present in the assemblage from St Andrew, York. Some of these have been listed

Fig. 227   Linear stickwork (S42–3, S45–6), heraldic fragments (S47) and miscellaneous painted fragments (S48–50) from Sempringham Priory. Scale 1:1

above (see also Fig.195, p.407). There were, in addition, 25cm^2 of an encircled quatrefoil stickwork edging pattern, with tiny circles in the interstices of the quatrefoil lobes (*S42*). A repeated quatrefoil motif occurs on pink glass (6cm^2). One unusual variation on a beaded edging pattern consisted of cross-hatched beads interspersed with two small scratched circles. All are probably from the 14th century. There was one 13th/14th century fragment of a running trefoil edge painted in outline on pot-metal green (*S43*).

There were several fragments from a common late 14th and 15th century border design which featured an ornate quatrefoil in the centre of a strapwork lozenge, placed within a rectangular pane, and with the spaces between the lozenge and the frame decorated with semi-circular lobes and serrated edges (for reconstruction see *S44*). These lobes (and possibly the central quatrefoils) are reserved in yellow stain. Another border design, featuring a multilobate flower reserved in yellow stain, dates to the 15th century. Two separate border designs were painted in outline, rather than stickwork, both on yellow pot-metal (*S45, S46*). Both may have featured in architecture of the 14th or 15th century.

Heraldry (Fig.227)

There are two pieces of an heraldic lion passant guardant (15cm^2; *S47*). The four birds described on p.470 under the heading of grisaille could, alternatively, have featured in heraldry between the late 13th and early 14th century. A portion from a crown may have belonged to a figure, but may equally have been a border motif of the type described in the section on Fishergate glass.

Miscellaneous painted fragments (Fig.227)

A small roundel was painted with a five-pointed star with wavy arms (c.20cm^2; *S48*). Such stars might be used to provide highlights in a background, for example, behind the 15th century Christ of the Lily. They might be used as a symbol of the Virgin, or in heraldry. Various leaf designs were also present (*S49*). There were a few fragments of large 14th century leaf (25cm^2 on pot-metal green and yellow). The leaves may have come from borders or background fill. They are unlikely to have come from a Tree of Jesse, as one would have expected the assemblage to contain a considerable amount of not only leaf, but stems, bunches of grapes, figural detail, including crowns, and perhaps inscription. As with the Fishergate assemblage, there was surprisingly little evidence for inscriptions from Sempringham Priory. Portions of black letter script, mostly probably late 14th/early 15th century, accounted for only c.40cm^2. At least one fragment bore a late 14th/15th century black letter inscription with 'ma' (*S50*). Although there are many possibilities as to what this came from originally, the name of the Virgin is an obvious possibility, as is the petitionary formula to pray for the soul (*pro anima . . .*) of benefactors and donors.

Painted glass with designs so small and partial that they could not be identified reliably accounted for 1,875cm^2.

Colour

The presence of coloured glass may be detailed as follows: ruby flashed 639cm^2; blue pot-metal 275cm^2; green pot-metal 103cm^2; purple/murrey 25cm^2; and pot-metal yellow 554cm^2. The most interesting aspect of the coloured glass from this site is not the painted decoration, but the relatively high proportion of fire-rounded edges: 35cm^2 red; 82cm^2 blue; 20cm^2 green; 175cm^2 pot-metal yellow. The fire-rounded edges imply cut-offs from the edges of sheets of glass made by the cylinder method of manufacture. Normally, one would not expect a high proportion of fire-rounded edges to have been used in glazing itself; rather, such a high proportion might indicate wastage from a glazing operation. If the coloured glass edges had been used in the windows it may be an indication of the economic desirability of using as much of the coloured glass as possible.

Shaped panes of plain glass

In addition to the painted pieces detailed above, there were 1,500cm^2 of plain glass, many examples of plain quarry glazing being evident and much of it bevelled. Glass manufacturing techniques were represented by 312cm^2 of glass, both white and coloured, which were definitely from the edges of crown glass sheets whilst 94cm^2 forms the centre or 'bullseye' from a crown sheet. There were 723cm^2 of cylinder sheet manufacture, again from both white and coloured sheets.

Discussion

The window glass from Sempringham Priory falls into three principal periods: early to mid 13th century, mid 14th century and late 14th/early 15th century. The early grisaille invites no comment other than that given above. The principal period of glazing, as demonstrated by this assemblage at least, was that of the mid 14th century. The fragments illustrate a suite of motifs and a form of window common enough in England at the time. These were 'band' windows with figures and historiated scenes set beneath ornate micro-architectural housings of canopies, mock-stonework and pinnacles. There would have been grisaille above and beneath these scenes, since both architecture and grisaille share the same edging pattern. The range of colour is wider than that used at Fishergate, perhaps an indication of the higher status of Sempringham within the Gilbertine Order and the ambitions of the 14th century rebuilding. If this assemblage is a true indication of the proportions of glazing by period, the limitations of that 14th century rebuilding are, perhaps, reflected in the fact that glazing was delayed until the middle of the century.

The uncertainty of funding is perhaps echoed in the later glass as well. High quality glass of the 15th century is exemplified by the work of Thomas of Oxford, who made the Winchester College chapel windows, and by John Thornton of Coventry and York whose influence can be discerned throughout the North of England and in the Midlands in the first half of the 15th century. It is a characteristic of this quality of work that seaweed diaper occurs predominantly on blue and red, the two most expensive colours to produce and

procure. The quantity of seaweed diaper painted on yellow pot-metal found at Sempringham, in proportion to the red in particular, may be an indication of the more reduced
circumstances in which the priory found itself in the late medieval period.

The only clue to provenance for any of this glass seems to be one postcard on which is
sketched the eastern end of the priory church, labelled with dimensions and initial letters,
and the words, 'Shrine glass small'. In the 1940s' account of the Sempringham excavation,
the site of the tomb of St Gilbert was thought to have been found in the medial wall between
the choirs of the nuns' and canons' churches, at the east end. This was the spot where
some of the original 12th century walling appeared to have been retained, whereas the
walls on either side were rebuilt in the 14th century. Fragments of statuary and vaulting
were found close by (Graham 1940, 80). So far as can be understood from the postcard
sketch, this is the site indicated as the source of the 'Shrine glass'. The problem is that it
is unlikely that there was a window in the medial wall, since it would have been an internal
division. The nearest windows would surely have been in the east walls of each choir, and
in the long side walls. If a collection of glass was discovered in the area of the 'Shrine', it
may have been coincidental, and was surely the result of Dissolution destruction debris
from the choir windows having been swept into a pile here. Graham did not mention glass
in her description of the tomb, and it seems most likely that the quantities were so small
that they did not merit mention. This, perhaps, explains the 'Shrine glass small' labelling
on the postcard.

In consequence, despite the importance of Sempringham Priory as the mother house
of the Gilbertine Order, the window glass which has been excavated from this site tells us
little about the glazing of the priory church, or of the iconographical or aesthetic preferences
of the Order. This serves to emphasise the importance of the window glass from the priory
of St Andrew, York.

Glass from Gilbertine Sites (Fig.228)

The following gazetteer summarises our knowledge of Gilbertine glazing to date. All information concerning foundation dates and type of institution is derived from Foreville and Keir 1987; and Golding 1995.

Alvingham, Lincolnshire

Priory, double house, founded 1148–69, possibly before 1154. No glass known.

Brachy, Normandy

Priory, canons only, founded before 1155, failed by 1184. No glass known.

Bullington, Lincolnshire

Priory, double house, founded c.1148–55. No glass known.

Cambridge

St Edmund's house of study, founded c.1290/91. No glass known.

Catley, Lincolnshire

Priory, double house, founded c.1148–54 or after 1166. No glass known.

Chicksands, Bedfordshire

Priory, double house, founded 1151–3. Five excavated fragments.

Chicksands Priory, Bedfordshire, was dedicated to St Mary and was a double house for nuns and canons. The initial endowment was made by Payn de Beauchamp, lord of the Barony of Bedford, and his wife the Countess Rohaise, widow of the first Earl of Essex. It is recorded in a document which may well be the foundation charter, dating to between 1151 and 1153 (Golding 1995, 217; Dugdale 1846, **6**, 2.950). The charter describes a group of nuns connected with the parish church which was already in existence at Chicksands. The priory was richly endowed and became one of the wealthiest of the Gilbertine institutions (Golding 1995, 218–19).

The core of the present house at Chicksands is built out of the medieval priory cloister ranges, although the church no longer exists. Six bays of medieval vaulting remain at ground floor level, and some of the roof structures are medieval. The house was altered and partially rebuilt in the Gothick style for General Sir George Osborn in 1813 by Wyatt (Pevsner 1968, 67–9; *VCHB* 2, 271–5).

Rose Graham noted that glass had been found at Chicksands in the burial ground to the east of the large cloister, along with coffins, bones and pottery (Graham 1901, 218; Fig.67f, *AY* 11/2). None of this glass has been traced, however. The Bedfordshire County Planning Department Archaeological Service recovered five small pieces of window glass from the burial ground in 1988. These fragments were of characteristic medieval potash composition, with grozed edges, but they had very little diagnostic paintwork. One fragment was from a 14th century leaf design and another was probably from early 14th century oak leaf grisaille. A collection of disparate pieces of medieval glass may be found in the oriel window of the western range of Chicksands Priory, but this was collected by General Sir George Osborn, who had it installed during or after the 1813 Wyatt alterations. Gamlen, writing in 1975, referred to the glass in the small oriel window as distinct from the main Osborn collection (Gamlen 1975, 9). He was certain that none of the Osborn collection had been excavated from the grounds of ruined buildings, rather that it had been collected from various sources, probably from local churches, and possibly from Oxfordshire and Buckinghamshire. This Chicksands glass has been discussed both by Gamlen (1975) and Marks (1976). None of the glass has been proven to have come from the medieval Gilbertine priory at Chicksands.

Clattercote, Oxfordshire

Leper hospital (before 1166) and priory for canons only, founded 1258–79. No glass known.

Dalmilling, Ayrshire

Priory, canons only, founded after c.1219, failed by 1238. Site abandoned. No glass known.

Fig.228 (facing page) Map showing the location of Gilbertine institutions in England and Scotland (after Knowles and Hadcock 1953)

1	Dalmilling	9	Mattersey	17	Haverholme	24	Fordham
2	Owton	10	Tunstall	18	Holland Bridge	25	Cambridge
3	Ravenstonedale	11	Sixhills	19	Holland Marsh	26	Chicksands
4	Old Malton	12	Nun Ormsby	20	Sempringham	27	Hitchin
5	York	13	Alvingham	21	Stamford	28	Clattercote
6	Watton	14	Bullington	22	Shouldham	29	Poulton
7	Ellerton	15	Lincoln	23	Marmont	30	Marlborough
8	Newstead	16	Catley				

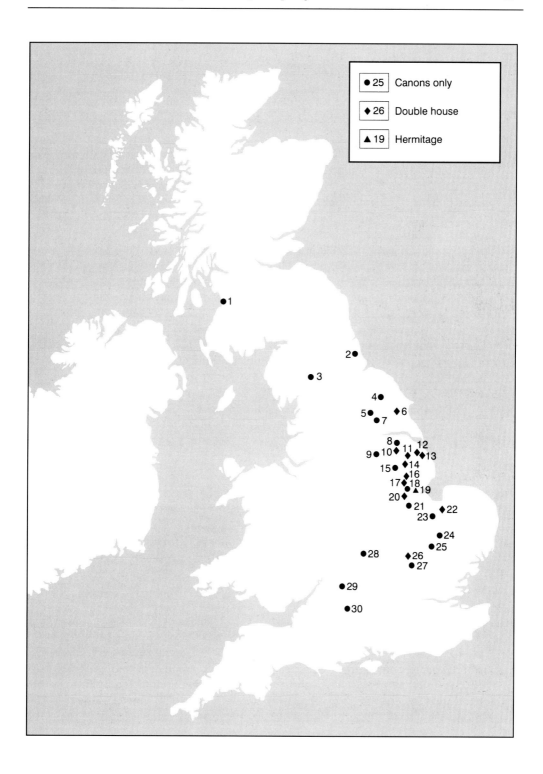

Ellerton, East Riding of Yorkshire

Priory and hospital, canons only, founded 1199–1203, or before 1207. Fragments and heraldic shields of the early 14th century, restored and releaded into north naive aisle of Selby Abbey, North Yorkshire.

The Gilbertine priory at Ellerton was a relatively late foundation of between 1199 and 1203, and made provision for the care of the poor. The founder was William son of Peter (of Goodmanham). The foundation charter suggests that Peter was associated with Geoffrey FitzPeter, who founded the Gilbertine house at Shouldham, and Hugh Murdac, who founded St Andrew's, York, 'since the grant was made for the salvation of their souls' (Golding 1995, 233). Indeed, William was a witness to the foundation of St Andrew's. Ellerton was intended to accommodate Gilbertine canons who were charged with the care and feeding of thirteen poor people. Peter, son of Peter de Mauley, made grants to Ellerton in the mid 13th century. One Alan de Wilton gave twelve acres to Ellerton in Howm (Holme-on-the-Wolds), five acres in West Coatham (Redcar and Cleveland), and some land in Habton (North Yorkshire) (*VCH Yorks* 1913, 251). The founder William Fitz-Peter's estates were acquired by the Hay family, who also took over the patronage of the priory and hospital and continued in that role until the late 14th century. Obits were to be sung for Germanus Hay, lord of the manor of Aughton, and Alesia his wife, in 1387 (Golding 1995, 234; *VCH Yorks* 1914, 252). In the later medieval period, however, bequests to Ellerton no longer mention the poor and infirm.

The present church at Ellerton was built in 1846–8 to replace the former parish church and it retained heraldic shields from the glazing of its predecessor until the Victorian church in turn was made redundant in recent times (K. Barley, pers. comm.). It now stands in a semi-dilapidated state. As the old parish church building had been the nave of the Gilbertine priory church, the painted shields which were transferred to the Victorian building may be supposed to have been Gilbertine glass (Graham 1901, 213). The glass was removed from Ellerton, cleaned and releaded by the York Glaziers' Trust under Peter Gibson, and placed in the north nave aisle of Selby Abbey, all with the aid of the Pilgrim Trust, Selby Civic Society and Selby Abbey Trust. The Ellerton glass is leaded into a window of three trefoil-headed lights, with three quatrefoils in the head. All the Ellerton glass has been leaded into either roundels or ogee quatrefoils and set on a ground of plain quarries. Whilst the heraldic shields appear to be original, the roundels into which they have been set may not be; the quatrefoils are constructed out of a jumble of fragments of medieval glass. Dr Peter Newton described the heraldic blasoning and suggested identifications of the bearers of the arms (Newton in Gibson n.d.). These notes on the heraldry, together with notes on the position of the glass whilst still in Ellerton church, were lodged with the York Glaziers' Trust by Peter Gibson (unpublished). Further research and consultation with the College of Arms has proved some of these identifications to be erroneous.

Fig.229   Stained glass from Ellerton Priory, restored and releaded into the north nave aisle of Selby Abbey, North Yorkshire. Reproduced by permission of Selby Abbey (© Judges Postcards Ltd, Hastings)

There are three superficially similar shields with lions rampant. The first shield (Fig.229) is (3b) Argent a Lion rampant Azure, placed on a roundel with a green ground and a red rim. The Argent ground is made up from a diaper with a common 14th century *rinceau* design of a trefoil in reserve from a thin wash, with curling stem, and tiny circles picked out of the background wash. The green roundel is made up, in the main, from a multi-lobate diaper in reserve, although there is at least one fragment of a different trefoil *rinceau* and an acorn. The red rim is unpainted. Newton identified these as the arms of Fauconberg (Gibson n.d.; but see below). The shield appears to be a complete survivor from the 14th century, whereas the surrounding roundel on which it is set is a composite of medieval and more modern pieces of glass. The shield was originally in the north wall of Ellerton church, in the third window from the east, set in a quatrefoil of fragments composed in the 19th century (ibid.).

The uppermost left-hand shield in the Selby Abbey window (4a) is Argent a Lion rampant Azure crowned Or, placed on a roundel with a red ground and a green rim (Fig.229). The uppermost right-hand shield (4c) is slightly smaller, the Lion rampant appearing noticeably smaller, also placed on a red roundel, but with a yellow rim. Newton suggested that these were the arms of Cleuisby, but there is no evidence for this identification (see below). The Argent grounds to 4a and 4c are each made up from a distinct form of *rinceau* different again to that of 3b; the ground of 4a has trefoils with pointed leaves, and that of 4c has a much more flowing design supplemented by many concentric curves and circles picked out from the background wash. The lions are very corroded, but original 14th century work, as is most of the Argent background material. At least one fragment of the background of 4a, in the top right-hand, is intrusive; the background to 4c includes an intrusive medieval fragment of fleur-de-lys in the top left-hand. The lions of 3b and 4c appear to have been drawn by the same hand, whereas that of 4a is distinct, with a more rounded, fleshy appearance to the head and limbs. Both shields were originally in the south wall of Ellerton church, 4a in the first window from the east, 4c in the third window from the east. Again, these shields were set in quatrefoils of glass assembled in the 19th century (Gibson n.d.). In these 19th century settings, however, it was noted that 4c was surrounded by parts of a red roundel. The present red roundel may therefore preserve an element of the original medieval setting for the shield.

There are two further shields which bear lions rampant. The first (2a) is Gules a Lion rampant Argent within a Bordure engrailed Argent, placed on a roundel with a green ground and red rim (Fig.229). These were identified as the arms of Mowbray by Newton (but see pp.493–4). The lion is very thin, although in execution it is very similar to those of 2c, 3b and 4c, especially in the treatment of the eyes and nose. The green ground is made up of several unpainted pieces, cross-hatching, varied foliate designs and at least two fragments with a trefoil *rinceau* on curling stems which have been painted to form the outer edge of a roundel. The shield is complete and dates to the 14th century. Newton observed it in the fourth window from the east of the north wall of Ellerton church. There is an anomaly concerning the setting of this shield which will be returned to after describing the second shield bearing a lion rampant.

This second shield (2c) is Or a Lion rampant Gules, the arms of de la Pole, according to Newton, placed on a roundel with light green ground and red rim (Fig.229). The field of the shield is made from a form of fern *rinceau* similar to that of 4c. The light green ground of the roundel is made up from a trefoil *rinceau* of the same design as that used for the field of 3b. This background has been cut to receive a shield and has a plain border on both the left and right sides of the painting, clearly intended as the medieval setting for a shield of this size and shape. Gibson noted this shield in the second window from the east of the south wall of Ellerton church. No photographs of these original settings seem to have survived, but extremely grainy photocopies of photographs were deposited with the York Glaziers' Trust. From these it appears that, until the shields were removed from Ellerton, the Mowbray shield (2a) was surrounded by far more pieces of a trefoil *rinceau* roundel than at present, in Selby Abbey. It also appears that whilst the two pieces of trefoil on curling stem on the left-hand side remain in an equivalent position, the right-hand side was occupied formerly by the trefoil *rinceau* which is now to be found on the left-hand side of the de la Pole shield (2c). The de la Pole shield had further pieces of this second trefoil design on the right-hand side. Judging by the size and shape, these are the pieces which remain with it now. These various fragments of roundel are 14th century, but it is no longer clear to which each belonged.

There are three heraldic shields of completely different blasonings. The first is (1b) Azure fretty Argent, on a roundel with a red ground and green rim. Newton identified these as the arms of Etchingham (Gibson n.d.). The red ground is, again, a trefoil diaper. Much of the 14th century glass is corroded, but it was noted that four pieces of the fret were modern (ibid.). This shield was to be found in the second window from the east of the north wall of Ellerton church. The second of this last group of heraldic shields is (4b) Argent three Asses or Horses heads erased Gules, on a quatrefoil with two ogee lobes constituted of mixed fragments of glass. These have been identified as the arms of Martin (Newton in Gibson n.d.; but see below). There is no clear distinction as to whether these are horses' or asses' heads. The Argent field is made up of a diaper of a similar design to that of 4a. This shield was set into the north window of the west wall of Ellerton church (ibid.). The jumble of background fragments includes several lengths of beading with stickwork stars between, and all reserved in yellow stain. There are a number of pieces of oak leaf and acorn quarry design, a rosette, a piece of diaper and a trefoil stickwork border design. Whilst most elements of the shield are 14th century, the jumbled fragments appear to be mainly 14th and 15th century.

The last heraldic shield is that of England with an azure label for difference denoting the eldest son of the monarch, that is, the heir apparent (cf. Brault 1997, 51). This is (6) Gules three Lions passant guardant in pale Or a label overall Azure, on a roundel with a green ground and white rim. The lions appear to be made out of pot-metal yellow. The label is diapered with a quatrefoil pattern picked out of a matt ground. The ruby ground is unpatterned. These are the royal arms of England prior to c.1340 when Edward III adopted the style and the arms of the kings of France, which he quartered with the lions of England. The shield is complete and dates to the first half of the 14th century, prior to c.1340; it is larger than the other shields. At Ellerton it appeared in the first window from the east in the north wall, within a medley of 19th century glass set in a quatrefoil (Gibson n.d.).

In addition to the heraldic shields, there are two roundels, one of which is an original 14th century composition (5b), the second of which has been reconstructed from 14th century fragments (5a). The first (5b) contains two oak leaves in reserve from a yellow ground and two corresponding leaves in reserve from a ruby ground. The four have been set in a cross and are surrounded by what appears to be a complete ring of grisaille edging pattern. The pattern consists of a lobed lozenge motif alternating with an 'S' design with trefoil terminals. Both the oak leaves and the grisaille ring are 14th century patterns, and are likely to be contemporary in this arrangement. This was the arrangement which survived from the 19th century, where it appeared in the north window of the west wall. Gibson believed this entire roundel to be more or less complete (ibid.). The outer ring of blue is a composite of painted and unpainted pieces, and must have been made for the resetting in Selby Abbey. The second roundel (5a) is a reconstruction made from medieval pieces and following the pattern of the first. This differs in having two oak leaves in reserve from a yellow ground opposed to two leaves in reserve from a green ground. The ring equivalent to the grisaille ring on 5b is made up from a number of odd fragments of grisaille and quarry glass, grozed to the correct shape. Only one piece appears in any way likely to have come from an original edging pattern similar to that of 5b. It is not at all clear from the surviving copies of the Ellerton church tracery lights that any of the glass which now surrounds the oak leaves was present in the 19th century; instead, large portions of plain beaded border were present when the roundel appeared in the south window of the west wall of Ellerton church (ibid.). Again, the blue outer ring is a composite which was made for installation in Selby Abbey.

Finally, the window in Selby Abbey contains five quatrefoils or tracery panels of jumbled medieval fragments. The first of these is (1a) oak and vine leaf grisaille from a quarry glazing with yellow-stained edge, or stickwork edging patterns. There is one finely drawn vine leaf on a curling stem in reserve which may have come from a Tree of Jesse, a rosette, two pieces of lozenge diaper and a fragment of masonry pattern. The quatrefoil is dominated by a large cross with flattened trefoil arms (cross patonce) in reserve from a yellow-stained ground. The second panel (1c) contains more oak and vine grisaille, with the same edging pattern as appears in 1a; here, however, it is clear that the edging pattern was curved, probably to fit tracery lights, and that the quarry lattice was bound by this stickwork pattern. There are two further, substantial pieces of finely drawn vine leaf such as might have been used for a late 14th/early 15th century Tree of Jesse. This panel also contains a rosette, two pieces of masonry pattern, a canopy pinnacle and the upper tower and crenellations of a castle, probably from a border pane. A larger piece of the heraldic fur vair or minever (which is the smallest form of vair), and a cross of the same pattern as that on 1a, also appear. The oak and vine leaf grisailles also appear in 2b, 3a and 3c, as do rosettes, oak leaves in reserve on a curling stem and further fragments of the heraldic furs vair or minever. A design of circlets of flowers is used in 3c, probably a late 14th/early 15th century textile pattern. There are two fragments of a distinctive vine leaf grisaille where the stem is twisted or plaited (3a and 3c). Two fragments of a 13th century double-headed upright trefoil with double side-curling leaves on a cross-hatched ground also appear in 3a and 3c. There is one complete quatrefoil in reserve in the centre of 2b. This panel differs from the other four quatrefoil tracery panels by including a piece of 14th century trefoil diaper or *rinceau*, and a human head. The head has a halo and curly hair, both highlighted in yellow stain, and the right hand is raised to the cheek. No identification of this saint or angel is possible without an attribute, but the style is of the first half of the 14th century.

With so little known about the buildings of Ellerton Priory, it is difficult to tie the glass into periods of construction. The similarity of the execution of the lions rampant on the shields, the shared repertoire of *rinceaux* diapers, the similarity in size of each of the shields strongly suggests that these were part of a contemporary programme. The only shield which is larger is that of the eldest son of the King of England. It need not be inferred from this difference in size that this shield belonged to a different glazing programme; rather the slightly larger dimensions may have denoted feudal superiority amidst an array of armigers.

The identifications of the shields are not as straightforward as Gibson's notes imply; whatever reasons Newton may have had for making the identifications, none are recorded. Further research and consultation with the College of Arms shows that alternatives are more likely for some of these identifications. The Dictionary of British Arms (*DBA*) is an 'ordinary' of arms relating specifically to identified arms in medieval material (both manuscripts and artefacts, the latter both movable and architectural) (Chesshyre and Woodcock 1992; Woodcock, Grant and Graham 1996). The *DBA* has been compiled in such a way that all the references associating a certain coat of arms with a given surname are listed, rather than subsuming them in a single identification; it is thus possible to gain an impression of the statistical likelihood of the identification (C.E.A. Cheesman, Rouge Dragon Pursuivant, pers. comm). Land-owning interests and social and political affiliations have also been taken into consideration when assessing the likelihood of a particular family being represented on the Ellerton shields. These arms appear to have been displayed in a coherent glazing programme, so there may have been connections between the people concerned.

The arms of the eldest son of the King of England are a useful starting point because they give us a date before which the shields must have been made, c.1340. It is unlikely that this is a retrospective reference to an heir to the monarch, since the lion passant guardant appears to be made out of pot-metal yellow and not yellow stain. Similarly, the crowns Or on the so-called Cleuisby arms are probably pot-metal rather than stained. This might suggest that the shields were made in the earlier part of the first half of the 14th century, rather than the 1330s, but this is by no means certain. These arms could refer, therefore, to Edward II whilst Prince of Wales (before 1307), or Edward III whilst heir to the throne (between 1312 and 1327). The label Azure, denoting the heir apparent, was changed to Argent during the lifetime of Edward, the Black Prince (who was not born until 1330; Brault 1997, 51; Brooke-Little 1970, 119). It is most likely, however, that the prince in question is Edmund Crouchback, Earl of Lancaster (died 1296), or his son Thomas, Earl of Lancaster (died 1322) (Chesshyre and Woodcock 1992). Both these used the arms of England differenced by an azure label, on which there frequently but not always appeared nine gold fleurs-de-lys (three on each point). On many artefacts on which the arms are shown, however, the fleurs-de-lys have disappeared through wear, or have been omitted due to the small scale of the object. This in turn encouraged the dissemination of the version without the fleurs-de-lys (C.E.A Cheesman pers. comm.).

The arms of Etchingham seem to be the least problematic of the smaller shields. The card-index for the *DBA* contains 24 references to this name in association with these arms. They are described and identified with William de Etchingham of Etchingham, Sussex, knight of the shire of Sussex, who died in 1290, and with his son and heir, also William, who died in 1326 (Brault 1997, 157). A younger son of William senior, Robert, succeeded his elder brother and may have borne these arms. William junior was summoned to serve against the Scots in 1298, 1300 and 1301 (ibid.). However, a Yorkshire family also bore these arms, namely the Caves of Cave, for whom the *DBA* card-index provides ten references (C.E.A. Cheesman, pers. comm.). This last identification may be thought the more likely if the connection with Ellerton were to be Yorkshire landholders rather than comrades-in-arms at the time of the Scottish wars.

The Fauconberg (Falconbridge or Fauconberge) arms are also relatively unproblematic. There were many different arms borne by members of the Fauconberg family in the late 13th and early 14th century. However, from the late 13th century onwards the senior line of the Fauconbergs used the arms of their maternal ancestors the Bruce or Brus family of Skelton, Yorkshire: Argent, a lion rampant Azure. This brings the connection far closer to Ellerton. It could be, therefore, that at the time that the shield was commissioned in the early 14th century, these were the arms of either Bruce of Skelton, or Fauconberg (illustrated in *VCH Yorks* 1914, 407; *VCH Yorks* 1969, 150). Brault (1997, 159) cites only one member of the Fauconberg family taking these arms, but later in the 14th century they became the generally used and recognised arms of the whole family. The only other is the Braytoft family, who are ascribed the arms with a certain regularity, but their interests were largely confined to their original county of Lincolnshire (C.E.A. Cheesman, pers. comm.). In conclusion, given the Yorkshire connection of the Fauconbergs, and the fact that their arms of c.1300 appear in the nave clerestory of York Minster (SXXVII), this would seem to be the most obvious identification.

It is interesting that although Alan de Wilton is recorded as having given land to Ellerton Priory, there is no documentation to prove that Alan de Wilton owned this land; it had been, and may have remained, the property of another of the Yorkshire branches of the Bruces (Golding 1995, 233–4).

The two shields which are very similar to that of the Fauconbergs, differing only in that the lions are crowned Or, were identified as possibly the arms of Cleuisby (Newton in Gibson n.d.), but there is no obvious reason for this. These precise arms are found ascribed only to 'Hanlo' and to 'S. Robert de Jauneby' (Chesshyre and Woodcock 1992). The first ascription comes from a 'roll' of arms giving the arms of the murderers of Thomas à Becket, preserved in a manuscript compilation called Calveley's book, now in the British Library (C.E.A. Cheesman, pers. comm.). These arms are, however, a reverse tincture of the arms of the Lord of Galloway. They are recorded in this reverse way and attributed to the Lord of Galloway in at least one Roll of Arms of the reign of Edward I (Brault 1997, 188). These arms were used by Devorguilla de Balliol (died 1290), daughter of Alan of Galloway. Devorguilla was married to John de Balliol of Barnard Castle, Durham. Their son, also John de Balliol, was crowned King of Scots in 1292, after Edward I had judged in his favour. He abdicated in 1296, during events which precipitated the Anglo-Scots wars, and left Edward I to assume the lordship of Galloway (ibid.). Two threads are recognisable in connection with the shields so far: families with landed interests in the close vicinity of York and Ellerton; and connections with the English armies mustered in the North during the Anglo-Scots wars.

There is, however, one further contender for the blasoning Argent, a lion rampant Azure crowned Or. This is Robert de Johnby of Northumberland, knight of the Shire of Cumberland (Brault 1997, 239). This knight was still living in 1319 and his inclusion in yet another Roll of Arms drawn up during the reign of Edward attests his presence in the muster.

The arms which are blasoned Or a Lion rampant Gules were ascribed to de la Pole by Newton. The *DBA* contains seven references for the ascription of these arms to individuals with that or a similar surname (Chesshyre and Woodcock 1992; Brault 1997, 349). This was not, however, the famous de la Pole family that rose to great prominence in the later 14th century and held the titles of Earl and Duke of Suffolk, but rather a prominent Welsh family better known as de Cherlton or Charlton, who held the Lordship of Powys centred on Pole or Poole (now Welshpool) in Montgomeryshire. If all the references for Pole/de la Pole, Cherlton/Charlton, and Powys are added together, the total number of references for these arms is 38 (Chesshyre and Woodcock 1992; C.E.A. Cheesman, pers. comm.).

Owain de la Pole, or Owain ap Gruffydd of Welshpool, Powys, Wales, was a prince of southern Powys and a banneret of Edward I's household (Brault 1997, 349). He bore these arms differenced with a label azure. Lewis de la Pole, his younger brother, bore them differenced by a band azure. The undifferenced arms were also borne by Ieuan ap Gruffydd (who has been identified with Owain de la Pole), Gruffydd ap Grewynwyn, father of the above, Roger le Bigod, Robert de Felbrigg and Robert de Musgrove. All may be identified through the Edward I Rolls of Arms (ibid., 481).

It should be added, however, that there are many other identifications for Or a Lion rampant Gules, among them the Norfolk family of Felbrigge (fifteen references in *DBA*); the family of Leigh of Leigh in Cheshire (nine references in *DBA*); and the 'attributed' arms of Randolph Meschines, the early post-conquest Earl of Chester, and the early, mythical kings of Scotland (Chesshyre and Woodcock 1992; Woodcock, Grant and Graham 1996; C.E.A. Cheesman, pers. comm.). The identification of these arms is, therefore, problematic.

The Mowbray shield is also problematic (Gules, a lion rampant Argent, within a bordure engrailed Argent). Whilst the undifferenced arms are certainly those of Mowbray, it has not been possible to trace anyone to whom the engrailed bordure can be attributed. The Mowbrays were of baronial status. The barony is one of four represented in the Heraldic Window of the north nave aisle of York Minster (nXXIII; c.1310–20). The first Lord Mowbray was Roger of Thirsk, North Yorkshire, whose son John, Lord Mowbray, became Sheriff of Yorkshire and Governor of York Castle in 1313 (Harrison 1927, 44). The lions of Roger de Mowbray alternate with the arms of his wife, Rose, daughter of Richard de Clare, Earl of Gloucester, in the borders of the early 14th century window nXXVI. It is John de Mowbray who is commemorated by this combination of arms. Mowbray shields of c.1300 appear in the north nave clerestory (NXXI and NXXV) of the Minster, in an early 15th century version in the choir clerestory (SX), and in the south aisle chantry chapel of Holy Trinity, Goodramgate. Roger de Mowbray's arms appear in a shield (not of glass) at Fountains Abbey (Brault 1997, 311). Roger fought against the Scots in 1291 and died in 1297. A younger son, also Roger, and brother of John, bore these arms and served at Perth in 1310 (ibid.).

Having considered reliable attributions to Mowbray, it would now appear wrong to identify the Ellerton shield as the arms of Mowbray. The Mowbrays only seem to have been recorded once with an engrailed border in the medieval period, and that was with a blue engrailed bordure. Much more usually one finds an indented border (also usually of some dark colour such as black), or — in the classic version of the arms — no border at all (C.E.A. Cheesman, pers. comm.). The prime candidate for the arms in Selby Abbey 2a appears to be Gray or Grey, for which *DBA* lists 27 instances (Chesshyre and Woodcock 1992). The particular Grey family in question was that associated with Chillingham in Northumberland; these arms are, for instance, recorded on the mid 15th century Grey monument in Chillingham parish church (Heslop and Harbottle 1999, 131); on the late 14th century roof bosses in the nave of Bothal church, also in Northumberland; as well as in the (lost) east window of St George's church, Stamford in Lincolnshire (Hebgin-Barnes 1996, 272–3 for antiquarian sources). The only other name recorded more than once for these arms in *DBA* is William Ridell or Rydell, given in Cotgreave's Ordinary c.1350 and in Calveley's book, in the roll of Becket's murderers (Chesshyre and Woodcock 1992; C.E.A. Cheesman, pers. comm.). Again, a North country connection seems to be the most likely explanation of the presence of these arms at Ellerton Priory in North Yorkshire.

The arms attributed to Martin by Newton were described as 'reconstituted' (Gibson n.d.). The meaning of this is unclear: whether made up from medieval elements that were not necessarily originally associated, or whether a corroded medieval shield had been restored to this standard. It has not been possible to locate any appropriate Martin arms of this description to date. Nothing of this description appears in the published volumes of the *DBA*. However, the card-index on which *DBA* is based includes a few coats of arms consisting of this design, though none of them is definitely found with this precise colour scheme. I am grateful to C.E.A. Cheesman (pers. comm.) for the following possible ascriptions:

John Charman, called Mockyng, seal, 1357: three Horses heads (no tinctures)

John de Horcy, seal, 1369: three Horses heads bridled (no tinctures)

John Horsey, seal, 1417: three Horses heads couped (no tinctures)

Adam Cossar, burgess of Stirling, seal, 1451: three Horses heads couped and bridled (no tinctures)

John Horsley, seal, 1457: three Horses heads couped (no tinctures)

Anonymous, Writhe's Book, c.1530: Argent three Nags heads couped Sable

John Horsey, monument, Yetminster (Dorset), 1531: three Horses heads couped and bridled (no tinctures)

The recurrence of surnames such as Horsey and Horsley in this list suggests that this may be a canting or punning coat of arms which identifies a family of such a name. It is also clear that none of the identifications stretch back to the period at which the glass was made. Other entries in the *DBA* card-index show that some Horseys at least used a shield in which the background was red, the horses' heads white, while others used one with a blue background. This discrepancy suggests a degree of variation and there may have been still others using a white shield with red heads (C.E.A. Cheesman, pers. comm.). The Ellerton identification, therefore, remains unknown.

It remains unclear what exactly links these arms, and why they should have been placed in Ellerton Priory in the early 14th century. There are certainly feudal links between some of the named families. At the time of the Testa de Nevill (compiled during the reign of Henry III, father of Edward I) members of the Brus family held seven knights' fees from the honour of Mowbray in Yorkshire, and Petrus de Fauconburg held one-fifth of a knight's fee from the same honour (Baines 1871–7, 510). One Roger Hay held two half knight's fees from the honour of de Brus in Yorkshire, and William de Balliol owed one-quarter of a knight's fee to this honour (ibid., 513). At least three of the possible identifications are to Yorkshire or Northern families. The relations which connected these families may have been a mixture of kinship and political affiliations as was common in 14th century displays of heraldry. This period, after all, has been described as that during which we see the maximum secular presence in ecclesiastical contexts. Whatever the particular reasons for the presence of these shields at Ellerton Gilbertine Priory, this provides a wider social and historical context to which we shall return in the general discussion below (pp.510–11).

Fordham, Cambridgeshire

Priory of St Mary Magdalene and St Peter, canons only, possibly founded between 1204 and 1227, possibly before. No glass known.

Haverholme, Lincolnshire (Fig.230)

Priory, double house, founded c.1137–9. Notes and illustrations from a rescue excavation in October 1962 made by M.U. Jones, supplied by Hilary Healey, lead came and painted window glass reported. Glass unlocated.

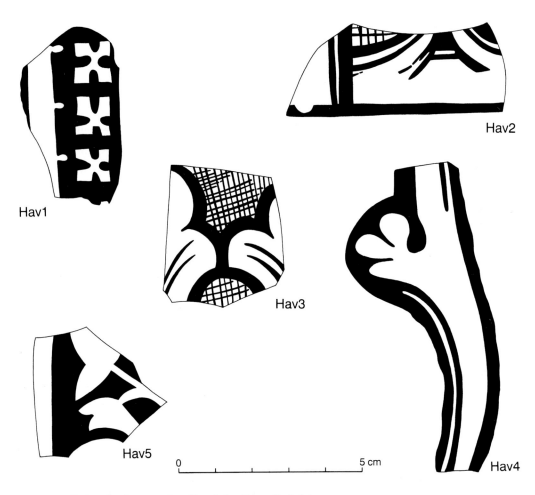

Fig. 230   Window glass fragments from Haverholme Priory. Scale 1:1

Haverholme Priory, Kesteven, Lincolnshire, was the second of the houses established for Gilbertine nuns, and was founded in 1139. The site of the priory was an island of boulder clay rising out of a marshy area formed by a fork in the River Slea, a few miles north-west of the Bishop of Lincoln's manor of Sleaford (Golding 1995, 202). The land had originally been offered by Bishop Alexander of Lincoln to the Cistercians of Fountains Abbey, in 1137. The Cistercians deemed the island unsuitable for agriculture and settled at Louth Park instead. The bishop subsequently offered the land to St Gilbert, although it may not have been his to give; two local lords, Halselin/ Hauselin and de Cauz, had to be compensated for the potential lost in the transfer of the property (ibid., 203). Haverholme Priory was very dependent on these and other local families for much of its existence.

A small quantity of window glass was recovered from trial trenching at Haverholme, undertaken by Peter Addyman in 1961. Further glass was found during excavations which took place between 1962 and 1964, supervised by Mr and Mrs W.T. Jones. Most of the glass came from a late deposit probably related to the demolition of the priory (M.U. Jones, pers. comm.).

Excavation took place on the south slope of the island and uncovered the partial layout of at least three buildings. These were interpreted as outbuildings lying south of the church and claustral ranges (M.U. Jones, typescript report). Although the Louth Park chronicle records that lay brothers were sent ahead of the original Cistercian party to construct the first buildings at Haverholme, the archaeology provided no distinction between Cistercian and Gilbertine phases (cf. Golding 1995, 202, n.45; Dugdale 1846, 5, 414).

One fragment from the 1961 trial trenching is painted with an edging pattern of crosses or quatrefoils which was common in the late 13th century and the 14th century, particularly the first half (*Hav1*). The majority of the fragments from the 1962–4 assemblage are pieces of 13th century grisaille. Cross-hatched grounds are common, although of varying thickness of line. It is clear, however, that many of the designs were contained within strapwork borders (*Hav2*), suggestive of a trellis-type arrangement of grisaille quarries, as existed in Lincoln Cathedral, or in geometrical arrangements whose leaded shapes were emphasised by these banded edges. This trait was used into the third quarter of the 13th century. The fragment which shows two trefoil heads side-by-side (*Hav3*) can be paralleled in an edging pattern found at Stowbardolph, Norfolk, and recorded amongst the grisailles at Salisbury Cathedral (Marks 1993, 131 fig.102b; 132, fig.104b). At least one trefoil has been painted on a piece of glass for which the cut-line follows the curve of the design (*Hav4*). A number of open and closed beading patterns are probably contemporary with this grisaille.

A smaller number of fragments appear to be of later date than the foregoing. Amongst these is a leaf design in reserve from a solid ground (*Hav5*). It was possibly used as part of a foliate border, probably side-alternating, or as a background diaper against which figures would be set, and dates to the very end of the 13th or the first half of the 14th century. One fragment may be part of the detail from an architectural canopy of the 14th century. At least two fragments remained encased in lead.

The fragments tell us little about the glazing of the priory and its buildings except, perhaps, that some of the outer buildings were either glazed from the 13th century, or received glass which had been taken out of the more significant buildings during a period of reglazing later in the history of the priory. Since there is so little represented, and what there is probably comes from Dissolution debris, this glass may only represent stray fragments deriving from elsewhere on the site.

Hitchin (New Biggin), Hertfordshire

Collegiate chantry/priory of St Saviour, canons only, founded 1361–2. No glass known.

Holland Bridge (Bridge End), Lincolnshire

Priory of St Saviour, canons only, founded c.1195–9. No glass known.

Holland Marsh, Lincolnshire

Priory of St Thomas the Martyr, canons only, founded c.1180, but more probably a hermitage. No glass known.

Lincoln

St Katherine's priory, canons only, founded c.1148 (including hospital of the Holy Sepulchre). No glass known.

Old Malton, North Yorkshire

Priory, canons only, founded c.1150. No glass known.

Marlborough, Wiltshire

Priory of St Margaret, canons only, founded c.1195–9. No glass known.

Marmont, Cambridgeshire

Priory, canons only, founded c.1204. No glass known.

Mattersey, Nottinghamshire

Priory, founded c.1185–92. Small portions in east window of north aisle of Mattersey parish church said to have come from the priory. No confirmation of original provenance.

Mattersey Priory was founded before 1192, probably by Roger son of Ranulf de Mattersey, and dedicated to St Helen (Golding 1995, 221). It may have been the last house to be founded during St Gilbert's lifetime. Mattersey may have been intended as a small house from the start; by c.1195 the Order limited the number of canons here to ten, that is, three less than the number stipulated by the Gilbertine constitution (Golding 1995, 222, cf.234, n.181). The founder's family were of the knightly class, but never had great wealth; Golding concludes that the endowment would have been limited (ibid., 222). At the time of the Dissolution there were only four canons and their prior.

Much of the layout of the site survives, centred around a small cloister. Although the plan and form of the church is unknown, it seems to have had a long aisleless nave with either a chapel to the south, or a chapter house. The eastern and southern ranges were vaulted at ground level, with the dormitory projecting to the east (Fig.67e, *AY* 11/2).

Fragments of stained glass in the head of the central cinquefoliated light of the east window of the north aisle (nI) of the parish church of All Saints, Mattersey, are believed to have come from the former Gilbertine priory church nearby (Graham 1901, 215). There are at least five fragments of a common 15th century border design of a strapwork lozenge, with a central quatrefoil in reserve from a yellow stained ground, and with seaweed leaves, again in reserve from a yellow stained ground, in each of the four corners of a rectangular pane. There are also at least two fragments of a crown border design, of approximately the same dimensions as the lozenge design. This shows a crown with some attempt at three-dimensional representation, with flowers decorating the band and long, elaborate strawberry leaves. Two shades of yellow stain were employed, the deepest being used for the decorative rosettes on the band of the crown. Stipple shading and white highlights are also used on the crown to denote depth and shadow.

The majority of fragments are decorated with a consistent 15th century quarry design, featuring a central boss with spokes. Both the main axial spokes and the short intermediary spokes incorporate ogee 'spade-like' leaves or points. The axial spokes are elongated versions, whereas the intermediary spokes are quite squat. With the exception of these intermediary spokes, the quarries resemble Type 16 in Newton (1979). There is a small quantity of drapery (c.40–50cm^2) painted with folds on blue pot-metal, which must have come from a fairly large-scale figure. Two roundels dominate the assemblage: one is the nimbed head of a figure, possibly a child; the other contains the monogram IHS. The head has short, curly hair in yellow stain, a simple nimbus with yellow-stained rim. There is no division of the nimbus to denote a member of the Trinity. The face is simply drawn in outline; only the right eye remains and it is looking up to the right. The most salient feature of this fragment is that a hand caresses or supports the chin of the head. Contrary to Graham (1901, 215), this does not appear to be the head of a female saint, but rather male. There are images in which the Christ Child caresses the chin of His Mother (cf. the 14th century Virgin and Child, in the east window of Eaton Bishop church, Herefordshire), but images which would provide the exact conjunction of hand and head seen at Mattersey are limited. The hand on the Mattersey fragment is at the wrong angle to be the subject's own hand, as one might see in a grieving angel (cf. York Minster sXXXVI, 3b; French and O'Connor 1987, pl.16e). It might possibly originate in a family group, like St Mary Cleophas, Alphaeus and family in the east window of Holy Trinity, Goodramgate, dated to 1471. It appears to be a demonstrative hand, denoting affection or speech, or drawing the viewer's attention to the nimbed figure.

The roundel with the sacred monogram IHS has gothic lettering in yellow stain, with some lightly drawn decorative *rinceau* detail, set on a ground of white grisaille composed of fairly simple rosettes. There are at least two other fragments of glass with yellow stain and floral decoration or rosettes which may have come from the edge of a robe, and one piece with a stylised fur pattern.

All these fragments could have come from a single 15th century window or an array of contemporary windows. There is no evidence internal to the assemblage to suggest that there is anything distinctively Gilbertine in the decoration or subject-matter, and nothing concrete with which to tie the glass to the priory site. The priory church lies about one and a half miles from the parish church. The north aisle of the parish church is Perpendicular in style, and there is no clear reason why the glass may not have originated in the parish church. Since the parish church had been appropriated to the Gilbertine Priory by October 1280 (*VCHN* 2, 1910, 141), the priory may have had some part in glazing this structure too. In style, there is little to distinguish these fragments from the glass-painting of neighbouring south Yorkshire or Lincolnshire, and there is very little extant medieval glazing in Nottinghamshire with which to compare it.

Newstead-in-Ancolne, Lincolnshire

Priory, canons only, founded 1171. No glass known.

Nun Ormsby (North Ormsby), Lincolnshire

Priory, double house, founded c.1148–54. No glass known.

Owton, Co. Durham

Priory, canons only, nominally founded c.1204, failed almost immediately. No glass known.

Poulton, Gloucestershire

Collegiate chantry/priory of St Mary, canons only, founded c.1348, Gilbertine from 1350. No glass known.

Ravenstonedale, Westmorland

Priory, canons only, founded mid 12th century, failed almost immediately. Continued until Dissolution as wealthy grange. No glass known.

Sempringham, Lincolnshire

Settled c.1131, priory of St Mary, double house, founded c.1139–47. Mainly mid 14th century glass held in Lincoln City and County Museum. For glass see pp.465–82.

Shouldham, Norfolk

Priory of St Mary and the Holy Cross, double house, founded 1193–1200. No glass known.

Sixhills, Lincolnshire

Priory, double house, founded c.1148–54. No glass known.

Stamford, Lincolnshire

Priory house of study, canons only, founded after 1266, possibly c.1303, but closed by 1334. No glass known.

Tunstall, Redbourne, North Lincolnshire

Priory, double house, founded before 1160, failed within a generation. No glass known.

Watton, East Riding of Yorkshire

Priory, double house, founded c.1150. Pieces of early 14th century glass now in the top of the central light of the nave south aisle of York Minster (sXXX).

Watton was a large foundation, made in 1150, and represented the first expansion of the Gilbertine communities beyond Lincolnshire. It was founded, along with the Gilbertine house at Malton, North Yorkshire, and the Premonstratensian Abbey at Alnwick (Northumbria), by Eustace FitzJohn, one of the greatest magnates of the 12th century in Yorkshire (Golding 1995, 215). The foundation may have been prompted by Eustace's second wife, Agnes, whose family had a close association with Gilbert of Sempringham. This was a double house established for nuns with thirteen canons to support them.

The site was excavated between 1898 and 1901 by St John Hope (1900; 1901). Excavation revealed suites of buildings arranged around two cloisters, connected by long corridors. These were interpreted, through use of the Gilbertine Rule, constitutions and Rite, as separate accommodation for the nuns and canons. Whilst each community had a chapter house, the monks had their own chapel, but the larger church was connected to the nuns' cloister and divided into two by a longitudinal wall. This was used by the nuns on one side and the canons on the other (Fig.67d, *AY* 11/2).

Given the extensive excavation of the site, and the fact that it became the richest of the Gilbertine houses, it is disappointing that so little remains of the former glazing. A very small quantity of fragments from Watton Priory have been leaded into a rectangular panel, set in the south aisle of York Minster nave (window sXXX). This includes some flashed ruby and pot-metal green glass. The central quarry features a form of quatrefoil, with trefoil terminals, all in outline on a plain ground. None of this informs us of the glazing of this once vast priory.

York, 46–54 Fishergate, North Yorkshire

Priory of St Andrew, canons only, founded c.1195–1202. Large amount of 13th and 14th century glass from excavations. For glass see pp.366–464.

Other glass associated with the Gilbertines

Finally, there is a small amount of glass from four Lincolnshire sites, which were associated with the Gilbertines, although they did not originate as Gilbertine monasteries as such. Heraldic arms attributed to St Gilbert were recorded in the chancel east window of the parish church of St Andrew, Cranwell, by 17th century antiquaries (Hebgin-Barnes 1996, 74; *VCHL* 1906, 186). Sempringham held land in the parish and the advowson of the church. Similarly, the shield of St Gilbert appeared in the chancel of St Peter, Norton Disney. The advowson had been granted to the Gilbertine house of St Katherine, outside Lincoln in the 12th century; it was then appropriated to Sempringham in 1306 (Hebgin-Barnes 1996, 228, n.4; *VCHL* 1906, 184, 188). The arms of Sempringham Priory also appeared in a window of St Denis, Kirkby Laythorpe; the priory had acquired the rectory of this parish before 1535 (Hebgin-Barnes 1996, 149, n.2; *VCHL* 1906, 18). Arms commemorating the three marriages of Margaret Everingham (d.1473), a woman who became a nun at Sempringham Priory, were once contained within the east window of the parish church of St Denis, Silk Willoughby (Hebgin-Barnes 1996, 255).

The paucity of glazing remains from other Gilbertine sites makes the two larger collections, from Sempringham Priory, Lincolnshire, and St Andrew, York, our only significant sources for this aspect of the furnishings of this unique English order.

Evidence for the Gilbertines

Historical evidence for the Gilbertine Rule

St Gilbert founded his first religious communities in order to accommodate women who had been inspired by the piety and spiritual rigour of the reforming monastic movement of the early 12th century. The women may have sought an eremitical life; Gilbert may have wished to support a male community. Whatever the aspirations, the result was that a community of female religious was established at Sempringham by 1131 (Golding 1995, 16–17). More followers were soon attracted to the austere and pious way of life pursued at Sempringham. A second house was established at Haverholme. The increased numbers of followers incurred greater responsibilities. However, 'Gilbert showed some reluctance to lead his communities and thus decided to cede them to the Cistercians' (ibid., 21).

Gilbert had spent time at Cistercian houses whilst on the Continent earlier in his life, and had been convinced that 'they were more perfect and stricter than others in their observance of the religious life' (ibid., 26). He travelled to Citeaux in 1147 but the Cistercians refused to admit the Lincolnshire women to their Order. Gilbert travelled on to Clairvaux in 1148 in order to discuss the formulation of a rule for his nuns, the priests, and communities of lay brothers and sisters required to fulfil their religious and economic needs. Whilst Elkins (1984) has argued that Gilbert and St Bernard of Clairvaux never met, Golding has argued that the Cistercian's personal guidance in the formulation of the Gibertine Rule is clear, whether directed through letter, deputising Cistercians in England or in person (Golding 1995, 31). The specific care of the Gilbertine nuns owed a lot to customs established at Augustinian and Premonstratensian houses, which had a greater experience with houses of religious women. On returning to Sempringham, Gilbert instituted canons for his communities; this restricted the role of the lay brothers, to whom he gave customs which were a modified version of those by which Cistercian *conversi* lived. The distinctive compostion of double houses of Gilbertine nuns and canons was the result. The Gilbertine institutes for canons 'are heavily dependent on models found in the Cistercian institutes' (ibid., 126).

A large number of the customs for the Gilbertine houses were devised in order to maintain the strict enclosure of the nuns to avoid unnecessary contact with the outside world and to secure strict segregation between the nuns and canons. This concern found its most accentuated form in the provision of turntables in the window-house by which means the nuns were to communicate with the canons; even here, only the most trusted and responsible members of each community were to be allowed to use this facility (Golding 1995, 127; St John Hope 1901, 28). The plan of Sempringham church clearly shows a medial wall creating a portion for use by the nuns and a portion for the canons (Figs.216–17, pp.466–7). Lay brothers were not to speak to or to hear the nuns except at mass; the canons only entered the nuns' church on fourteen of the most solemn feasts of the year, and then in strictly ordered procession. Curtains were to be hung about the nuns' cloister and at the church door in order to prevent them catching a glimpse of the canons. According to the Gilbertine Rule, 'Both the layout and the structure [of their conventual buildings] emphasised an isolation of all senses except hearing, and even that was strictly regulated' (Golding 1995, 128). The irony is that Gilbertine women ended up more strictly enclosed than their contemporaries, including the later Cistercian nuns, and Cistercian abbesses had greater access to power than Gilbertine women.

The inspiration of the Cistercians, nonetheless, was to remain a strong influence in the foundation of both the Gilbertine Rule and liturgical rite (King 1955; Woolley 1921). This is obvious in the textual stipulations concerning the physical appearance of Gilbertine houses. One of the Gilbertine Institutes forbids unnecessary ornament and the use of figural representations, allowing only the use of wooden crosses, and can be compared with the *Cistercian Exordium Parvum*.

Sculpturae, vel picturae superfluae in Ecclesiis nostris, seu in officinis aliquibus Monasterii ne fiant interdicimus, quia, dum talibus intenditur, utilitas bonae meditationis, vel disciplina religiosae gravitatis saepe negligitur. Cruces tamen pictas, quae sunt ligneae habemus.

(*Coenobia Anglicana Ordinis Sancti Gilberti de Sempringham* vol.IV, t.II, part II, 784; King 1955, 398)

We forbid that there be superfluous sculptures or paintings in our churches or in any other of the Monastery buildings, because while people are looking at such things, the usefulness of good meditation and the discipline of religious gravitas is often neglected. We do however allow painted crosses which are wooden.

Sculpture vel picture in ecclesiis nostris seu in officinis aliquibus monasterii ne fiant interdicimus, quia dum talibus intenditur, utilitas bone meditationis vel disciplina religiose gravitatis sepe negligitur. Cruces tamen pictas que sunt lignee habemus.

(*Exordium Parvum Ordinis Cisterciensis* XXVII; Norton 1986b, 324)

We forbid there to be sculptures or paintings in our churches, or in any other buildings of the monastery, because while people are looking at such things, the usefulness of good meditation and the discipline of religious gravitas is often neglected. We do however allow painted crosses which are wooden.

Furthermore, the rubrics in the Gilbertine missal and some of the ordinances in the Gilbertine ordinale are taken directly from the *consuetudinarium* of the Cistercians, in some cases word for word (King 1955, 400). Gilbert died in 1189 and was canonised in 1201/2. Nine double monasteries and four houses of canons only had been founded in his lifetime. After his death, only two nunneries were founded, the remaining institutions were set up for canons only (Foreville and Keir 1987, xxxvi–xxxvii). However, the Order that he left behind came under considerable pressure to justify its continuing existence. Elkins (1984) has argued that the *Vita* of St Gilbert, written after his death, deliberately emphasised the role of St Bernard of Clairvaux in advising and approving Gilbert's stay at Clairvaux. The *Vita* probably overstated the reality of Bernard's involvement, but did so in order to legitimise the origins of the Gilbertine Order. Thus, Bernard's considerable spiritual and theological authority was added to the argument in support of the Gilbertines as a distinct and worthy institution. This period in the Order's history may provide a context in which to understand the remains of the first priory at Fishergate, and the pattern of furnishings, including the glazing, which archaeological investigation has revealed.

Influence of the Gilbertine Rule upon the glazing schemes

Material culture studies are concerned with all aspects of the relationship between the material and the social . . . The aim is to achieve a model capable of representing the complex nature of the interaction between social strategy and artefactual variability and change (Miller 1985, 4).

It was suggested above that the initial glazing programme for the priory church and chapter house at Fishergate included little or no figural or historiated glass. Coloured glass illustrating Christ, the saints and historiated scenes may only have been introduced from the mid to second half of the 13th century, at about the time the first alterations to the priory were made (Period 6b/c) (pp.139ff, *AY* 11/2).

Is there any further evidence for believing that the original glazing of the Gilbertine priory church of St Andrew, York, may have employed little or no figural glass? Can the archaeological evidence from this house suggest a history which would otherwise escape us?

Simplicity: a positive aesthetic option

The archaeological evidence for the original priory buildings at Fishergate suggests that they were relatively plain compared with contemporary religious establishments in York, for example, the Benedictine priory of the Holy Trinity, Micklegate. The plan of St Andrew's church is reminiscent of cruciform churches with aisleless nave and transepts, each with a single eastern chapel (125–31, *AY* 11/2). This is the form taken by early Augustinian churches and the earliest stone churches of the Cistercians in the British Isles, such as Waverley. It has been argued that, whether by design or economic constraint, the form of the original St Andrew's priory church reflected that current at least 50 years before its foundation (ibid.). Further to this, the painted wall plaster is considered to have been conservative in its design (ibid., 305–6). It has been argued that, in the context of the time at which St Andrew's was founded, and the crisis of identity for the Order which followed Gilbert's death, the York house may have been chosen as an exemplar of an austere ideal to which the Order, retrospectively, aspired.

It is known that in the 12th century and in the first decade, at least, of the 13th century, the Cistercians were encouraged to eschew figural decoration in their churches. A preference for geometric and vegetal patterns is evident in floor tiles as well as window glass. White was used for painted wall decoration (for example at Fountains Abbey) as well as being the principal colour in grisaille glass. The symbolism of grisaille and the patterns which glazing schemes share with tile, in particular, have been studied in relation to themes of order, number symbolism, light and its equation to whiteness and purity, vegetal and floral symbolism. Zakin (1979) has found vivid exegesis of these motifs in the writings of St Bernard of Clairvaux whose works formed part of the core contemplative texts of Cistercian religiosity. He used imagery of light and whiteness to symbolise God and truth. The trilobed, fruiting trefoil (known as the *herba benedicta*) was a variant of the lily, symbolic of the Trinity, purity and Mary. In the Sermons on the Song of Songs, Bernard uses flowers as a symbol of spring and resurrection, blossoming and bringing forth fruit.

> *Truth, however, is a beautiful lily, remarkable in its brightness . . .* [it is] *eternal light, and its splendour and form is the essence of God . . . But notice that the signs of the Resurrection are like this year's flowers, blossoming in a new summer under the power of grace. Their fruit will come forth in the end at the future general resurrection and it will last forever. As it is said: 'Winter is over, the rain is past and gone. Flowers appear in our land'* (Sancti Bernardi opera, I, Sermons super Cantica Canticorum, trans. Zakin 1979).

Bernard refers to Christ as:

> *the first and chiefest Flower of the human race . . . the Rose of Sharon, and the Lily of the valleys (Cant. 2: 1); He then appeared as the first Flower of the Resurrection* (trans. Eales 1895, 351).

The particularly apposite use of the lily in conjunction with light as analogy for God's being is brought out in a sermon on the virtues:

> *An exquisite lily . . . is Truth; for its brightness is that of the Eternal Light, the unspotted mirror of the Power of God, and the image of His goodness (Wisd. 7: 26). It is assuredly a lily which our earth has produced by a new benediction, and prepared before the face of all peoples, a light to lighten the Gentiles (Luke 2: 31, 32)* (trans. Eales 1895, 428–9).

Bernard emphasised pattern and order in all things and obedience to God's law, the ultimate Order.

Examination of Cistercian ideals as expressed in architecture and art often links Bernard's work to the metaphysical aesthetics claimed for Gothic builders such as Abbot Suger of St Denis. The basis of such thought was the Platonic proposition that material forms were a pale reflection of a purer idea, and that the truth could only be reached by contemplation of the ideal which could disengage essential knowledge from those material settings (Leff 1958, 13). Contemplation of the ideal led the soul to a rediscovery of what it must originally have known. The Neoplatonists of the 12th century sought to trace natural things back to a divine source and believed that this spiritual reality in things was accessible to the human soul. Ultimately, contemplation allowed the soul to return to God, the Logos, the original whose idea it was.

An assessment linked to these ideas, however, risks presenting St Bernard's aesthetics as 'ascetical in an exclusive sense or contemplative in a simplistic sense' (Stiegman 1984). The first problem with such an interpretation is that asceticism is equated with renunciation of worldly wealth. Clearly, the English Cistercian houses thrived on vast landholdings and the wool production they supported. Whilst individual monks renounced all worldly possessions, the rebuilding of Rievaulx Abbey was a very grand and expensive exercise. Meredith Lillich (1982) has suggested that some Cistercian grisailles could be as costly as coloured glass. The second problem is that simplicity is a relative term in this context, implying a negative comparison, whereas Bernard's adoption of ascetical language may have represented a postive aesthetic option (Stiegman 1984, 1).

Stiegman claims that the context of Bernard's writings is a contemplative system proposed by the saint, which contrasts with other systems such as that of the Pseudo-Dionysius expounded by Suger, which was acknowledged as the means by which the mass of the population might form their spiritualities (Eco 1986, *passim*; Gage 1982, 1995, 40–69). Instead, as Bernard argues in his *Apologia*, 'We who have left the condition of the ordinary laity no longer have the aesthetic needs of their piety [*Nos vero qui iam de poplo exivimus* . . .]' (*Apologia* 28; Stiegman 1984, 5; cf. Rudolph 1990, 280–1). At least half the remaining text of the *Apologia* is concerned with Cistercian interiority. Stiegman argues that the Cistercian pursuit of *notitia sui*, or self-knowledge, has the dimension of an aesthetic principle in Bernard's writings. Bernard contrasts his conception of self-knowledge with *curiositas*, a dissipating curiosity for outward things (Rudolph 1990, 110–15). 'What Bernard calls curiosity is not intellectual vitality, but an outward movement that lessens concern for God's presence in the soul' (Stiegman 1984, 7).

The soul is the Cistercian criterion of created beauty. If attainment of spiritual, or personal, authenticity comes in the search for the true self, then Cistercian notitia sui *may be spoken of as a principle of authenticity* (Rudolph 1990, 8).

For Bernard, the search for true knowledge, self-knowledge, the return to God, could not be achieved without divine help, that is through grace. To achieve grace 'involved not proof but a condition of life in which the will to love God was the *sine qua non* of knowing Him' (Leff 1958, 135). Thus the monastery was for Bernard a workshop, in which the religious worked towards humility, compassion for others (*caritas*), and contemplation (looking upon the truth) culminating in ecstasy, the union with God (ibid.; Hufgard 1989, 66–101). Thus the practices of monasticism, as discourses by which the subject interprets him or herself, may be thought of as technologies of the self (Foucault 1988; Asad 1987; 1993, 125–67). It is the constitution of Christian subjectivities which must lie at the centre of our understanding of the physical form and decoration of the religious house.

The disciplinary practices of medieval religious communities regulated, informed and constructed religious subjects, the object being to create obedient wills. Mere observation and imitation of exemplary Christian lives was not enough for the Cistercians. To become a Christian subject was not to be the product of mere readings of symbols, but took re-organisation of the inner self. The will to obedience is a potentiality, a process of power

— the power of volition. Every aspect of the monk's life was subject to disciplining processes, aimed at creating perfection of will, perfection of soul. Discipline acted on the soul through the body: through dress, speech, table manners, physical work and gesture — posture and movement. Written texts which were chanted, recited, read, attended to and meditated upon were part of the disciplining programme and essential to interpretation of the physical environment within which the monks moved (Asad 1987, 170–1 and *passim*; 1993, 125–67 *passim*). External things were only useful insofar as they promoted the regulation of internal impulses and desires. The regulated environment of pattern encouraged an inward-looking discipline rather than the dissipating curiosity aroused by ornate and figurative environments against which Bernard of Clairvaux had railed.

It has been argued that the plan of the first priory church at Fishergate consciously evoked the simplicity of an earlier age and that the Gilbertines were keen to present their Order as aspiring to the spiritual asceticism already established by the Cistercians in the 12th century (pp.156–7, *AY* 11/2). The simplicity of decoration and conscious avoidance of figural images in the early glass may indicate that the canons made a real attempt to follow the spiritual and contemplative rigour of their contemporaries. The difference, however, is that as canons the Gibertines had contact with the secular world around them and were not 'dead to the world' in the way that the Cistercians nominally were. The particular impetus behind the choice of glazing and decorative schemes may lie in the fact that, following Gilbert's death, his houses of canons alone had to fight hard to justify their continued existence (as opposed to those canons who were attached to double houses and served the spiritual requirements of communities of religious women) (Elkins 1984). The foundation and construction of the Fishergate priory coincided both with the compilation of the *Vita* of Gilbert and his canonisation in 1202. The austerity of form and furnishing at Fishergate were not echoed at Sempringham in the 13th century, although the 12th century arrangements would have remained at that time. Haverholme is the only other site which has produced almost solely 13th century grisaille. As a small assemblage, however, it cannot be claimed to be diagnostic or representative.

Whatever spiritual ideals were embodied in the original priory buildings at Fishergate, they were evidently being eroded by the second half of the 13th century. This is the period during which we see definite evidence for figural and coloured glass. The necessity to maintain their precinct and buildings may have made it easy for the canons to accept the patronage of Bishop Burghersh. His intervention in the affairs of the community may be just one particular reflection of a wider process of secular intervention in the sacred spaces of churches which has been identified by Martindale (1992; and see pp.510–11).

From this perspective, the choice of a simple church form, simple architectural detail, simple mural decoration and largely grisaille glass at St Andrew's, Fishergate, may be seen as more than a happy coincidence of aesthetic preferences and economic stringencies: it was the conscious provision of an environment which helped to shape the spiritual discipline of the canons.

Conclusions

This study set out to collate and examine the remains of the glazing of the Gilbertine priories of England. The intention was, firstly, to publish all known Gilbertine glazing evidence for the first time, secondly, to determine the dating and stylistic affinities of the various assemblages, and thirdly, to determine whether or not there might be some consistency in the glazing preferences or priorities of the Order, in its iconography or patronage.

This study has shown that medieval window glass has been recovered from very few Gilbertine sites. The largest assemblages are from St Andrew's Priory, Fishergate, the mother house of St Mary's Priory, Sempringham, and the shields and fragments from the small priory at Ellerton, outside York, now to be seen in Selby Abbey. Smaller collections have been found at Haverholme (Lincolnshire), Mattersey (Nottinghamshire), Chicksands (Bedfordshire) and Watton (Yorkshire). The dates of all these assemblages and their component groups have been determined as far as possible above (pp.483–502).

In terms of the production of the glass, it is perhaps unsurprising that the stylistic affinities of the Sempringham glass are with other sites in Lincolnshire, whilst the stylistic affinities of the Fishergate glass, insofar as they can be discerned from fragments, are with other contemporary work in York. The Fishergate glass does not rank amongst the best quality of glass-painting in the city but was clearly influenced by it in the *rinceau* motifs used, attempts at three-dimensional representation, micro-architecture and other details. The glass is too fragmented to be attributable to specific craftsmen who might have been responsible for individual windows or suites of windows in the city's churches. It seems probable, then, that the Gilbertines employed local artisans rather than maintaining teams of artisans within the Order.

Lillich has argued that:

> *the arts of the medieval monastery are different from others — different not only from the arts of the palace and the bourgeois home, but from those in service of the cathedral and the parish church. The uses and purposes of art in monasteries are different in kind, and the demands made upon the arts by monks are more severe and more pervasive . . . The mark of monastic patronage should be most easily discerned in iconography: the subjects chosen and the particular forms of those subjects* (Lillich 1984, 207–8).

No shared subjects or forms of subjects have been discernible across the entire corpus of Gilbertine window glass, but the quantity which has survived through excavation is fragmentary relative to the overall area which must have been occupied by the windows of these churches and conventual buildings.

Only in the case of the York priory of St Andrew can the case be made for possible intentional selection in the glazing of the first priory buildings; namely a preference for plain glass with either foliate motifs or patterned through the leading of repeated geometric shapes. This selection was diluted by the intrusion of figural designs in the second half of the 13th century or possibly towards the close of that century. A comprehensively different overall glazing accompanied the rebuilding of the priory in the early 14th century and continued into the mid 14th century. This was fully coloured glazing, displaying figures beneath canopies which mirrored contemporary architectural nichework. There were probably historiated scenes, and heraldic devices were either used in a general way to frame these images or in heraldic shields.

Early–mid 13th century trefoil motif grisaille was also recovered from Haverholme Priory and, to a far more limited extent, from Sempringham Priory. Glass of this type is amongst the most commonly found on excavated monastic sites. There can be little doubt that grisaille was once far more extensively used in the British Isles than the present examples in situ would suggest. Consequently, the full repertoire of grisaille motifs which may once have been employed in Britain is unknown. Until a corpus of such designs is collected from excavated assemblages we cannot know if individual religious Orders had preferences for particular designs or suites of motifs.

A case has been made for the original glazing of the priory of St Andrew in York being consistent with a retrospective design in the plan and form of the church itself, and a deliberate and overall simplicity in its decoration. Apart from what is stipulated in the institutes of the Order (see p.504), there is no convincing evidence thus far that any Gilbertine church or convent was so austere in its aesthetics at this date or after. The reason for the singular appearance of the priory for canons at York may be found in the political context in which the Order found itself at the end of the 12th century, and in the immediate aftermath of Gilbert's death. The most significant Gilbertine text of this time, the *Vita* or hagiographic Life of St Gilbert, emphasised the influence of the Cistercians, and particularly of St Bernard of Clairvaux in the foundation of the Rule (Elkins 1984). It can be argued that the Gilbertines were striving to create an identity for their Order, and in so doing re-invented themselves with more of a Cistercian-inspired origin and ethos than had previously been the case.

The majority of the Gilbertine glazing evidence dates to the early to mid 14th century. This includes not only the Fishergate material, but the substantial amount from Sempringham Priory and from Ellerton Priory. The glass from both Fishergate and Sempringham suggests band windows which featured figures standing beneath architectural canopies and narrative scenes interspersed with naturalistic grisaille. There is limited evidence for heraldry of this date from both sites. The Ellerton glass is dominated by heraldry of the first half of the 14th century. A case has been made for the 14th century glazing of the rebuilt priory at Fishergate reflecting a change in spiritual priorities, and a more secular aesthetic having been embraced. The evidence from Ellerton certainly seems to reflect secular alliances or allegiances. This may be seen as part of a wider secular penetration of religious spaces as described by Martindale (1992).

Whilst it would be unwise to over-emphasise a distinction between sacred and secular which the people of the medieval period themselves may not have recognised, the mid 14th century does seem to represent the greatest extent of this process. The process is the more remarkable, and of particular interest to archaeologists, for being unremarked in contemporary written sources (ibid., 143). Secular interest was often manifested in parish churches and monasteries by the erection of tombs, sometimes in conjunction with liturgical furniture such as Easter Sepulchres. Surely the most pervasive display of secular interest in the church environment, however, was heraldry and the donation of glass windows. Thus we see the great change in aesthetic and spiritual environment in the early 14th century at St Andrew's, Fishergate, and a mid 14th century glazing programme at Sempringham. The 14th century also saw Sempringham admit a number of wealthy corrodians to its precincts (Platts 1985, 50; p.197, *AY* 11/2). Whilst Burghersh physically occupied portions of the Gilbertine precinct in York, heraldry or at least heraldic devices entered the glazing repertoire in the church. Heraldry made the concerns of the contemporary feudal elite very visible to their peers: concern of status, feudal hierarchy, lineage, legitimacy, inheritance, marriage, political alliances and obligations. The early 14th century heraldic shields from Ellerton Priory, just outside York, are the best examples of this phenomenon in the Gilbertine context. This can be seen as more than merely 'fashion'; it was part of a process by which spiritual and temporal authority reinforced one another. Whether the shields represent a group of Northern lords drawn together through mutual interest as lords and vassals, or as comrades-in-arms in the course of a muster, they would have been constant reminders to both the religious and any laity who used the church, of the power of those represented.

This study of the glazing of the one peculiarly English monastic Order has underlined the extent to which we must understand historical context before we can fully understand the choices of subject and subject form in the glazing of religious houses. The archaeology of these houses did not emerge from some ideal set of circumstances. Compromise and economic and moral exigencies were part of the everyday running of the houses. The nuns, canons, lay brothers and sisters of the Order sought to follow their particular religious discipline within these changing circumstances. This study has attempted to bring together the various sources which may inform us about those circumstances.

Conservation

H.I. Alten, J-F. De Laperouse, M.A. Little, J.P. Maish, S. Rees and J.A. Spriggs

Introduction

The large amount of waterlogged window glass excavated at 46–54 Fishergate posed a considerable conservation challenge. It was necessary to develop and implement a successful treatment to clean, dehydrate and consolidate large numbers of fragments rapidly, while incurring minimal loss or damage to the material. The treatment needs of the glass, the expertise and number of people working on the project, and the equipment available for use in the laboratory had all to be taken into account. A mass treatment approach to this material was considered appropriate and possible after treatment alternatives were reviewed.

The Fishergate glass consisted of approximately 900 small finds groups each containing one to 50,000 glass fragments in varying states of decay. The glass was removed from a damp, high-silica content soil matrix consisting primarily of crushed and deteriorated window glass and other demolition materials. Following established wet site procedures (Spriggs 1980), glass was layered with damp poly-ether foam or placed in polythene bags with water and stored in airtight polythene tubs. The glass had been bagged and recorded according to archaeological context, information which had to be retained during the treatment process.

Temporary storage

The 'temporary' storage lasted up to four years for some of the material. The limited space and suitably skilled labour to treat so much material neccesitated dividing the glass collection into manageable batches. The storage of such vulnerable material over a protracted period was a concern, and regular checks were made to ensure that the glass was not allowed to dry out. Algal and fungal growth in the wet storage environment was a recurring problem since the use of biocides was precluded for fear that their predominantly alkaline nature might attack the silica component of the glass. When microbial growth was suspected the water and packaging materials in the storage containers were changed.

Long-term wet storage can lead to the problems of continued, and possibly increased, deterioration. Small amounts of water very quickly turn alkaline as constituents within the glass are leached out. At pH 9 the solution begins to attack the silica network. Alkaline etching, or destruction of the silica matrix, theoretically leaves a smooth surface. In reality, medieval window glass in situ is covered in salts which have precipitated out of solution and adhere tenaciously to the glass, shielding parts of it from attack and thereby creating an unevenly etched or roughened surface (Adams 1984; Newton 1985; Perez y Jorba et al. 1980).

When water removes alkalis from the glass surface, stresses are created at the glass/corrosion interface. These stresses are relieved in dry medieval glass by cracking and surface spalling, but the strong polarity of water, plus its high surface tension, will keep the glass structure physically intact despite its weakened state. Removal of this support through air drying either causes the leached areas of glass to shrink and collapse or causes flaws in the glass to become visible. Either way, the appearance and strength of wet glass is drastically altered when it is dried out. Air drying results in increased structural fragility, cracking, surface lightening and powdering, and occasionally the appearance of opaque white spots (Alten 1986; 1988).

Despite all efforts some of the glass was dry or showed signs of microbial activity by the time it was finally treated.

Burial environment

Medieval window glass is composed principally of silica, the network former, to which potash is added to lower the melting point during manufacture. To this mix is also added a stabiliser, usually calcium or magnesium oxides, to render the glass insoluble in water during everyday use. The exact composition of the glass will affect its performance in use and will also affect its state of preservation in the burial environment (Newton and Davison 1989, 14).

During burial, water is a major factor in deterioration. The water diffuses into the glass and reacts with oxygen to produce hydroxyl ions. There is an exchange of ions which is often described as leaching. The hydroxyl ions migrate out with the alkali cations. The rate of leaching of the alkali slows down as the surface layer also becomes hydrated. As the silica content decreases there is an increased tendency to form a crust. This leached layer may be protective and, if left in situ, the reaction rate may reduce over time (Adams 1984, 195). Leaching can be slowed down, but the surface appearance can be deceptive and leaching may still be going on below the surface. The surface layer has a different appearance and different properties to the glass below. It shrinks as smaller protons replace larger alkali ions. Stress at the glass/corrosion interface will usually be relieved by cracking, especially upon drying of the glass. The resistance of glasses to such stress-corrosion is related to the co-efficient of thermal expansion of the glass, which is related to the alkali content. Tummala (1976) found that medieval glass had a high thermal expansion co-efficient and poor durability to water because of its high-potash content. Thus, high-alkali medieval glass displaying this phenomenon may be untreatable (Newton and Davison 1989, 155).

The leached layer is usually a dark opaque crust often replicating the original surface. It is caused by the precipitation, on and in the glass surface, of compounds of iron and manganese from the attacking solution (ibid., 154). Ferrous sulphide, produced by microbial organisms and bacteria introduced before or during burial, can also cause

Fig.231   Quarry from 46–54 Fishergate, front (left) and back (right). On the back the outline of the lead came can be seen as the preserved surface of the glass free of pitting

blackening. Factors affecting the rate of leaching during burial are thought to be the soil type, the amount and fluctuation of water present, and the pH of the surrounding environment. Most of the Fishergate window glass was found in dumps containing mixed building debris dating from the destruction of the priory. The presence of broken-up limestone and calcareous lime-mortar (Ashurst and Kelly 1989) would suggest a mildly alkaline pH for the deposits. Other contexts from the site produced a pH in the range 7·6 to 8·4 which would confirm this view. The contexts containing the glass were not deeply stratified and were mostly beneath the floors of the modern glass factory that stood on the site for over 100 years. The largest group of Gilbertine glass was from context 2114 which lay at a depth of only 20cm beneath the modern concrete floor. Prior to the construction of the modern glass factory, the site lay in open land (Stonewall Close) used as orchards. The glass has therefore been exposed to two rather different burial environments since its deposition: firstly, well aerated and wet (though well drained) with a high humic content; and secondly, much drier, warmer and sealed from the atmosphere. The latter environment would tend to favour the preservation of glass rather than the former, but the change in burial conditions would be likely to exacerbate the damage already done.

It should always be borne in mind that some of the deterioration observed in the Fishergate window glass may well have occurred in use. The type and nature of deterioration in 'standing' window glass is well documented (e.g. Perez y Jorba et al. 1980), but only now can it be differentiated from post-burial damage (Cox and Cooper 1995) (see pp.535–8). That the glass had suffered weathering whilst in use was evident from a number of near-complete quarries that showed circular pitting on external surfaces, but with a protected border where the lead came had been (see Fig.231). For further examination of long-term weathering effects see pp.535–6, 539–40).

Burial experiments on modern, medieval, Saxon and Roman replicate glasses (Fletcher 1972) have shown that an alkaline environment will attack the medieval and Saxon replicates much quicker than an acid environment. Only the Saxon replicate was affected by an acid environment (Newton 1981, 44). Complexing agents in the soil, such as are found in peats and humic horizons, can cause rapid lead extraction in potash-lead-silicate glass and increase the potash extraction (Newton and Davison 1989, 151).

Elemental mapping of Fishergate glass samples carried out using energy-dispersive X-ray analysis (Alten 1986) indicated the possible presence of sulphur in the corrosion layers. It is most likely that this was in the form of calcium sulphate (gypsum), a common corrosion product on degraded glass (Newton 1975, 64; Newton and Davison 1989, 159). This would undoubtedly form part of the grey/white incrustations obscuring the surfaces of much of the Fishergate glass (see Fig.232, p.516).

Treatment procedure

The challenge was to apply theoretical studies and practical experiences to the treatment of this large assemblage of glass. Treatment would entail compromises and a balancing of approaches, but would not jeopardise the stability of the artefacts. At the time of the Fishergate excavation very little had been published on stabilisation treatments for wet archaeological glass. Conservators who were known to have worked with this material were interviewed. The treatment included one year of experimental research on Fishergate glass samples, and mass treatment involved five steps: cleaning, dehydration (dewatering), consolidation, drying and storage. A process approach was adopted to work through the material efficiently while maintaining some individualisation of treatment. The proposed procedure advanced material through the following stages on a daily basis: cleaned fragments advanced to dehydration, then to consolidation, drying and storage. Although treatments were systematically scheduled, in reality the materials were so varied that schedules could not be adhered to rigidly. For example, fragments did not have the same amount of accretions to be removed, and these accretions did not always react in the same way with the cleaning solution.

Cleaning

The dirt and incrustations on the Fishergate glass fragments were partly calcareous (owing to proximity to stone, mortar and building debris) above the original glass surface, and often much harder than the underlying enamel and glass. When the surface dirt dried

Fig. 232   Small find context group 2670 of glass fragments before (above) and after (below) treatment

it congealed and consolidated to the surface forming an extremely hard, cement-like concretion which could contract and peel off some of the glass surface. Mechanical cleaning was considerably easier on wet glass that had never been dried.

Mechanical cleaning alternatives in the literature included brushes, swabs, wood sticks, scalpels, glass-fibre brushes, ultrasonic tanks, airbrasives, adjustable water jets and pulsed laser radiation (Asmus 1975; Lee et al. 1982; Reisman and Lucas undated a and b; Robinson et al. 1985). Mechanical cleaning of individual glass fragments is extremely time consuming. A quicker, more efficient bulk cleaning method was needed.

There is little published information on chemical cleaning of archaeological glass, but unpublished conservation reports cited good results using formic acid as a cleaning agent. Formic acid, mineral acids, acid and basic solutions of di- and tetra-sodium EDTA, and sodium hexametaphosphate were tested to measure their effectiveness in removing incrustations without damaging the glass or the red/brown enamel painted decoration. Chelation was ineffective in removing deposits and acid EDTA solutions attacked the red enamel paint on the glass. However, organic acids, adjusted to pH 3, effectively removed incrustations in 30 to 90 seconds.

A second test was designed for a visual comparison of the effect of various solutions on glass surfaces. Partially protected polished cross-sections were immersed in hot concentrated solutions and subsequently examined microscopically under reflected light. The di-sodium EDTA solution readily attacked the glass surface. However, organic acids did not affect the glass surface. Atomic absorption investigations showed that the amount of alkaline leaching is extremely small at 10ppm after 24 hours of immersion, for a glass sample in 10% formic acid.

The cleaning method developed for the glass from Fishergate involved a combination of chemical and mechanical techniques. The glass had to be cleaned when it was wet and the incrustation relatively soft. Entire small find groups were carried through the treatment process simultaneously. Soil was rinsed off, sometimes in the plastic bag. The glass withstood short ultrasound baths well. Rinsing was combined with ultrasonic cleaning for some of the glass fragments. Afterwards the glass was sorted by colour, deterioration and decoration. During sorting, superficial dirt was removed from the glass surfaces using stiff hogshair brushes. Fragments needing additional cleaning were placed in a screen basket and immersed in a dilute (pH 3) formic acid solution. The rate of reaction was monitored because the mechanical action of violent bubbling could dislodge surface decoration on the glass. After approximately 90 seconds, the basket was removed and placed in a bath of clean water for rinsing. Scalpel cleaning was used only on very tenacious accretions.

After more than two years in storage before treatment commenced, accretions on the glass began to dry before the glass could be treated, becoming more intractable. Fragments often had to be removed from a treatment group for additional mechanical cleaning with scalpel or glass-bristle brush. This problem was exacerbated as the years went on.

Dehydration, consolidation and drying

The choice of a consolidant was difficult. The hygroscopic and alkaline nature of glass keeps most adhesives and consolidants from forming strong, lasting bonds to the surface. Deterioration will continue if water is trapped under a consolidant or water vapour diffuses through the consolidant. Many consolidants will reduce the transparency of glass. Examination of the dehydration process suggested that irreversible structural collapse may occur upon removal of the liquid. Therefore, it was essential that the glass remained in a liquid until conservation treatment was completed. The consolidant needed to act as a bulking agent, to be hydrophobic and transparent, to have minimal shrinkage during drying, and to have a refractive index close to that of glass. Materials which have been used in the past include soluble nylon, cellulose nitrate, polyethylene glycol (PEG) 400 and 6000, polyvinyl acetate resins and emulsions, acrylic resins and dispersions, and silanes. These materials have been used singly or in combination for the desired effect. Of these treatments, five treatment options were assessed visually, by weight to dry weight ratio (Fitz 1981; Alten 1988), and by sample breakage after treatment. It should be noted that although PEG solutions have been used as a consolidant on wet glass by some conservators, the hydrophilic nature of PEG makes it a questionable consolidant for a material which is attacked by water. PEG is not a transparent consolidant, but does satisfy the requirements of a bulking agent. It was not experimented with because it seemed to be intrinsically damaging for the glass.

1 Polyvinyl acetate emulsion: Wet glass samples were immersed in 50% polyvinyl acetate (PVA) emulsion in distilled water followed by air drying. PVAs have a higher shear strength than acrylics and have refractive indices (1·45–1·47) close to that of soda glass. Some strength was added to the glass by the PVA, but very badly deteriorated pieces continued to break apart. The low glass transition temperature (28° C) of the PVAs caused consolidated fragments to stick to their storage container. The polymer is prone to cold flow and dirt attraction. Water may not have been completely removed from the consolidated glass.

2 Acrylic dispersion: Wet glass samples were immersed in 10% (as supplied) Primal WS-24 (3·6% solids) followed by air drying. No strength seemed to have been imparted to the glass samples by the acrylic dispersion, nor had the pieces been visually enhanced. Consolidated glass actually weighed less than unconsolidated air-dried glass, suggesting that Primal WS-24 has a detrimental effect on the glass. The acrylic colloidal dispersion is slightly alkaline (pH 6·8–8·8). It should be noted that in treatment with water-based emulsions or dispersions, where consolidation and dehydration occur more or less simultaneously, there is less control and less certainty that water has been completely removed from the glass. If any water remains within the glass, it could rapidly cause deterioration because of the small volume of water in relation to the large volume of glass (Roberts 1984).

3 Acrylic resin: Glass samples were dewatered through two ethanol baths prior to immersion in 1% Paraloid B-72 (a methacrylate co-polymer) in toluene. Samples were dried on mylar in a toluene environment. Experimentation showed that higher concentrations of the acrylic resin, 5–10%, strengthened the glass to an acceptable level. However, acrylics bond poorly to glass over time and care must be taken that acrylics do not trap water inside glass. This procedure has the advantage of separating dehydration from consolidation. The glass transition temperature of acrylics (Tg 40° C) is high enough to avoid surface tackiness.

4 *Silanes*: Wet and dewatered glass samples were immersed in 100% (as supplied) Dow-Corning Z6070 (a methyl trimethoxy silane) and then air dried for six weeks on teflon coated mylar. The water-repellent nature of methyl (trialkoxy) silanes should decrease the extent to which water attacks the glass. The chemical structure of methyl trimethoxy silanes suggests that they will be stable over time. Experimentation to date seems to substantiate the stability of this class of silanes. The silane alone did not impart much strength to the glass. Samples immersed in the silane directly from water were slightly stronger than samples which had been dewatered through two one-hour ethanol baths, but still were not sufficiently strengthened (D'Alessandro 1984; Errett et al. 1984; Grissom et al. 1981; Plueddemann 1982; Vogel et al. n.d.).

5 *Silane and acrylic resin:* Wet and dried glass samples were immersed in 100% (as supplied) Dow-Corning Z6070 followed by immersion in 1% Paraloid B-72 in Z6070. Samples were dried in a toluene environment on teflon-coated mylar and left to cure for six weeks. The silane coupling agent combined with Acryloid B-72 was the most successful consolidant for the deteriorated archaeological glass. The presence of the silane increased the penetration of the acrylic resin. However, silanes are difficult to work with because they are relatively expensive, dangerous to handle, and are usually unobtainable in small amounts. Silane treatment is not reversible. It is important to note that removal of any of the consolidants would cause irreversible structural damage to the glass.

Experimental results and research suggested that the ideal consolidation treatment for waterlogged glass involves a combination of methyl trimethoxysilanes and acrylic resins (Alten 1988). Initially fragments were treated with the silane and acrylic mixture but, in general, bulk consolidation of the Fishergate glass did not use this treatment for practical reasons. The health risks and expense involved in handling silanes were considered too great. A safer consolidation method, which perhaps imparted less internal strength to the glass, was combined with a stable, supportive storage system to allow long-term preservation of the material.

As bulk treatment of the glass progressed, after chemical cleaning, several hours of rinsing in distilled water, and an overnight soak in distilled water, the glass was dehydrated in two 24-hour baths of acetone prior to consolidation. The separation of dehydration from consolidation attempted to ensure that water was completely removed from the glass prior to impregnation. Experimentation had shown that it was very important for the glass to remain in a liquid medium until treatment was completed (ibid.).

For consolidation, the glass was immersed under partial vacuum overnight in 10% Paraloid B-72 in toluene. Upon removal from the consolidant, the fragments were stood on edge, on corrugated silicone release paper, to dry. The use of slower evaporating toluene promoted the retention of consolidant in interior spaces and produced a matt surface finish. If desired, silanes may be introduced at a later time to selected glass fragments. The fragments treated with the silane-acrylic mixture will be monitored over time for changes different from those seen in fragments consolidated with the acrylic resin alone. To date, the silane-acrylic consolidated glass seems to be stronger than the glass consolidated with acrylic resin alone, having less noticeable fragmentation in storage.

A number of problems were encountered during the course of the treatment. Lack of a large enough vacuum chamber meant glass could only be impregnated in small groups. Despite batch treatment, it was noted that approximately 10% of the glass fragments required individual attention during the earlier stages of cleaning (Little 1988).

Drying tests

On the assumption that the glass would all have to be dried free of water at some stage during the conservation process, some simple drying tests were set up in order to observe how the glass reacted as it was dehydrated (Alten 1988). The glass could be conveniently divided into three groups representing different degrees of hydration: glass almost black in colour, glass less dark and semi opaque, and clear glass.

Air drying

A sample piece from each group was dried gradually over a two-hour period under two 100 watt light bulbs. The greatest damage was observed within the first four minutes on the fully opaque piece. This and the semi-opaque sample lightened considerably in colour, showed fine surface cracking, and what were described as 'white spots' (Alten 1988, 280). The lightening and powderiness of the surface of the opaque and semi-opaque pieces may be due to loss of surface water from pits where calcium and sodium salts were deposited during the decay of the glass. The fine cracks were thought to be due to the shrinkage of the hydrated silica layer as the water was removed. The shrinkage could also have worsened cracks already present.

The opaque white spots which appeared after drying have not been mentioned before in the literature but have been noted by other conservators (Alten 1988), and are mentioned by Newton (1989, 157) as being something already present on dry glass. Alten thinks these could be the result of air in internal cracks causing diffusion of light or deposition of salts upon interior cracks (Alten 1988, 281).

Air drying appeared to be detrimental in varying degrees to all three categories of glass, although it should be noted that thermal shock from the proximity of a hot light source may well have contributed to the damage observed.

Solvent drying

As an alternative to air drying, solvent drying was investigated, to test if it would be less damaging to replace the water with a liquid with a lower surface tension, so that as it evaporated from the glass less damage would be caused. Three pieces from each group were put through two successive one-hour baths of ethanol and then dried. On the surface of the opaque glass more hairline cracks appeared and it became crumbly and granular with a cream colour. All translucency was lost in the semi-opaque glass, and the surface became patchy granular and cream-coloured with a fine network of cracks. Underneath this surface, clear bumpy glass was found and there appeared to be little adherence between this and the weathered outer surface. In the clear glass, any defects in the surface such as cracks became surrounded by a 'whitish halo' and a metallic or opalescent sheen appeared along the broken edges. Overall the clear glass was stable.

Results

From these simple tests on so few samples the results indicated that drying alone, even using solvent dehydration, would cause unacceptable damage to much of the collection. The visual changes recorded during the tests suggested that even the better preserved, translucent and 'stable' glass would have a better appearance if consolidated prior to drying.

Examination and analysis

A number of examination techniques were applied to samples of glass to identify further the nature of the decay.

Cross-section analysis

A number of cross-sections were made and recorded photographically at ×33 magnification (Alten 1986). Extensive cracking and surface pitting were observed on the blackened and opaque pieces which were decolourised and contained dirt, indicating that the damage was done prior to excavation. Other cleaner cracks were observed in the centre of the cross-sections which may have formed during the drying process. The better preserved and less opaque glass samples showed similar types of damage, but to a lesser degree.

SEM analysis

The cross-sections were examined by Scanning Electron Microscope (a Link AN 10,000 dispersive X-ray analyser; Alten 1986). The aim was to see if the composition of the glass determined the nature and extent of its decay. The clear and semi-opaque samples had both calcium and potassium present, whereas the opaque glass was found to have only calcium. The lack of potassium in the latter was thought to be the cause of the greater degradation of this sample. Elemental mapping at ×27 magnification of the opaque sample showed concentrations of various elements in separate parts of the glass compared to a clear glass sample which showed an even elemental distribution. A dendritic structure around a pit in the opaque sample at ×80 magnification showed a high concentration of manganese and a corresponding decrease in concentrations of silica, calcium, phosphorous and iron. Another dendritic structure in a semi-opaque piece was analysed at ×200 magnification and showed also the presence of lead and aluminium. These dendrites were thought to be evidence of bacterial attack owing to the presence of manganese and sulphur, as documented elsewhere (Newton 1989, 154; Perez y Jorba et al. 1980), and the bacterial attack could have been occurring on the glass before burial. This might account for the differing states of corrosion of the glass from the same burial environment (Alten 1988, 283). See pp.525–40 for results of further analysis carried out by G.A. Cox.

Storage

Planning for the proper storage of archaeological material is an important step in its treatment. Planning for the storage of the thousands of glass fragments excavated at 46–54 Fishergate posed a number of difficult problems. Whatever system was used, it had to satisfy at least four basic requirements. Firstly, the materials used for construction of the storage containers had to be stable and acid-free to avoid any adverse chemical interaction with the consolidated glass. Secondly, the possibility of physical damage to the glass fragments due to abrasion had to be minimised. Thirdly, the system had to be organised so that the glass would be kept in its small find groups. Fourthly, construction had to be as economical as possible, in terms of materials costs, time spent for manufacture and space utilisation in storage.

A number of storage container systems were investigated: re-utilisation of the archae-ologists' plastic storage boxes and bags, in-house manufacture of acid-free cardboard trays, and commercial manufacture of special plastic trays with compartments for individual fragments. Acid-free, 4-ply cardboard trays, with strips of acid-free board along the perimeter, covered with lightweight cotton muslin which cushioned the glass fragments and prevented their movement on the trays, were preferred. They satisfied all four requirements. The trays were stacked in 4-ply acid-free cardboard storage boxes which were mass-produced by a local firm. Conservators made the cardboard trays. Acid-free cardboard strips were stapled to the trays using corrosion resistant steel staples. Loops of cotton ribbon were inserted in the borders to facilitate lowering and lifting the trays into and out of the boxes.

An assembly-line operation produced the trays as quickly as possible; it took approximately fifteen minutes to make a tray from start to finish. Time constraints resulted in the adjustment of the original goal to store all glass fragments on these trays. Groups of ten fragments or less were packed within clip-top polythene bags, with supporting 'jiffy-foam' inserts. It was hoped that a small number of fragments would not damage each other.

Approximately 250 trays were made, loaded with glass, and labelled. The entire collection of glass is stored in 50 boxes which take up about 6 metres of shelving when stacked four deep. Almost 250 working-hours were spent in this final stage of the treatment.

Documentation

Documentation of the Fishergate glass treatment posed a number of problems because so much material was treated at a relatively rapid pace. Treatment documentation would normally consist of photographs or drawings before, during and after treatment, along with condition and treatment reports. This level of documentation was impractical for the quantity of material treated. The small find groups into which the glass had been assigned during excavation could contain from one to 50,000 unrelated glass fragments. Photographs taken of single fragments or groups of fragments proved to be extremely time consuming. The severely deteriorated condition of most fragments required experimentation to produce readable photographs. Images were obtained using reflected light, transmitted light, and technical illustration. Beta backscatter radiography (Knight 1989) was also explored as an option, and produced some promising results (Maish 1987). Visual documentation was both time consuming and labour intensive. To expedite treatment, the decision was made not to photograph or draw glass fragments unless an unusual condition was noted. This decision was made with the understanding that the publication illustrations would augment the treatment record.

Written documentation was simplified because, for the most part, a single treatment was used on all of the glass. A 'shell' report containing the constant information, such as the general condition description and treatment procedure, was prepared on computer. Variable information, such as the small find number, context and treatment date, was placed in a separate computer file. Using Mail Merge, a word processing function, the treatment report for each small find group can be generated.

The treatment reports were generic. Deviations in treatment, such as an extended amount of time in an acid bath or additional mechanical cleaning, were noted in the treatment log. These logs, which were initially used to keep track of the treatment in progress, were retained as an integral part of the treatment record.

Conclusion: evaluation of the treatment methodology

Treatment of the Fishergate glass began in 1985, and by 1989 all of the 900 small find groups had been treated and stored. There were two significant drawbacks to the treatment system. First, the amount of time it took to complete the project was greatly underestimated. As there were no standard procedures to follow, it was impossible to estimate the time required in advance of work commencing. Secondly, the treatment required dedicated laboratory space and equipment, and this could not always be guaranteed. Equipment and space utilisation for this project had to fit in with the work schedules and space requirements of concurrent laboratory projects.

In evaluating the glass treatment, a number of positive points can be made. First, the vast majority of the glass responded well to the treatment, and in those fragments which did not, which remained fragile after consolidation, it appeared that the deterioration process had been halted at least. The long-term stability of the glass had also been assured. Secondly, the treatment was implemented as rapidly as possible, and because a single treatment system had been initiated, consistency of the treatment was ensured. Thirdly, the treatment system was easy to learn and flexible enough to adapt to individual working styles and modifications in the procedure.

A survey of the Fishergate glass collection was undertaken in September 1995, almost exactly ten years after the conservation of the glass began. Each of the 50 or so boxes in which the glass is stored was opened, and an examination made of the way in which the packaging system had lasted and performed, as well as an assessment of the condition of the glass itself.

Despite fairly heavy use, the boxes, card frames and other packaging were still structurally sound and performing the function for which they were designed. The only observable sign of ageing was yellowing of the PVA-based adhesive used to afix Plastozote foam padding strips inside the boxes. The muslin-covered trays had successfully prevented movement of the fragments, and virtually no edge abrasion was noted. Only one fragment, positioned on the lowest of a stack of four trays had become broken, though it was unclear whether or not this could have been due to pressure from above. Two other pieces in another box had suffered a little fragmentation on one edge, possibly due to abrasion. None of the pieces grouped in 'minigrip' bags and stored together with card separators in storage boxes appeared to have suffered any ill effects. The conclusion of the survey was that the consolidative treatment that the glass received had provided sufficient strength and cohesion to protect the glass during ten years of study and storage, and that the storage system itself had performed well.

The Technical Examination of the Gilbertine Glass from 46–54 Fishergate

By Dr G.A. Cox, Department of Physics, University of York

Introduction

A total of 33 fragments of glass from 46–54 Fishergate were made available for scientific study, several of which proved to be of considerable interest. They were selected with three principal objectives in mind: one, to further the understanding of how medieval window glass weathers; two, to study the influence of the local environment on the mode of decay; and three, to ascertain whether the alkali content of certain anomalously durable fragments was soda or potash. Two examples of multi-layered ruby glass were included in order to examine their structure.

It is evident that by the time of the Dissolution of the priory in c.1538, the glass in its windows had been exposed to attack by the atmosphere for up to 350 years. Following the destruction of the windows, the glass fragments then suffered further weathering for about 440 years — but in a totally different environment: fallen masonry, building rubble and damp soil. It could be expected, therefore, that in favourable cases it might be possible to distinguish the weathering of the glass resulting from its exposure to these two markedly different environmental conditions. In order to appreciate how, in principle, this may be realised, it is first necessary to summarise the differences in morphology of the weathering crusts which form when poorly durable glass decays in the atmosphere as opposed to an archaeological context.

Long-term weathering of glass

Medieval window glass is a complex material, typically composed of ten or more principal constituents (conventionally represented in terms of their oxides), in addition to minor concentrations of colourants and impurities. Its mode of decay is also complex, being critically dependent upon the environment, but the essential features are now reasonably well understood (Geilman 1956; Cox et al. 1979; Newton 1985; Gillies and Cox 1988a, 1988b; Cox and Ford 1993).

A prerequisite for glass to corrode is the presence of water, or its vapour. Hydrolytic attack of the glassy network occurs at nonbridging oxygen sites ($\equiv$SiOR), whereby protons, H^+ ions (which probably enter the glass in hydrated form, H_3O^+), are exchanged for alkali ions, R^+, typically K^+ or Na^+ (Doremus 1975; Ernsberger 1980; Paul 1990; Scholtze 1991). In order to maintain charge neutrality, the latter and other mobile species, for example Ca^{2+} and Mg^{2+}, migrate towards the surface of the glass where they participate in further chemical reactions.

Groundwater invariably permeates archaeological sites in Britain and readily attacks glass. If the flow rate of water through the site is low, the pH-value of the aqueous solution in contact with the glass increases as the extraction of alkali (leaching) proceeds. At pH > 9, dissolution of the glassy network ensues, consequent upon ≡Si–O–Si≡ bonds being broken. The entire glass then rapidly breaks down (El-Shamy et al. 1972). When the solubility limits of silica, alumina and other constituents of the glass are exceeded at the reaction zone (corrosion front), precipitation of new phases occurs, which has the effect of regulating the pH and eH (oxidation potential) of the attacking solution. Cyclic reaction conditions thus prevail. Hence, the weathering, or corrosion, crusts which build up on the surface of glass that decays in the presence of groundwater have a layered structure (Lutze 1988; Cox and Ford 1989). A common feature of such crusts, especially in the immediate sub-surface regions, is the presence of lustrous, black deposits of manganese-rich compounds. Mn^{2+} ions, present in soils as a breakdown product of silicate minerals, are soluble in water, but are thermodynamically unstable. Under anaerobic conditions they readily enter the porous crusts in solution in groundwater. However, local increases in the oxygen content of the environment, caused for example by microbial activity (Marshall 1979), convert Mn^{2+} ions to higher oxidation states, which result in the precipitation of insoluble manganese compounds. The chemical behaviour of manganese in soils is notoriously complex (Collins and Buol 1970). The dark coloured appearance of the surface of excavated glass (particularly if it is poorly durable) is commonly caused by the presence of these phases (Raw 1955; Geilman 1956; Cox and Ford 1993; Cooper et al. 1993).

Window glass that decays in situ in the atmosphere does so under very different conditions. Rain, condensation and periods of high humidity cause alkali and other ions to be leached from the glass, but the surface does not remain permanently wet. As it dries, the pH of the solution in contact with the glass increases, which results in the surface being attacked. Ions leached from the glass react with gases in the atmosphere, but especially with carbon dioxide and sulphurous gases (the detailed mechanisms are not fully understood), the end products being weakly soluble carbonates, sulphates and double salts; simultaneously, the leached surface regions become progressively richer in hydrated silica (Gillies and Cox 1988a, 1988b). Since cyclic conditions of the type previously described do not prevail, the weathering crusts do not have a layered structure; instead, they have a compacted, granular appearance. Extensive areas of corrosion and pits commonly develop on the surface of the glass. As the pits expand laterally and deepen, the sample is reduced in thickness, a process which, if unchecked by conservation measures, ultimately results in its destruction. The atmospheric corrosion of in situ medieval stained glass is by no means restricted to Britain; it occurs widely throughout the continent of Europe and has been well documented. A brief review of the literature on this subject, together with illustrations of weathered surfaces, has been published (Newton and Davison 1989, 159–64).

Fig.233   Sample YFG12iii, showing a corroded surface with micropits, i.e. atmospheric weathering. Scale 2:1

Details of the sample fragments examined

Visual inspection of the fragments provided for examination showed that their degree of weathering varied considerably: nine were in a remarkably good state of preservation with naturally polished surfaces still evident, for example, YFG26; at the other extreme were three fragments in which no pristine glass survived, for example, YFG1. As summarised in Table 8, the remaining 21 fragments had suffered localised or more extensive weathering. The appearance of YFG12iii in the 'as received' state is shown in Fig.233, where the physical condition of its surfaces may be seen. This sample (and four others) proved to be of exceptional interest, as will be explained on p.536.

The mean thickness of the specimens which had retained their natural surfaces, irrespective of whether or not they were corroded, was 3·0 ± 1·6mm. Evidence for differential rates of weathering was apparent in a number of cases, YFG17 providing a good example. Its enamelled surface was deeply, but irregularly, eroded, whilst the opposite face, although blackened and corroded to some extent, was overall in a better physical state. The reasons for such differences are rarely apparent, since past environmental conditions to which the glass has been exposed can normally only be surmised.

Table 8 Details of specimens

Note: White glass implies not deliberately stained, but has a pale green tint caused by the presence of iron as an impurity

Context	Sf no.	No. of specimens	Specimen number	Colour of glass	Description
3194	3457	3	YFG1, YFG2, YFG3	Probably white	Dark brown/black surfaces with irregular white patches. Highly corroded throughout; exceptionally light in weight. No decoration visible.
3180	3045	3	YFG4	White	Patchy areas of dark brown corrosion, but some glass visible. One surface more corroded than the other.
			YFG5	Mid-green	One surface with brown/black patches; the other with areas of pale green iridescence. Suggestion of micropits on one (external?) surface.
			YFG6	Amber	Both surfaces black; thin corrosion crusts, but colour of glass visible. Four linear streaks of red/brown decoration. Micropits on external surface.
3283	4085	1	YFG7	White	Both surfaces pale brown and lightly corroded. Colour of glass visible.
3163	2179	2	YFG8i; YFG8ii	Multi-layered ruby	Good, uncorroded surfaces with slight iridescence (Fig.234, p.535).
3180	3045	1	YFG9	Dark blue	Good surfaces with slight corrosion, mainly near edges.
3002	425	1	YFG10	Light blue	Heavily corroded surfaces with bright yellow, iridescent layers, which readily exfoliated.
3163	2183	1	YFG11	White	Good surfaces; brown line grisaille decoration. Micropits on external surface.

Table 8 *(contd)*

Context	Sf no.	No. of specimens	Specimen number	Colour of glass	Description
2001	9171	5	YFG12i	White	Good surfaces; brown, curved-line decoration. Specimen is light in weight for its size.
			YFG12ii	White	As YFG12i; very fragile weathering crusts.
			YFG12iii	White	As YFG12i; micropits on external surface. Specimen in 'as received' state is shown in Fig.233 (p.527).
			YFG12iv	White	As YFG12i.
			YFG12v	White	Brown/black corroded surfaces; one corner of the specimen has flaked. Hatch-line decoration in brown.
3000	2082/3	2	YFG13i	White	Good surfaces; traces of brown line, grisaille decoration. Micropits, mainly isolated, on external surface. Specimen is shown in section in Fig.235, p.537.
			YFG13ii	White	Good surfaces; traces of brown line, grisaille decoration.
3012	558	1	YFG14	White	Good surfaces with areas of brown, curved line decoration. Micropits on external surface.
2001	9175	2	YFG15	White (blue/green tint)	Very good condition. Surfaces have 'etched' appearance. Brown line decoration. Quarry fragment.
			YFG16	White	Good, iridescent surfaces: one with brown decoration, one with yellow stain. External surface with suggestion of micropits and also black, patchy areas.
3030	456	1	YFG17	White	Internal surface with remains of brown decoration; much corroded. External surface also much corroded, but retains natural polish. Specimen light in weight. Quarry fragment.

Table 8 (*contd*)

Context	Sf no.	No. of specimens	Specimen number	Colour of glass	Description
2060	1193	1	YFG18	White (blue/green tint)	One good surface, one with a thin layer of corrosion.
3012	553	2	YFG19i, YFG19ii	White (blue/green tint)	Thin, black, flaking corrosion on both surfaces. Very fragile.
2000	2067	1	YFG20	White	Internal surface has thin layer of black corrosion; brown, curved line decoration. External surface has similar appearance. Fragile; light in weight.
2001	9174	1	YFG21	White	Good surfaces with slight iridescence. Fern *rinceau* decoration. Thin, but substantial.
3180	3045	1	YFG22	Blue	Very good condition with largely unweathered surfaces. Decorated in brown with V-fold drapery.
2114	3609	4	YFG23, YFG24, YFG26	Blue	Excellent, uncorroded condition.
			YFG25	Blue	As YFG23; but one surface with slight iridescence.

The pH-values of three samples of damp soil from the site were as follows: context 3180, 8·4; context 3194, 7·6; context 3283, 7·7. These correspond to moderately alkaline conditions.

For the purpose of examining the samples, their fragile crusts, where present, were consolidated with a 5% solution of 'Acryloid' B72 in acetone. Individual samples were then sectioned and embedded in a cold-curing epoxy resin, followed by polishing with diamond paste to a 0·5µm finish. This procedure revealed the detailed morphology of the weathering crusts and exposed flat surfaces of glass suitable for chemical analysis. Those samples of art-historical importance (YFG6, 15, 16, 21 and 22) were polished at an edge (an area of approximately 1mm^2) to expose unweathered glass whilst causing minimal damage.

Sectioned samples were first subjected to Fourier transform-infrared (FTIR) microspectroscopy to characterise the material forming their weathering products. They were then coated with carbon and examined in a scanning electron microscope (SEM) to reveal the microstructure of the crusts. An X-ray analyser fitted to the SEM permitted the chemical composition of the glasses to be determined by electron-probe microanalysis (EPMA). Details of the equipment are given in Notes (p.568). By carrying out 'spot' analyses of the sectioned specimens along a linear traverse at 20µm intervals, commencing at the surface and progressing into the interior of the glass, the concentration profiles of the principal constituents could be plotted. In this manner, the effects of leaching by groundwater could be determined. Similarly, salts in solution which had diffused into the weathering crusts could also be detected and their concentration profiles established.

Discussion of results

Composition and physical structure of the glass

The chemical compositions of the 30 fragments in which pristine glass survived are given in Table 9. It is evident that they were all of the potash-lime-silica type ('forest glass'), which is entirely consistent with their date of manufacture. The mean composition of the samples and the standard deviation of individual components are also given. One fragment of mid-green glass, YFG5, had a high copper content (CuO = 2·98%), which had a pronounced effect on the mean and standard deviation of this component. Data are given in Table 9 which include and exclude this specimen. So close are the compositions of YFG12i and YFG12ii that it is probable they were originally parts of a larger piece of glass which fragmented when the window was destroyed. Similarly, YFG19i and YFG19ii may have a common origin, as may YFG23, YFG24 and conceivably YFG26. Lack of homogeneity of the glasses, together with expected statistical variations in the analytical data, are sufficient to account for the differences in the analyses. It should be mentioned that the concentration of cobalt in the blue glasses was not measured on account of X-ray spectral interference caused by iron, present as an impurity in all of the specimens. Only

Table 9 Composition of the glass. Note that samples YFG1–3 are not included as no pristine glass remained

Key: * Multi-layered specimen, white base glass analysed; ** Excluding YFG5; † Including YFG5; nd denotes not detected

Specimen number	Weight % of oxide											
	Na_2O	MgO	Al_2O_3	SiO_2	P_2O_5	K_2O	CaO	MnO	Fe_2O_3	CuO	PbO	Total
YFG4	2.6	7.1	1.3	52.2	5.7	15.2	14.2	0.96	0.35	0.05	0.19	99.85
YFG5	2.8	6.5	1.3	50.4	5.7	12.4	15.2	0.87	0.66	2.98	0.39	99.20
YFG6	2.9	7.8	0.9	50.0	5.2	16.7	14.1	1.35	0.28	0.13	0.10	99.46
YFG7	2.0	3.4	3.6	56.6	3.7	6.5	21.2	1.62	0.49	0.05	0.07	99.23
YFG8i*	3.7	6.9	1.5	52.7	5.5	10.3	17.2	1.00	0.43	0.16	0.03	99.42
YFG8ii*	2.8	4.9	1.8	55.6	4.6	14.4	13.8	0.62	0.69	0.10	0.17	99.48
YFG9	3.0	6.5	1.2	52.5	5.6	16.0	12.4	0.70	0.65	0.44	0.37	99.36
YFG10	4.9	8.3	1.1	55.8	4.0	10.5	12.4	1.21	0.85	0.24	0.18	99.48
YFG11	3.0	7.5	1.3	50.0	6.4	17.9	11.9	1.01	0.60	0.11	0.09	99.81
YFG12i	1.7	5.2	1.9	45.7	6.1	17.8	19.4	0.51	0.92	nd	0.28	99.51
YFG12ii	1.8	5.2	2.0	45.8	6.3	17.5	19.3	0.55	0.85	nd	0.27	99.57
YFG12iii	2.5	4.7	1.7	48.3	5.5	16.6	18.8	0.58	0.82	0.05	0.18	99.73
YFG12iv	2.0	7.7	1.9	50.6	5.2	15.8	14.3	1.33	0.52	0.12	0.13	99.60
YFG12v	3.0	4.9	1.9	48.0	5.4	15.7	19.3	0.53	0.70	0.10	0.06	99.59
YFG13i	2.8	8.6	0.9	50.5	5.8	15.0	14.0	1.29	0.40	0.10	0.07	99.46
YFG13ii	3.2	5.3	1.8	48.0	5.6	15.7	18.7	0.40	0.61	0.08	0.05	99.44
YFG14	2.9	7.6	1.4	49.3	6.1	17.4	12.6	1.00	0.45	0.41	0.33	99.49
YFG15	1.3	5.2	1.5	55.1	4.6	17.4	12.1	0.92	0.51	0.06	0.32	99.01
YFG16	1.9	3.4	3.0	56.0	3.3	7.2	22.9	1.08	0.40	0.06	0.16	99.40
YFG17	2.0	6.7	1.4	54.1	4.8	13.0	15.4	0.72	0.56	0.07	0.82	99.57
YFG18	1.4	5.4	1.5	53.5	4.5	17.7	13.6	0.88	0.40	0.04	0.64	99.56
YFG19i	4.2	8.0	1.1	54.3	5.0	12.7	12.3	1.27	0.28	0.09	0.16	99.40

Table 9 (*contd*)

Specimen number	Weight % of oxide											
	Na_2O	MgO	Al_2O_3	SiO_2	P_2O_5	K_2O	CaO	MnO	Fe_2O_3	CuO	PbO	Total
YFG19ii	4.1	8.2	1.2	54.1	5.0	12.9	12.5	1.14	0.24	0.06	0.13	99.57
YFG20	1.9	3.4	3.2	56.3	3.3	7.2	22.5	1.13	0.47	0.08	0.05	99.53
YFG21	2.3	3.6	2.9	54.8	4.5	7.7	21.9	1.19	0.34	0.09	0.19	99.51
YFG22	3.9	7.1	0.9	56.8	3.2	14.0	11.1	1.06	0.86	0.19	0.26	99.37
YFG23	3.1	7.1	1.7	55.5	3.7	14.8	11.2	0.94	0.88	0.15	0.34	99.41
YFG24	3.1	7.1	1.8	55.4	3.7	14.6	11.4	0.94	0.80	0.18	0.26	99.28
YFG25	2.6	3.4	1.3	60.1	3.1	5.8	21.6	0.69	0.56	0.07	0.13	99.35
YFG26	2.9	7.0	1.7	55.1	3.8	14.7	11.6	0.90	1.11	0.21	0.23	99.25
Mean (n=30)	2.7	6.1	1.7	52.8	4.8	13.7	15.6	0.95	0.59	0.12** 0.21†	0.22	
σ_n	0.8	1.6	0.7	3.5	1.0	3.6	3.8	0.29	0.21	0.10** 0.52†	0.17	

small amounts of cobalt would be expected (about 0·05%), since this colourant acts as a powerful stain.

The wide variability in the concentrations of the principal constituents is consistent with the date of production of the glass. Although the glassmakers might possibly have been working to a recipe, it has to be remembered that quality control of raw batch materials did not exist at the time of manufacture of this glass and their purity was quite erratic. Of note are the following ranges: potash 6·5–17·9%; lime 11·1–22·9%; silica 45·7–60·1% and magnesia 3·4–8·6%. As a general observation, the more durable glasses are those with silica contents in excess of about 55%, especially when combined with a low to moderate potash content, i.e. 5 to 15% — for example, YFG20 to YFG26 inclusive. Particularly notable in this respect is YFG21, a thin, white fragment with an iridescent surface, but otherwise in an excellent state of preservation. Although durable 12th century potash glasses are known, for example, in nearby York Minster, they are uncommon (Gillies and Cox 1988a, 80 and table 1). This point will be returned to when the Fishergate durable blue glasses are discussed. The reason why some medieval potash glass proves to be durable, whilst other contemporaneous material of similar composition shows obvious signs of weathering, is rarely clear; factors which may have a bearing include poor surface homogeneity of the glass, surface roughness, built-in stresses due to inadequate annealing and the presence of damage to the surface caused, for example, by wind-borne particles whilst the glass was in situ in a window. Specimens of durable potash glass in Austrian churches dated to the 14th and 15th centuries have been described, but they differ in type from the Fishergate samples discussed here (Schreiner 1988, table 1) and hence are not strictly comparable. In the case of glass of archaeological origin, a given sample may have been 'shielded' by fallen masonry or protected within a demolition dump, whilst neighbouring fragments suffered unhindered attack by groundwater.

The structure of the glasses, as revealed by low-power optical microscopy of polished sections, showed features expected in glass of this date, notably, inclusions of unmelted batch, gas bubbles (seed), and the presence of cord and ream (inhomogeneous regions with differing refractive indices). Typically, the bubbles were elongated in a direction parallel to the surface and occurred in linear formation, indicative of the cylinder process for producing flat glass having been used (Newton and Davison 1989, 91–3). Iron in the ferrous state (Fe^{2+}), present as an impurity, imparted a distinct green tint to the 'white' glass.

Multi-layered ruby glass

The production of ruby window glass in the 12th and 13th centuries presented problems. A pot-metal uniformly stained with copper proved to be so optically dense that it transmitted relatively little incident light. The imaginative solution to this problem was to manufacture multi-layered glasses consisting of very many narrow layers of red and white glass (Newton and Davison 1989, 96). Two of the samples of Fishergate glass that were examined were of this type, YFG8i and YFG8ii. The latter was studied in detail. This fragment, of 3·43mm thickness, consisted of two regions: a multi-layered one extending

Fig.234   Multi-layered ruby glass (YFG8ii). Linear magnification × 90

for 1·95mm, followed by a further 1·48mm of white glass. Thus some 57% of the total thickness of YFG8ii was made up of alternating red and white layers. Fig.234 reveals the intricate, fine structure of this specimen, seen here in section, with layers bending back upon themselves. Research carried out in York and elsewhere to determine the method of producing these glasses has so far failed to provide a clear understanding of the manufacturing techniques involved (Spitzer-Aronson 1975, 1977).

Weathering of the glass

The appearance of the 33 samples varied widely (Table 8), reflecting the extent of weathering. At one extreme were those fragments which showed little evidence of having weathered, merely a slight surface iridescence; at the other were those where no glass was visible, indeed in some (YFG1 to YFG3) none was present, the glass having been attacked to the point of total destruction. As previously mentioned, the composition of individual samples (Table 9) and the environmental conditions to which they had been exposed are probably sufficient to account for their gross weathering behaviour. Research carried out in the Department of Physics, University of York, into the corrosion of medieval stained glass has failed to show a connection between the colour of the pot-metal and its weathering characteristics (unpublished).

On a finer scale, low-power optical microscopy revealed the expected layer structure of the weathering crusts present on the poorly durable specimens. Depending upon factors additional to the ones referred to above, for example, microcracks, cord and ream in the glass, or the presence of inclusions, the morphology of the layers varied in a remarkably complex manner, each specimen having developed its own unique layer structure. Fig.235 shows a polished section of the corroded, near-surface region of YFG13i, where the morphological details are clearly visible. As previously described, manganese ions, originally in solution in groundwater, have diffused throughout the layers of corrosion, which in this case appear to radiate from a point on the surface; insoluble manganese compounds have subsequently been precipitated as black deposits with a fern-like appearance. Comparable examples of this phenomenon are known in samples of decayed potash glass from other archaeological sites (Raw 1955; Geilmann 1956; Cox and Ford 1993).

However, sample YFG13i was of interest for other reasons. It was one of five fragments (the others being YFG6, YFG11, YFG12iii and YFG14) which showed convincing evidence of having weathered in the atmosphere whilst they were in situ in the windows. This took the form of approximately circular pits of varying sizes on the surface of the glass, but mainly within the range 0·1 to 0·4mm in diameter. These may be seen on sample YFG12iii in Fig.233 (p.527), where numerous such pits are apparent. They are more readily visible in section in Fig.235, where two pits of this type on YFG13i have merged as they deepened and spread laterally. It is significant that they occurred only on what would have been the external (non-decorated) surface of the glass; this was the case on all of the samples where micropits of this type were noted. Infrared micospectroscopy of the granular, compacted weathering products present within the pits revealed them to be rich in amorphous, hydrated silica, $SiO_2.xH_2O$, almost certainly derived from the network of the original glass. Additional features of the infrared spectra revealed the presence of carbonate and phosphate functional groups (absorption peaks at approximately $1430cm^{-1}$ and $1040cm^{-1}$, respectively), probably arising from CO_3^{2-} and PO_4^{3-} ions in solution in groundwater having diffused into the crusts whilst the glass was buried. The occurrence of carbonates in material of archaeological origin is well documented (Courty et al. 1989, 172–9). A detailed account of these most interesting specimens has been published (Cox and Cooper 1995).

Surprisingly, sulphates such as gypsum, $CaSO_4.2H_2O$, or syngenite, $K_2Ca(SO_4)_2.H_2O$, both commonly found on the surface of atmospherically weathered glass, were not detected in the granular material within the pits, although their presence could have been expected (Geilman et al. 1960; Collongues and Perez y Jorba 1973, 1974; Collongues et al. 1976; Bettembourg 1976; Fitz et al. 1984, 123–6 and table 3; Marschner 1985, 134–5; Gillies and Cox 1988a, table 6). A probable explanation for their absence, even if originally present, is that during the period the specimens were buried, sparingly soluble salts, such as gypsum, would have been leached out of the weathering products by groundwater.

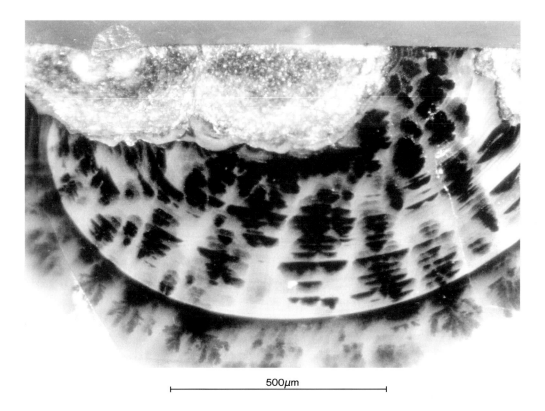

Fig. 235   Sample YFG13i in section showing layers of corrosion, Mn-rich inclusions and micropits

Aqueous leaching of the glass

'Spot' chemical analyses of sections of several samples, carried out at regular intervals commencing at the surface and following a linear traverse into the interior of the glass, enabled the concentration profiles of selected components to be determined. The objective was to establish which ionic species had been leached from the surface regions through contact with groundwater; conversely, it also provided information on which ions in solution in groundwater had diffused into the weathering crusts. It will be appreciated that the natural, aqueous dissolution of glass involves counter diffusion processes.

The resulting data showed that the sub-surface regions of the samples were almost entirely devoid of alkali (Na_2O and K_2O) and magnesia (MgO), and that a silica-rich barrier had formed at the interface (reaction zone) between the unaltered glass and the weathering crust. Further, the concentration profiles of CaO and P_2O_5 were strongly correlated throughout the thickness of the weathering crusts, reaching maximum values at the surface. This is indicative of these constituents being chemically combined, probably in the form of a calcium phosphate (several are known), such as hydroxyapatite $Ca_5(PO_4)_3OH$, or one of its derivatives (Cooper et al. 1993). Phosphates commonly occur on archaeological sites, partly as a result of past human and animal activities (Courty et al. 1989, 186–9). It is suggested that this is the explanation for the enhanced levels of phosphorus in the surface regions of the crust material. The calcium, too, may have originated from the environment or, conceivably, it may have been leached from the glass. The increased concentration of manganese in the sub-surface regions (Fig.235) is similarly explained by its having entered the decomposing glass from the surroundings. Analagous weathering behaviour has been observed in medieval potash glasses recovered from other archaeological sites; for example, concentration profiles for the constituents of the corrosion crusts present on glass fragments excavated at Rievaulx Abbey (glass compositions comparable to those recorded in Table 9) have been published (Cox and Ford 1993, fig.4).

Comparisons with glass in York Minster

The windows of York Minster contain a wealth of medieval stained glass, many pieces of which have been examined in the Department of Physics, University of York, and provide useful comparative material in the present context (Cox et al. 1979; Gillies and Cox 1988a; 1988b). Glass displaying a wide range of durability occurs in the windows of this building, but of particular relevance is the highly durable blue in the nave clerestory tracery lights dating to the late 12th century, and the 14th century material in the nave windows, much of which is now in a weathered condition.

In appearance, the well-preserved blue glass from Fishergate, samples YFG22 to YFG26, is remarkably similar to that of the highly durable, 12th century glass of this colour in the nave clerestory of York Minster (French 1971), a number of pieces of which have been analysed (Cox and Gillies 1986). Other closely related examples of this material were recovered during excavations at York Minster (Phillips 1985, frontispiece and 159). Further fragments of similar glass have been excavated in Britain at Old Sarum and Winchester (reported by Newton 1977); the relevant analytical data have been published (Cox and Gillies 1986, appendix B). However, in sharp contrast to the durable Fishergate glasses, which were of the potash-lime-silica type, the specimens from the other sources mentioned above were exclusively soda-lime-silica glasses ($Na_2O > 12 \cdot 1\%$; $CaO < 10 \cdot 1\%$; $SiO_2 > 66 \cdot 8\%$), the high soda and silica contents being largely responsible for their exceptional stability.

Sample YFG22 is representative of this small group of durable blue glasses from St Andrew's Priory. Its X-ray emission spectrum produced by EPMA is shown in Fig.236 (p.539). Each 'peak' is associated with the characteristic X-radiation emitted by a constituent element within the specimen when it was subjected to the electron beam. It can be seen that YFG22 has a high silicon content ($SiO_2 = 56 \cdot 8\%$) and that the amount of

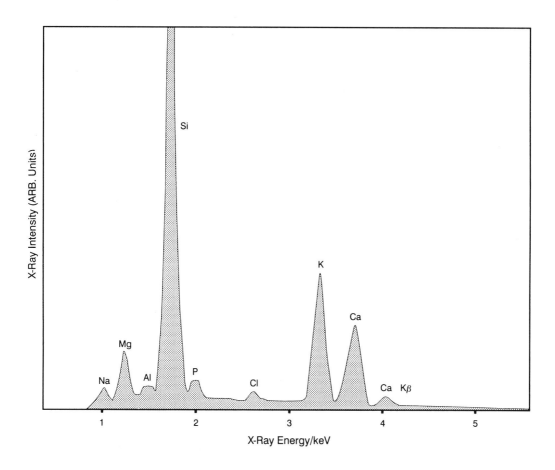

Fig. 236 X-ray emission spectrum of YFG22 (one of the durable blue glasses). The spectral region at higher energies where peaks for the heavier metals manganese, iron, copper and lead appear has been omitted. All peaks are K_α except where stated.

potassium present ($K_2O = 14\cdot0\%$) outweighs that of sodium ($Na_2O = 3\cdot9\%$); a prominent calcium peak ($CaO = 11\cdot1\%$) is also evident.

The composition of YFG25 is somewhat anomalous. Of the samples examined, it had the highest silica ($SiO_2 = 60\cdot1\%$) but the lowest total alkali content ($Na_2O = 2\cdot6\%$; $K_2O = 5\cdot8\%$). Rather than regarding this simply as a potash glass, it is possibly better described as being of the 'mixed alkali' type with a high silica content. As previously mentioned, durable, medieval glasses occur in York Minster, and elsewhere, but are uncommon; thus it can be appreciated that specimens YFG22 to YFG26 are of especial technological interest.

Whilst considering the atmospheric weathering of glass, it is instructive to compare the behaviour of YFG13i (and the four other samples, referred to on p.536, which had developed pits on their surfaces), with near-contemporaneous material in York Minster. Many chemically different weathering products have been identified on the surface of glass that has undergone long-term weathering in the atmosphere, of which hydrated silica is but one. On the basis of the composition of the five samples (Table 9) with micropits on their surface containing predominantly hydrated silica, parallel examples of this mode of decay could be expected to be found on specimens of similar composition in York Minster. The fact that such examples have been recorded further supports the contention that the pits observed on the Fishergate glass are, indeed, the result of atmospheric attack (Cox and Cooper 1995, table 2).

Summary and conclusion

The specimens of Gilbertine glass from St Andrew's Priory that were subjected to technical examination proved to be of interest and importance. They were all of the potash-lime-silica type and, therefore, typical of most of the window glass produced in western Europe from about the 12th to the 14th century. However, the chemical composition of individual fragments varied considerably. This was reflected in their wide-ranging durability; indeed, several examples showed an uncommon degree of resistance to weathering.

Of particular interest were those specimens which provided evidence, in the form of surface pitting, of having weathered in the atmosphere whilst they were in situ in the windows prior to their destruction, followed by further decay caused by subsequent exposure to groundwater. Possibly for the first time, these fragments provide an indication of the physical condition of at least some of the ecclesiastical window glass in Britain at the time of the Dissolution of the monasteries.

Thus, contrary to popular belief, rising levels of air pollution during the past 250 years or so, associated with the burning of increasing quantities of fossil fuels, cannot solely be responsible for the deterioration of in situ stained glass. By the mid-16th century, the weathering of poorly durable medieval window glass would appear to have reached the stage where visible signs of its decay were unmistakable.

Key to Painted Decoration and Glass Type Codes

A   13th century grisaille

A1   Upright trefoil on cross-hatched ground
A2   Upright trefoils with strapwork
A3   Either distinct quarries or side fronds of A1 or A2
A4   Crossed trefoils
A5   Side-curling trefoils
A6   Double-headed trefoils
A7   Split and twisting stemmed trefoils
A8   Trefoils with berries
A9   Trefoils with internal lines
A10 Other variations on trefoils on cross-hatched ground

B   Late 13th/early 14th century grisaille

B1   Small trefoils on plain grounds
B2   Quatrefoil with pointed lobes
B3   Quatrefoil with rounded lobes
B4   Quatrefoil with serrated lobes
B5   Strapwork at quarry edge
B6   Oak leaf and acorn grisaille

C   Patterned quarries

C1   Oak leaf and trefoil framing design
C2   Oak leaf and acorn
C3   Rose quarries
C4   Lily or rosebud
C5   Quarry edge or framing design including trefoil
C6   Similar with other design

D   Diaper

D1   Frond fern *rinceau*
D2   Thistle *rinceau*
D3   Leaf and frame with trefoil design
D4   Spade leaf *rinceau*
D5   Multi-lobate or early seaweed diaper
D6   Cross diaper
D7   Circles and lozenges

D8   Other design

E   Other vegetal and floral decoration

F   Architecture

F1   Canopy gables and crockets
F2   Canopy gables and internal detail; other roofline features (turrets)
F3   Merlons
F4   Columns, capitals and bases, shafting detail, including shading
F5   Small crockets on their own
F6   Cusping on its own
F7   Tracery designs on their own
F8   Buttresses, shafts and canopy finials

G   Figures

G1   Human heads or details from head (e.g. hair, eyes)
G2   Drapery
G3   Human hands and arms
G4   Human feet
G5   Wings (angels or birds)
G6   Other

H   Linear stickwork and geometric borders

H1   Open beading
H2   Open beading with central dots
H3   Open beading interspersed with small beads
H4   Open beading interspersed with small linked circles
H5   Beading with central dots interspersed with linked circles
H6   Circles interspersed with small circles
H7   Circles with small central beads interspersed with small circles
H8   Circles with small central beads interspersed with linked circles
H9   Circles with small central beads and

dots interspersed with linked circles

H10   Alternating open beads with central dots and circles with small internal circles and dots interspersed with linked circles

H11   Alternating circles and crosses interspersed with small circles

H12   Quatrefoils

H13   Quatrefoils interspersed with small circles

H14   Quatrefoils interspersed with triangles

H15   Alternating beading and encircled quatrefoils interspersed with small circles

H16   Alternating crosses and encircled quatrefoils interspersed with small circles

H17   Encircled quatrefoils interspersed with triangles

H18   Circles interspersed with parallel upright lines

H19   Saltires interspersed with cross-hatching

H20   Indented or zig-zag line interspersed with circles

H21   Crescents interspersed with open beading

H22   Hooped corners

H23   Miscellaneous beadwork

J   Heraldry

K   Colours

K1   Red

K2   Blue

K3   Green

K4i   Yellow pot-metal (inc. amber)

K4ii   Yellow stained

K5   Pink

L   Shaped panes

L1   Roundels painted with flowers

L2   Roundel spacer shapes

L3   Curved shoulder or borders

L4   Rectangular glaziers' strips

L5   Triangles and quarries

L6   Rectangular and square panes and quarries

L7   Quarry apexes

L8   Irregular shapes

M   Miscellaneous fragments

M1   Miscellaneous painted fragments whose designs are undiagnostic or unrecognised

M2   Miscellaneous unpainted fragments

Catalogue of Illustrated Fragments

The catalogue numbers follow consecutively those on Microfiche **2:B12**, *AY* 11/2. Each entry ends with the glass type code and information about any grozed or re-used edges on the fragment. This is followed by the area of glass in cm², context number and small find number, prefixed sf. The period, prefixed P, and phase number appear in brackets. A list of phases containing window glass appears on pp.559–61.

G = grozing; 1G = one grozed edge etc. R = re-used edge

46–54 Fishergate (1984–6.9)

13th century grisaille

174 White glass. Lead stains. The design is in reserve, an upright trefoil with small head and pendant trails within the stem, with one sideways curling trefoil to the right. The paintwork for both this and for the large cross-hatching is crude. A1, 2G, 19cm², 4070 sf680 (P7a 443) (*Fig.168*)

175 Grey/green tinted white metal. Upright trefoil with inner stem definition flanked by unbroken curling trefoils. Fine cross hatching in between. Paint unevenly spread. A1, 2G, 21cm², 2001 sf9173 (P7a 225) (*Fig.168*)

176 Apex of a quarry. Design is of the upper half of a grisaille quarry in strapwork. The trefoil is a stiff upright form with pendant trails in the stem. On a medium-fine cross-hatched ground. One line crossing diagonally and forming the bottom edge is lead stained, releading? A2, 2G, 25cm², 4070 sf735 (P7a 443) (*Fig.168*)

177 White glass. Design has an upright stiff trefoil lying diagonally across the rectangle, but the grozing may imply that this was a quarry shape proper with the trefoil central. The head is small and tight, the stem has no pendant trails. The stem curls round the trefoil in a tight oval. Very fine cross-hatching. A2, 4G, 18cm², 3002 sf451 (P7a 331) (*Fig.168*)

178 White glass with blue/green tint. Grozed to a right angle. Painted with the corner of a strapwork design, with a side-flowering medium-sized trefoil on a very pale cross-hatched ground. A3, 1G, 13cm², 3000 sf2128 (u/s) (*Fig.168*)

179 Painted with crossing trefoils on very fine cross-hatched ground. Two complete and two partial grozed edges. A4, 4G, 36cm², 3009 sf547 (P7a 331) (*Fig.169*)

180 Friable white glass painted with two trefoils, possibly crossing, with a curling stem, on a very fine cross-hatched ground. A4, 3G, 57cm², 3030 sf456 (P8 333) (*Fig.169*)

181 White glass. Painted with a curling trefoil and large cross-hatched ground with thick lines. A5, 4G, 20cm², 3163 sf2167 (P7a 331) (*Fig.170*)

182 White glass. A double-headed trefoil with large pendant trail in the stem, a round terminal to the cusp, on cross-hatched ground. A quarry 120 × 55mm max. A6, 4G, 53cm², 3000 sf2281 (u/s) (*Fig.170*)

183 White glass. Possible border piece of a double-headed trefoil with a loop between filled with fine cross-hatching. A6, 2G, 10cm², 3163 sf2172 (P7a 331) (*Fig.170*)

184 Painted with a squat upright trefoil on cross-hatched ground. A6, 1G, 13·5cm², 2005 sf31 (P7a 225) (*Fig.170*)

185 White glass. Painting is probably the head of a double-headed trefoil, but small. There is a curling stem reaching to the mid-point of the head and a small circular design here. The linework is very accurate and the cross-hatched ground very fine. A6, 2G, 10cm², 3009 sf542 (P7a 331) (*Fig.170*)

186 White glass. Painted with partial double-headed trefoil and stem or strapwork on cross-hatched ground. A6, ¬, 14cm², 3030 sf456 (P8 333) (*Fig.170*)

187 White glass. Painted with a very large trefoil on large cross-hatching. A7, 1G, 25cm², 3215 sf3372 (P7a 331) (*Fig.171*)

188 Thick cross-hatched side-facing trefoil with curling stem to the right. A7, 5G, 26cm², 3180 sf3045 (P7a 331) (*Fig.171*)

189 Piece with medium-fine cross-hatching and a group of berries. A8, ¬, 8cm², 3002 sf306 (P7a 331) (*Fig.171*)

190 Semi-translucent yellow glass. Painted with trefoil with stamens off curling stem on cross-hatched ground. A9, ¬, 10cm², 3163 sf2363 (P7a 331) (*Fig.171*)

191 Painted with an upright trefoil and side foils, with stamens, in reserve from matt ground. A9, 1G, 10cm², 3163 sf2167 (P7a 331) (*Fig.171*)

192 Decoration in brown matt paint, cinquefoil with inner circle on cross-hatched ground. A10, 2G, 1R, 13cm², 2001 sf6 (P7a 225) (*Fig.171*)

193   White glass. Design in reserve. A diagonal length of strapping for a quarry edge, within which is an upright cinquefoil in the form of stiff leaf on a cross-hatched ground. A10, ¬, 7·5cm², 5000 sf2104 (u/s) (*Fig.171*)

194   White glass. A crude upright trefoil on large and thick cross-hatched ground. A10, 1G, 32cm², 3163 sf2414 (P7a 331) (*Fig.172*)

195   White glass. The opening of a large trefoil, an upright multi-foil (six lobe). A10, ¬, 10cm², 3163 sf2414 (P7a 331) (*Fig.172*)

196   Three partial and one complete lobes and circle at centre of quatrefoil on fine cross-hatched ground, the marks of the cross-hatching seen on the outline of the flower. This may be a border pattern, but note that the grozing crosses the pattern diagonally. One side definitely has lead stains. The grozing is very close together rather than the usual wide spacing of grozing on thick, early glass. Could be releading. A10, 2G, 6cm², 2028 sf90 (P7a 329) (*Fig.172*)

197   Border defined by cut-lines and grozing, with a linear zone of cross-hatching in the central area. Possibly a small foliate motif on one of the broken edges in reserve. A10, 2G, 6cm², 3283 sf4085 (P6a 319) (*Fig.172*)

Early 14th century grisaille

198   Lead stains. The design is of two downward flowering trefoils on a plain ground. One trefoil with berries. B1, 3G, 12·5cm², 3030 sf456 (P8 333) (*Fig.172*)

Late 13th/early 14th century grisaille

199   White glass, blue/green tint. Two fragments which join. Grozing on all sides. Lead stains. Painted with the strapwork edge and three lobes and two cusps of a quatrefoil with round lobes. Possibly releaded. B3, G, 36cm², 3030 sf456 (P8 333) (*Fig.173*)

200   Translucent, blue/green tinted. Grozing forms corners of squares. Painted with quatrefoil in outline, with pointed lobes. B2, 4G, 59cm², 2001 sf57 (P7a 225) (*Fig.173*)

201   White glass. Painted with the edge of strapwork and two partial and one complete round lobes. The cusp has a rounded terminal and the base has a cross-hatched triangle in place of the tear reserved on other examples of this kind. The ends of the cross-hatched lines can be seen as brushstrokes superimposed on the paint of the border. B3, 1G, 23cm², 3030 sf456 (P8 333) (*Fig.173*)

202   Transparent yellow/green tinted white glass. Large grozing, corner, painted with

roughly surfaced enamel, strapwork and one lobe. B4, 2G, 7·5cm², 2114 sf3609 (P7a 225) (*Fig.173*)

203   White glass. Painted with an oak leaf and strapwork. B6, 1G, 19cm², 3163 sf2365 (P7a 331) (*Fig.174*)

204   White glass. Painted with stem and base of oak leaf, showing undulating line within stem. B6, ¬, 7·5cm², 3163 sf2178 (P7a 331) (*Fig.174*)

205   Almost opaque. Grozed to a corner, with strapwork, the beginning of a *rinceau* and the stem for oak leaf grisaille. B6, 2G, 11cm², 3163 sf2181 (P7a 331) (*Fig.174*)

206   Fine, almost opaque glass, white. Painted with curves and lines. B6, ¬, 6cm², 2000 sf4940 (u/s) (*Fig.174*)

207   Lead staining. Painted with the stem of the oak leaf grisaille beside a running tendril with trefoil heads and dots alternating either side of it. B6, 1G, 8cm², 3163 sf2139 (P7a 331) (*Fig.174*)

208   Oak leaf. B6, ¬, 10cm², 3180 sf3045 (P7a 331) (*Fig.174*)

209   Oak leaf outline. B6, 1G, 20cm², 3163 sf2414 (P7a 331) (*Fig.174*)

210   Painted with oak leaf and an acorn with cross-hatched base. B6, 1G, 16cm², 3163 sf2190 (P7a 331) (*Fig.174*)

211   White glass. Painted with an acorn, strapwork and part of a leaf. B6, ¬, 8cm², 3000 sf2128 (u/s) (*Fig.174*)

212   Lead stain. Painted with an acorn in outline. B6, 1G, 5cm², 3000 sf2082 (u/s) (*Fig.174*)

Patterned quarries

213   Edge of a pane painted with framing lines and trefoil terminal, highlighted in yellow stain. C5, 1G, 3·5cm², 2001 sf6 (P7a 225) (*Fig.175*)

214   Two fragments. Painted with an acorn on a long stalk, the base made up of cross-hatching, the lower half of an oak leaf, a trefoil terminal. Some yellow staining. C2, ¬, 7·5cm², 2062 sf2670 (P7a 225) (*Fig.175*)

215   Transparent white glass. Painted with a partial oak leaf in fine outline and trefoil terminal in yellow stain. C1, ¬, 3cm², 2001 sf6 (P7a 225) (*Fig.175*)

216   Transparent white glass. Painted with a rose of five petals with cross-hatched yellow stained centre. Between the main petals are yellow stained subsidiary petals, with short stems. C3, ¬, 4cm², 2001 sf6 (P7a 225) (*Fig.175*)

217   Fine consistent transparent white glass. Seeds visible within the metal, a darkened lead stain. Painted with a quarry edge, stained; a stem shoots from the edge and a flower like a lily is featured with some yellow staining. C4, 1G, 8cm², 2001 sf6 (P7a 225) (*Fig.175*)

218 Same type of glass as *216*, with a stained trefoil terminal, possibly a subsidiary petal and a spade-like terminal may be part of the same sort of design. C4, ⌐, 2cm², 2001 sf6 (P7a 225) (*Fig.175*)

219 Some stain at the edge. The paintwork could define the curve of a canopy, but being outlined by thin lines could be foliate. There is a finely outlined design within. Resembles some of the fine quarry lily designs and grisaille. C4, 1G, 5cm², 2081 sf2896 (P7a 225) (*Fig.175*)

220 Fine translucent white glass, painted with the interstices of two petals and yellow stained piece between. C4, ⌐, 2·5cm², 2114 sf3609 (P7a 225) (*Fig.175*)

221 White translucent glass. Painted cut-line, yellow staining and painted quarry edges and some internal painted design. C5, 2G, 6cm², 2114 sf3609 (P7a 225) (*Fig.175*)

222 Consistent transparent white glass. Trefoil terminal and stained edging. C5, 1G, 7cm², 2001 sf6 (P7a 225) (*Fig.175*)

223–4 Four fragments which join together, painted with portions of oak leaf in very fine outline, and with quarry edge. Some evidence for yellow staining. C1, ⌐, 6cm², 2062 sf2670 (P7a 225) (*Fig.175*)

225–6 Fine translucent white metal-painted with fine oak leaf. C1, ⌐, 1cm², 2114 sf3609 (P7a 225) (*Fig.175*)

227 Acorn in matt brown paint, strapping of quarry with yellow stain. C2, ⌐, 1·5cm², 2001 sf9174 (P7a 225) (*Fig.175*)

Diaper

228–30 White glass, translucent. Scratched fronds, fine wash, scratches and curves in ground. D1, ⌐, 6cm², 2114 sf3609 (P7a 225) (*Fig.178*)

231 Translucent, apparently pot-metal yellow. Painted with a fine wash from which a *rinceau* of circular flowers has been picked; fine stems and background decoration of curls and circles have been scratched out. D2, 2G, 10cm², 2001 sf6 (P7a 225) (*Fig.178*)

232 Lead staining. Mid-green pot-metal. Decoration is in reserve from a wash of enamel paint, picked out as spade-like leaves, from a central stem, with little circles scratched out from the background. D4, 3G, 10cm², 3163 sf2180 (P7a 331) (*Fig.178*)

233 Flashed ruby glass. Painted in reserve, a border round the edge, multi-lobate within. D5, 3G, 15cm², 2062 sf3208 (P7a 225) (*Fig.178*)

234 Painted in reserve, multi-lobate or seaweed diaper. D5, 3G, 12cm², 3002 sf306 (P7a 331) (*Fig.178*)

235 Flashed ruby glass. Painted in reserve with stickwork, a border at the edge. Diaper pattern. D7, 1G, 2·5cm², 2001 sf6 (P7a 225) (*Fig.179*)

236 Flashed ruby glass. Painted in reserve with stickwork. D7, ⌐, 4cm², 2114 sf3609 (P7a 225) (*Fig.179*)

237 Ruby flashed translucent glass. Slight lead staining. Painted with a thin wash from which circles and concave-sided diamonds have been formed, with scratched decoration within. D7, ⌐, 4cm², 2001 sf6 (P7a 225) (*Fig.179*)

238 Blue/grey glass. Painted in reserve with stickwork. Edge of a diaper pattern. D7, 1G, 6cm², 2001 sf9173 (P7a 225) (*Fig.179*)

239 Flashed ruby glass. Painted in reserve with stickwork. D7, ⌐, 2cm², 2114 sf3609 (P7a 225) (*Fig.179*)

240 Flashed ruby glass. Painted in reserve with stickwork. Edge to diaper pattern. D7, 1G, 3cm², 2001 sf6 (P7a 225) (*Fig.179*)

241 Opaque glass painted in reserve with stickwork along the edge to diaper pattern, possibly used in architecture. D7, ⌐, 6cm², 2063 sf2214 (P7a 225) (*Fig.179*)

242 Opaque in parts, flashed ruby. Painted in reserve with stickwork. D7, ⌐, 2cm², 2114 sf3609 (P7a 225) (*Fig.179*)

243 Fine white, translucent glass. Painted with a right angle quarry edge. Pale wash from which a leaf has been reserved and detail scratched out. D3, 2G, 4cm², 2114 sf3609 (P7a 225) (*Fig.179*)

244 Blue/grey pot-metal. Decoration in reserve in matt brown paint, possible diaper of lobed foliage with stickwork detail of background curls and outline of leaves. D3, 1G, 4cm², 2001 sf9172 (P7a 225) (*Fig.179*)

245 Almost opaque, possible trefoil diaper in reserve from a matt ground, with scratched curved highlights. D8, ⌐, 4cm², 2001 sf9172 (P7a 225) (*Fig.179*)

246 Grozed edge with painted cut-line, painted cross diaper. D6, 1G, 4cm², 2114 sf3609 (P7a 225) (*Fig.179*)

247 Translucent pot-metal, deep green. Painted with a wash divided into small lozenges, each with a circle scratched out of it. D8, ⌐, 1·5cm², 2114 sf3609 (P7a 225) (*Fig.179*)

Vegetal and floral decorated fragments

248 Translucent green apex of quarry. A leaf in reserve from a plain ground. E, 2G, 12cm², 2001 sf9172 (P7a 225) (*Fig.180*)

249 Opaque, white. Grozed to a sharp point. Quarry. Painted in reserve, a trefoil with elongated middle lobe and central vein. E, 2G, 18cm², 2001 sf57 (P7a 225) (*Fig.180*)

250 Opaque, apex. Leaf design in reserve from plain ground. Central boss and stamens

painted in line. E, 3G, 10cm², 2001 sf9172 (P7a 225) (*Fig.180*)

251   Opaque. Grozed to produce a curved shoulder. Painted in reserve, a vine leaf, probably from a running stem with alternate leaves. E, 4G, 16cm², 8023 sf1834 (P7c 804) (*Fig.180*)

252   Green-tinted white glass, translucent. Painted with leaf design in reserve from enamel ground. E, ¬, 10cm², 2114 sf3609 (P7a 225) (*Fig.180*)

253   Painted with the central vein and side veins of a leaf with a row of dots showing the position of a leaf indent. In reserve. E, ¬, 14.5cm², 2114 sf3609 (P7a 225) (*Fig.181*)

254   White glass. Three sides of a quarry present, with lead stains. Painted with an undulate line to one side and a leaf to the other in reserve. Possibly releaded. E, 3G, 12cm², 3163 sf2172 (P7a 331) (*Fig.181*)

255   Pink to ruby glass. Painted with a fringed leaf design and double-veined stalk. E, 2G, 7cm², 3163 sf2181 (P7a 331) (*Fig.181*)

256   Mid-blue/grey pot-metal painted with a semi-circular cut-line and a foliate design in reserve. E, 1G, 8cm², 2114 sf3609 (P7a 225) (*Fig.181*)

257   Fine white glass. Within a curved border, a multi-lobate shape and a single curve with yellow stain behind, probably floral. E, ¬, 3.5cm², 2062 sf3471 (P7a 225) (*Fig.181*)

258   Translucent light–mid green. Painted with a circle and radiating stamens, as flower. E, ¬, 2.5cm², 2114 sf3609 (P7a 225) (*Fig.181*)

259   Translucent fine white glass. Painted cut-line. Quarry apex. The strapwork is painted and yellow stained on the reverse. Apex of the quarry has a fleur-de-lys type design in reserve but with veins. The space below seems to be curved and is in reserve. E, 1G, 5.5cm², 2062 sf3471 (P7a 225) (*Fig.181*)

Figural fragments (heads)

260   White glass. Only the left eye of a face remains with some hair defined at the tip and either shading or a beard at the bottom. G1, ¬, 5.5cm², 3180 sf3045 (P7a 331) (*Fig.182*)

261   Opaque. One curved edge of grozing defines the top of the head. A pair of eyes, looking to the figure's left. High arched brows, lids in fine line and some shading between. The hair is finely detailed at the front. May be yellow stained on the back. G1, 1G, 6cm², 3163 sf2357 (P7a 331) (*Fig.182*)

262   The curls of the hair are detailed with the right eye and top of nose. The curve of the hairline round the side of the face is echoed in short strokes on the back. G1, 1G, 4cm², 5060 sf2536 (P8 527) (*Fig.182*)

263   White glass. Painted with the left side of a face, with long hair and large open eye looking to the left. Slight shading under the

eyebrow. G1, 1G, 3cm², 3163 sf2178 (P7a 331) (*Fig.182*)

264   Painted with a small-scale face, showing both eyes, nose and part of mouth. Some slight shading can be seen around the eyes. G1, ¬, 2.5cm², 3163 sf2172 (P7a 331) (*Fig.182*)

265   Two fragments. Painted in reserve, with the left hand side of a face, featuring the chin, nose and hair. The hair may have had shading. The hair defines the right side of the head and neck. It is thickly painted giving a depth to the strokes causing slight ridges. The ear and chin are painted, the mouth droops. The chin is speckled with dots like stubble shading. G1, ¬, 2cm², 3163 sf2178 (P7a 331); G1, 1G, 5cm², 3180 sf3045 (P7a 331) (*Fig.182*)

266   Translucent white. Painted with a series wavy lines, perhaps representing hair, and yellow stained. G1, ¬, 4cm², 2114 sf3609 (P7a 225) (*Fig.182*)

267   Transparent white, slightly amber glass. Painted with the lower half of a face and neck in reserve and outline in matt brown. Face flanked by long, wavy hair in thick outline; part of the mouth and chin are shown. The neck is contoured with lines similar to drapery folds. G1, 1G, 30cm², 2001 sf6 (P7a 225) (*Figs.183–4*)

268   White glass with green tint. Design in reserve and drawn detail. A figure of the Christ Child in the Virgin's arms. The paint has a texture as a result of uneven application and very free brushstrokes, although thin washes are used in places to emphasise the folds of the child's drapery. Grozed all around. G1, 1G, 31cm², 3180 sf3045 (P7a 331) (*Fig.183*)

269–70   White glass. Painted with a mass of curly flowing hair defining the face which is full frontal. A band with rings bound round it crosses the forehead. Only the left eye is wholly visible, with a thin line above the brow. On the reverse, the area covering the hair above and below the band are shaded, an oval outline of the face is traced, as are the outlines of the eyes. Shading makes the hair appear golden brown. G1, 1G, 14.5cm², 3180 sf3045 (P7a 331) (*Fig.183*)

Figural fragments (hands and feet)

271   Left hand painted in reserve. The hand is stretched out, palm towards the viewer, the fingers long and tapering. G3, 2G, 5.5cm², 3180 sf3045 (P7a 331) (*Fig.185*)

272   Blue/green tinted white glass. Paintwork is very feathery. Defines three fingers and a thumb, elegant pose. The thumbnail is drawn. G3, 3G, 5cm², 2114 sf3609 (P7a 225) (*Fig.185*)

273   Design is of a hand, in reserve, of very small scale with fine, tapering fingers. G3, 1G, 3cm², 3163 sf2190 (P7a 331) (*Fig.185*)

274   Translucent white glass. Curved grozed edge, painted with thick concentric lines with sporadic parallel lines sticking out from them. Some shading. Possible halo or fingers. G3, 1G, 9·5cm², 2114 sf3609 (P7a 225) (*Fig.185*)

275   Translucent. Grozed around the shape. Painted with the design of a hand in reserve with the details of the nails painted in. G3, 1G, 7cm², 2001 sf9173 (P7a 225) (*Fig.185*)

276   White metal. Painted with a tight buttoned sleeve, one full hand and part of a second. A purse beneath. Details picked out in yellow stain which has gone copper blue/green round the edges and opaque black in parts. G3, ¬, 12cm², 2114 sf3609 (P7a 225) (*Figs.185, 187*)

277   White metal. Several very fine slivers of glass painted with part of a laminated saboton with rivets, from the foot of a knight. Outline and yellow stain highlights. G4, 4.5cm², 2114 sf3609 (P7a 225) (*Figs.185, 187*)

278   White glass. Painted with a foot. There are five digits all painted with nails from a side view. G4, 2G, 7cm², 3163 sf2190 (P7a 331) (*Fig.185*)

279   Translucent. Painted with the design of a hand or foot in reserve with the details of the nails painted in. G4, 1G, 4cm², 2114 sf3609 (P7a 225) (*Fig.185*)

Figural fragments (drapery)

280   Decoration showing fall of drapery, fairly vermicular with careful shading unlike any other piece in corpus. Stipple shading? Small-scale imagery. G2, ¬, 3·5cm², 3174 sf3354 (P6c 325) (*Figs.187, 189*)

281   White glass. Painted with lines and a hook of drapery folds, and deepened by smear shading. G2, ¬, 1·5cm², 3163 sf2178 (P7a 331) (*Fig.189*)

282   Translucent, thick ruby flashing. One grozed edge with white cement from the came concreted to the inner face. Painted with drapery folds and creases, gathered in by a belt. Some light shading. G2, 3G, 31cm², 2001 sf6 (P7a 225) (*Fig.189*)

283   White glass. Painted with very bold and simple drapery hook. Slight shading. G2, 2G, 11cm², 3163 sf2178 (P7a 331) (*Fig.189*)

284   Translucent, deep ruby or murrey (pot-metal) colour. Painted with two sharp hooked folds. G2, 1G, 12cm², 2001 sf57 (P7a 225) (*Fig.189*)

285   Flashed ruby glass. Painted with swathes and a hook fold, some shading. Probably drapery, shoulder. G2, 2G, 15cm², 3163 sf2190 (P7a 331) (*Fig.189*)

286   Light–mid green with yellow tint, painted with drapery folds, one fairly hooked, shading. Shaped as a shoulder and arm. Back-painting adding depth. G2, 1G, 9·5cm², 2114 sf3609 (P7a 225) (*Fig.189*)

287   Translucent rich amber yellow. Probably an arm or leg. Painted with drapery including some back-painting for depth and shading. Lead stains. G2, 1G, 11cm², 2114 sf3609 (P7a 225) (*Fig.189*)

288   Yellow pot-metal, translucent glass. Painted with drapery folds and shading. G2, 2G, 5cm², 2114 sf3609 (P7a 225) (*Fig.189*)

289   Green/blue tinted white glass. Painted with strong thick lines, some converging, with some thin wash shading. On the reverse back-painting is very thin, shows as white wash, brushstrokes visible. G2, ¬, 10cm², 2114 sf3609 (P7a 225) (*Fig.190*)

290   Painted with a series of tapering lines, some forming very sharp Vs, some shading in-between. 12th century. G2, 2G, 5cm², 3180 sf3045 (P7a 331) (*Fig.190*)

291   White glass, lead staining. Painting depicts strong drapery folds with light shading and back-painting. G2, 1G, 14cm², 3163 sf2178 (P7a 331) (*Fig.190*)

292   Green glass. The painted lines may have been bunched stems of curling foliage. On the reverse some patches of smooth surfaces on glass show clear signs of linear markings which may be resultant from the manufacturing process. G2, ¬, 16cm², 4048 sf515 (P7b 444) (*Fig.190*)

293   White glass. Painted with possible drapery lines, cutting across the pane. Some shading beside each line. Backpainted smear shading on the reverse. G2, 2G, 20cm², 3163 sf2182 (P7a 331) (*Fig.190*)

Figural fragments (miscellaneous)

294   White glass. Painted in outline and internal detail as a bird wing. G5, 1G, 6cm², 2163 sf2178 (P6b 215) (*Fig.191*)

295   White glass, possibly with yellow stain. Painted in reserve, a series of rows of overlapping feathers, with some wash shading towards the left grozed edge. Very small-scale imagery. G5, 1G, 5cm², 2081 sf2896 (P7a 225) (*Fig.191*)

296   Semi-opaque, ruby flashed. Painted with two lines and some short strokes curving one way for one line and another way for the next. G5, ¬, 2cm², 2001 sf57 (P7a 225) (*Fig.191*)

297   Yellow stained. Painted with overlapping scales or feathers. G5, 1G, 4cm², 3163 sf2414 (P7a 331) (*Fig.191*)

298   White glass. Painted cut-line, with a small circle with radiating wavy lines. Decorated sword chape or strap-end? G6, 1G, 3cm², 3180 sf3045 (P7a 331) (*Fig.191*)

299 White glass. Painted with fine wash and a plain strip; the wash painted with two comma-shaped tails probably indicating ermine. G6, 3G, 4·5cm², 3180 sf3045 (P7a 331) (*Fig.191*)

300 White glass, yellow stained to a light yellow. Design is in reserve, between two strawberry leaves and with a linear design below. Crown. G6, ¬, 5·5cm², 3180 sf3045 (P7a 331) (*Fig.191*)

301 White glass, highlighted with yellow stain. Design in reserve, small strawberry leaves. G6, ¬, 3cm², 2001 sf9171 (P7a 225) (*Fig.191*)

Architectural fragments

302 Two fragments. Fine transparent white glass. Inner edges grozed, possibly in order to accommodate a figure. Design picked out of a matt paint. Yellow stain. F2, 1G, 5cm², 2114 sf3609 (P7a 225); F2, 2G, 9cm², 2001 sf6 (P7a 225) (*Fig.192*)

303 Opaque. Decoration in matt paint; crockets on canopy. F1, ¬, 3cm², 2001 sf9173 (P7a 225) (*Fig.192*)

304 Transparent white glass. Canopy, decorated with painted outlines and yellow stain. F2, ¬, 9cm², 2001 sf6 (P7a 225)(*Fig.192*)

305 White glass. The paintwork consists of a central triangular zone filled with a light wash from which a linear fern design has been picked and a cusped circle. This is bounded by thick lines on one side of which is a linear motif employing an undulating line similar to that found in late 13th/early 14th century grisaille stems. The corresponding zone on the other side of the triangle has a thin wash. Both these areas have been washed with yellow stain on the reverse. None of the paintwork or scratching is very precise. Architectural, but linked with *rinceau* backgrounds. F2, 1G, 28cm², 2114 sf3358 (P7a 225) (*Fig.192*)

306 White glass. Painted with parallel horizontal lines, yellow stained, shaded. Pinkish shaded wash. F8, 1G, 2cm², 2114 sf3609 (P7a 225) (*Fig.192*)

307 Small crocket, in reserve and yellow stained. F5, ¬, 4cm², 2114 sf3609 (P7a 225) (*Fig.192*)

308 White glass. Design in reserve. Internal detail of a canopy. Some drawn detail of foliage. F2, ¬, 3cm², 2005 sf2067 (P7a 225) (*Fig.192*)

309 White glass. Design in reserve. Internal detail of a canopy. Some drawn detail of foliage. F2, ¬, 3cm², 2005 sf2067 (P7a 225) (*Fig.192*)

310 White glass, bevelled and transparent. Crocket design in reserve highlighted in yellow stain, with painted detail. F1, 1G, 6cm², 2001 sf9171 (P7a 225) (*Fig.192*)

311 Semi-translucent white glass, painted with a small version of H13 scratched and a cusp in reserve. Very small scale. F6, 1G, 3·5cm², 2114 sf3609 (P7a 225) (*Fig.192*)

312 Semi-translucent white glass with faint yellow stain crocket. F5, 1G, 3·5cm², 2114 sf3609 (P7a 225) (*Fig.192*)

313 Translucent white painted with stickwork design on plain background, looks like the cusping of a window, or similar tracery. F7, ¬, 2·5cm², 2114 sf3609 (P7a 225) (*Fig.192*)

314 Blue pot-metal glass. The former paintwork can be seen in glancing light and was composed of several converging lines, one set with a series of crescents in descending order of size. K2, 3G, 10cm², 3030 sf473 (P8 333) (*Fig.193*)

315 White glass. Painted in reserve and stickwork. Part of canopy cusping or other architectural tracery. F2, 2G, 8cm², 2001 sf1881 (P7a 225) (*Fig.193*)

316 White glass. Painted in reserve. An architectural cusp. F6, ¬, 4cm², 2005 sf2067 (P7a 225) (*Fig.193*)

317 White glass. Painted with parallel horizontal lines, yellow stained, surmounted by concentric lines, shaded. Pinkish shaded wash. F4, 1G, 7cm², 2114 sf3609 (P7a 225) (*Fig.193*)

318 Translucent glass, probably stained yellow. Painted with lines resembling buttress offsets. F8, 2G, 5cm², 2114 sf3609 (P7a 225) (*Fig.193*)

319 Pot-metal amber or yellow stained. Grozed on all edges. Decoration in reserve on matt brown ground. F4, 5G, 17cm², 2001 sf9173 (P7a 225) (*Fig.194*)

320 White glass. Design painted in outline. A bell or capital with one band of undulating line decoration. F4, 3G, 16cm², 3163 sf2363 (P7a 331) (*Fig.194*)

321 Painted with the bell, astragal and shaft of a capital. As the grozing of the top edge cuts through the bell, perhaps a medieval releading. F4, 2G, 8cm², 2039 sf104 (P7a 329) (*Fig.194*)

322 Fine, smooth white glass. Transparent where not going opaque. Painted with an outlined merlon, with cross loop. Smear shading. F3, ¬, 12cm², 2000 sf4940 (u/s) (*Fig.194*)

323 White glass, semi-translucent. Painted with a cross with round terminals to each limb and a rectangle in the corner, with some shading beneath merlon. F3, ¬, 10·5cm², 2262 sf2670 (P7a 225) (*Fig.194*)

324 White glass. Some back-painting or spill. In reserve, a turret corbelled out or with a domed roof. Cross-slit window and the sides are shaded. F2, 2G, 8cm², 3025 sf396 (P10 335) (*Fig.194*)

Linear stickwork patterns and geometric borders

325   White glass. Painted with plain open beading in reserve. H1, 2G, 4cm², 3009 sf547 (P7a 331) (*Fig.195*)

326   White glass. Plain open beading in reserve, with parallel bands in reserve. H1, 1G, 3·5cm², 3163 sf2363 (P7a 331) (*Fig.195*)

327   Opaque glass. Open beading in reserve with internal dots. H2, 1G, 5cm², 3180 sf3045 (P7a 331) (*Fig.195*)

328   Opaque glass. Plain open beading interspersed with dots, all in reserve, and stickwork. H3, 1G, 2·5cm², 3163 sf2415 (P7a 331) (*Fig.195*)

329   White glass, with open beading interspersed with pairs of linked circles, in reserve and stickwork. H4, 1G, 5·5cm², 3180 sf3045 (P7a 331) (*Fig.195*)

330   Opaque glass, with open beading with internal dots interspersed with pairs of linked circles, in reserve and stickwork. H5, 2G, 4cm², 2001 sf57 (P7a 225) (*Fig.195*)

331   Opaque, slightly murrey/pink glass, with circles interspersed with pairs of smaller circles in stickwork. H6, 1G, 2·5cm², 2114 sf3609 (P7a 225) (*Fig.195*)

332   Semi-opaque, yellow-tinted white glass. Circles with internal beading interspersed with pairs of circles in stickwork. H7, ¬, 3·5cm², 2114 sf3609 (P7a 225) (*Fig.195*)

333   Opaque glass, with circles with internal beading interspersed with pairs of circles in stickwork. H7, 2G, 3cm², 2001 sf57 (P7a 225) (*Fig.195*)

334   Semi-opaque. Transmitted light shows streak of ruby. Decorated with circles with internal beading interspersed with pairs of linked circles. H8, 3G, 4·5cm², 2062 sf3471 (P7a 225) (*Fig.195*)

335   Opaque glass, with circles with internal beading and further internal dots interspersed with pairs of linked circles in stickwork. H9, 2G, 3·5cm², 2001 sf9173 (P7a 225) (*Fig.195*)

336   Mid-green pot-metal, some back-painting. Grozed to a sharp curve. Open beading with internal dots alternating with circles with both internal beading and further internal dots, interspersed with pairs of linked circles in stickwork. H10, 2G, 7cm², 3163 sf2190 (P7a 331) (*Fig.195*)

337   Opaque glass, circles alternating with crosses with circular terminals with pairs of circles between in stickwork. H11, 2G, 8cm², 2114 sf3609 (P7a 225) (*Fig.195*)

338   Opaque, quatrefoils in stickwork. H12, 1G, 3cm², 3163 sf2190 (P7a 331) (*Fig.195*)

339   Opaque, slightly murrey/pink glass, quatrefoils interspersed with pairs of circles in stickwork. H13, 1G, 4cm², 2114 sf3609 (P7a 225) (*Fig.195*)

340   Opaque, deposit on the reverse could be yellow staining. Quatrefoils interspersed with pairs of triangles in stickwork. H14, 1G, 3cm², 2114 sf3609 (P7a 225) (*Fig.195*)

341   Red flashed glass, quatrefoils within circles alternating with open beading interspersed with pairs of circles in stickwork. H15, 1G, 3·5cm², 2114 sf3609 (P7a 225) (*Fig.195*)

342   Red flashed glass, quatrefoils within circles alternating with crosses with circular terminals, interspersed with pairs of circles. H16, 2G, 6·5cm², 2001 sf9174 (P7a 225) (*Fig.195*)

343   Red flashed glass, quatrefoils within circles alternating with crosses with circular terminals, interspersed with pairs of circles. H16, 2G, 3cm², 2001 sf9174 (P7a 225) (*Fig.195*)

344   Pink glass, quatrefoils within circles interspersed with pairs of triangles in stickwork. H17, 2G, 6cm², 3180 sf3045 (P7a 331) (*Fig.195*)

345   Opaque glass, circles interspersed with pairs of vertical lines in stickwork. H18, 1G, 3cm² (u/s) (*Fig.195*)

346   Murrey/pink glass, with saltire crosses between cross-hatched panels in line and stickwork. H19, 2G, 6cm², 2114 sf3609 (P7a 225) (*Fig.195*)

347   Opaque. Painted with a linear band with zig-zag line in reserve, and rough circles picked out with stickwork. H20, 1G, 14cm², 3030 sf460 (P8 333) (*Fig.196*)

348   Translucent white glass. Grozing and lead stains. Painted with long portion of border pattern with crescents and circles in reserve. H21, 2G, 15cm² 3163 sf2178 (P7a 331) (*Fig.196*)

Heraldic decoration

349   White glass. Four fragments make an almost complete fleur-de-lys. The paintwork is rather crude, the design in reserve. J, 7G, 45cm², 3030 sf456 (P8 333) (*Fig.197*)

350   White glass. Design is reserved from a matt wash of fairly thick brown enamel paint. The lower half of a fleur-de-lys of a standard form found in the Fishergate material. Fairly crude definition with a plain band tying the elements together. Whereas the top leaves are differentiated, those of the bottom are not. Uncertain as to whether there could be any yellow stain on the reverse due to opacity. Shape tapered to fit the lower leaves. Probably a border design. J, 3G, 25cm², 3002 sf430 (P7a 331) (*Fig.197*)

351   Two fragments, translucent, concretions on the grozed edges. From a broad matt wash, two fleurs-de-lys of the same size are reserved. The paintwork is quite thin in parts, so that overlaps in the strokes can be seen as double thickness, spoiling the design. Pos-

sibly some light yellow staining. J, 3G, 21·5cm², 2062 sf3208 (P7a 225) (*Fig.197*)

352   White glass, translucent, either entirely yellow stained or a golden yellow pot-metal. Fleur-de-lys in reserve with an added detail to the leaf. J, 1G, 5cm², 2114 sf3609 (P7a 225) (*Fig.197*)

353   Broad lead stain. Decoration in red/brown outline on cross-hatched ground, heraldic lion passant guardant in outline. J, 1G, 9cm², 2062 sf3433 (P7a 225)(*Fig.198*)

354   White translucent glass. Could be yellow/ green pot-metal rather than yellow stain. Painted with quarry apex but grozing cuts across the design as well. Lion or leopard's paw in reserve. J, 2G, 4cm², 2114 sf3609 (P7a 225) (*Fig.198*)

355   Semi-translucent white glass with a quarry edge. Leopard or lion's mouth in reserve on yellow stained ground. Tongue formed by stickwork. J, 1G, 3·5cm², 2114 sf3609 (P7a 225) (*Fig.198*)

356   Translucent yellow stained or pot yellow, lion or leopard's paw in reserve. Individual claws visible, hairy fetlock. J, 1G, 2·5cm², 2114 sf3609 (P27a 225) (*Fig.198*)

357   Translucent white glass. Painted with the leg of a beast in reserve, probably yellow stain. J, 2G, 2.5cm², 2114 sf3609 (P7a 225) (*Fig.198*)

358   Translucent white glass. Two legs and paws of a leopard or lion rampant or passant guardant. J, 1G, 3·5cm², 2114 sf3609 (P7a 225) (*Fig.198*)

359   Translucent, yellow stained, portion of a crown in reserve with line detail. J, 2G, 6cm², 2001 sf57 (P7a 225) (*Fig.198*)

360   Translucent white glass. Painted with lower left hand corner of crown in reserve with two partial trefoil uprights. Small painted details as the others. Faded yellow staining visible as slight green swathes. J, ¬, 3·5cm², 2114 sf3609 (P7a 225) (*Fig.198*)

361   Translucent. Painted with the left side of a crown (as worn) and yellow stained, with line detail. J, 1G, 3cm², 2114 sf3609 (P7a 225) (*Fig.198*)

Miscellaneous painted fragments

362   Flashed ruby? Painted with carefully spaced lines which could be black letter script in reserve. K1, ¬, 7cm², 3215 sf3372 (P7a 331) (*Fig.200*)

363   White glass, possibly stained. Painted with circles and lines, probably a holy book held by a saint. Two fingers may be shown. M1, 3G, 10·5cm², 3163 sf2363 (P7a 331) (*Fig.200*)

364   Mid–light green pot-metal. Decoration in reserve and painted detail, geometric. Possible buckle or holy book, held by a saint. K3, 3G, 9·5cm², 3180 sf3045 (P7a 331) (*Fig.200*)

365   White glass painted with a possible stem design with angled rhomboid dots in outline. M1, ¬, 4cm², 3180 sf3045 (P7a 331) (*Fig.200*)

366   Translucent glass, painted with almost geometric shapes in outline, kites, ellipses, with a diagonal hatched ground. M1, 1G, 11·5cm², 3009 sf538 (P7a 331) (*Fig.200*)

367   Translucent glass, painted with almost geometric shapes in outline, kites, ellipses, with a diagonal hatched ground. M1, 1G, 2cm², 3009 sf538 (P7a 331) (*Fig.200*)

368   White translucent glass. Painted with outline and shading on reverse. M1, G, 11cm², 2081 sf2923 (P7a 225) (*Fig.200*)

369   Translucent white glass, possibly some yellow staining or back-painting. Painted with rectangle and lines, possible merlon or book and clasp. M1, 1G, 11cm², 2114 sf9025 (P7a 225) (*Fig.200*)

370   Yellow stained. Painted with a decorated circle in reserve. The circle has a square at the centre, and gadrooning round it as found on other architectural details. Possible shoe detail. M1, 2G, 17cm², 3163 sf2178 (P7a 331) (*Fig.201*)

371   White glass. Translucent. Painted with wavy lines. M1, ¬, 3·5cm², 3163 sf2179 (P7a 331) (*Fig.201*)

372   White glass with green tint. Painted with linear arrangement in outline, some shading and yellow stain. Buckle? M1, G, 6cm², 3163 sf2179 (P7a 331) (*Fig.201*)

373   Translucent pot-metal yellow. Painted with almost symmetrical design. Possible architectural canopy crocket in reserve. M1, 2G, 10cm², 3163 sf2182 (P7a 331) (*Fig.201*)

374   Opaque glass, bevelled. Possible architectural crocket in reserve. M1, 1G, 6cm², 2005 sf11 (P7a 225) (*Fig.201*)

Possible glaziers' marks

375   Translucent white glass, shaped as pentagon. Stippled with a cross bar shape reserved or scratched out. M1, 1G, 18cm², 2062 sf2670 (P7a 225) (*Fig.202*)

376   White glass. Fragment with stipple shading from which an angular mark has been scratched out. Some painted lines. M1, 1G, 8cm², 3163 sf2190 (P7a 331) (*Fig.202*)

Shaped panes of plain glass

377   Blue/green metal. Iron corrosion on a grozed edge. Rectangular pane. L4, 4G, 20cm², 2001 sf9172 (P7a 225) (*Fig.204*)

378   Rhomboid or glazier's strip with one diagonal edge. L4, 4G, 23cm², 2001 sf9174 (P7a 225) (*Fig.204*)

379   Angled L shape, one edge with a very shiny slightly bevelled glass. L8, 6G, 17cm², 2001 sf9172 (P7a 225) (*Fig.204*)

380 Green-tinted white glass, lead stains. Curved with a pointed terminal to one side. L3, 4G, 28cm², 3030 sf460 (P8 333) (*Fig.205*)

381 Opaque. Curved shoulder pane. L3, 3G, 12cm², 2001 sf9171 (P7a 225) (*Fig.205*)

382 Curved shoulder pane. L3, 3G, 9cm², 3180 sf3045 (P7a 331) (*Fig.205*)

383 Flashed ruby glass, grozed to an irregular pentagon with two concave sides. Possible spacer for circular panes. K1, 5G, 16cm², 2001 sf9171 (P7a 225) (*Fig.205*)

384 Blue/green metal. All edges grozed, irregular pentagon. L6, 5G, 38cm², 2001 sf9173 (P7a 225) (*Fig.205*)

385 Ruby flashed glass. Lead stains. Quadrilateral with two opposing concave sides. Spacer for roundel. L2, 3G, 19cm², 3030 sf456 (P8 333) (*Fig.206*)

386 Ruby flashed glass. Quadrilateral with two opposing concave sides. Spacer for roundel. L2, 3G, 28cm², 3030 sf456 (P8 333) (*Fig.206*)

Roundels

387 Design in reserve, quatrefoil with rounded lobes, stamens extending from a central circle. Colour irretrievable. L1, G, 29cm², 3002 sf423 (P7a 331) (*Fig.210*)

388 Decoration in reserve in red/brown enamel, quatrefoil with central circle and radiating stamens. The stamens radiate from parallel lines in each petal/lobe. Set in lead cames. L1, G, 28cm², 2001 sf9159 (P7a 225) (*Fig.210*)

389 Probably white glass. Part of roundel with quatrefoils with pointed tips to the lobes, in reserve with line detail. L1, 1G, 18cm², 3030 sf467 (P8 333) (*Fig.210*)

390 Lead stains. Two fragments of a roundel painted with three lobes with pointed cusps. L1, 2G, 20cm², 3030 sf456 (P8 333) (*Fig.210*)

391 Partially grozed to a semi-circle, one stretch of fire-rounded edge. Painted with a broad outline, circle within which the design of a flower is in reserve. Fine stamens. L1, 1G, 8cm², 2001 sf6 (P7a 225) (*Fig.211*)

392 Semi-translucent white glass, may have slight blue/green tint. Grozed to a semi-circle, no particular evidence to suggest that the straight edge is secondary. Flower in reserve with internal detail. L1, 1G, 8cm², 2114 sf3609 (P7a 225) (*Fig.211*)

Shaped panes of white glass

393 White glass. Slight lines visible on inner surface. In two fragments which make a double pointed shape. L5, G, 27cm², 3012 sf553 (P7a 331) (*Fig.207*)

394 White glass. Grozed to a right-angled point with lead stains. May have been a square quarry originally. L6, 2G, 21cm², 3030 sf456 (P8 333) (*Fig.207*)

395 White glass, formerly square pane just under 7 × 7cm. L5, 3G, 37cm², 3030 sf460 (P8 333) (*Fig.207*)

Sempringham Priory, Lincolnshire (26–7/1987)

Grisaille and bird fragments

S1   Painted with upright trefoil on a fine controlled cross-hatched ground. A1, ¬, 21cm² (*Fig.218*)

S2   Painted with side-curling trefoil. A5, ¬, 13cm² (*Fig.218*)

S3   Painted with head, front body and wing of a bird in reserve and with internal line detail. G5, G, 15·5cm² (*Fig.218*)

S4   Painted with wing tip, back leg and tail of a bird in reserve and with internal line detail. G5, G, 4·5cm² (*Fig.218*)

Fragments of decorated quarry

S5   An almost complete quarry painted with a central quatrefoil leaf design in outline with a plain ground and edged with strapwork design. B2, 4G, 71·5cm² (*Fig.219*)

S6   Painted with oak leaf grisaille with one edge of strapwork. B6, ¬, 14·5cm² (*Fig.219*)

S7   Painted with oak leaf and acorns with fine cross-hatched cups and an associated beaded stickwork border. B6, 1G, 20cm² (*Fig.219*)

S8   Painted with a simple rose on curling stems, with a beaded stickwork border. C3, ¬, 22cm² (*Fig.219*)

Diaper fragments

S9   Painted *rinceau* pattern of a repeated trefoil, with finely fringed stickwork lobes and tendrils. D8, –, 10cm² (*Fig.220*)

S10   Fine border decorated with a running trefoil, executed in stickwork on blue and green. D8, 3G, 7cm² (*Fig.220*)

S11   Partially opaque white glass. Painted with running pattern of trefoils on a curling stem in reserve and stickwork. Trefoils with rounded lobes. D8, 2G, 9·5cm² (*Fig.220*)

S12   Painted with large-scale circle and concave lozenge diaper pattern in stickwork. D7, ¬, 25·5cm² (*Fig.220*)

S13   White glass, painted with cross diaper, outline and stickwork. D6, 1G, 6cm² (*Fig.220*)

S14   Rose-coloured pot-metal. Painted with a cross diaper of thin double lines, with the spaces divided into quatrefoils. D6, ¬, 5cm² (*Fig.220*)

S15   Painted with larger scale diaper with a painted leaf form. D8, ¬, 13·5cm² (*Fig.220*)

S16   Yellow pot-metal. Painted with a vine leaf or seaweed diaper in reserve. Fine veins painted in dilute paint. D5, 2G, 12cm² (*Fig.221*)

S17   Pale yellow pot-metal. Painted with fluid seaweed diaper in reserve. Some cross-hatching used to enhance depth. One cut edge. Friable. D5, 4G, 34cm² (*Fig.221*)

S18   A small fragment painted with finely scratched oak leaf and acorn detail, possibly from a background. D8, ¬, 6cm² (*Fig.221*)

Figural fragments

S19   Painted with a small head, the eyes looking right and framed by hair. G1, ¬, 5cm² (*Fig.223*)

S20   Painted with part of the head of Christ encircled by the crown of thorns. G1, ¬, 28cm² (*Fig.223*)

S21   Very finely painted with small-scale drapery with tight, vermicular folds. It includes a detail that might be a censer bowl or ointment jar, possibly suggesting that it is the figure of St Mary Magdalene. G2, ¬, 16cm² (*Fig.223*)

S22   Partially opaque. Painted with a succession of wavy lines and some light shading. Chainmail? Some traces of yellow stain on the reverse, following the painted lines. G6, 1G, 21cm² (*Fig.223*)

S23   Painted with a textile detail. G2, ¬, 20cm² (*Fig.223*)

S24   Painted with a small detail of hair. G1, ¬, 7·5cm² (*Fig.223*)

S25   Painted with a small detail of hair. G1, ¬, 7·5cm² (*Fig.223*)

S26   Green pot-metal. Painted with feathers in reserve, with edges highlighted in reserve and careful smear shading. Fragment of a fire-rounded edge left. G5, 3G, 12cm² (*Fig.223*)

Architectural fragments

S27   Painted architectural form with stickwork gable and pointed trefoils in the spandrels. F2, ¬, 12·5cm² (*Fig.224*)

S28   Opaque, painted with an architectural arrow slit in reserve, with trefoil terminals. Lead stain on reverse. F3, 2G, 12cm² (*Fig.224*)

S29   Arched top of a painted rectangular side shaft with quatrefoil in reserve. F4, G, 8·5cm² (*Fig.224*)

S30   Well-preserved painted ring and lower portion of a foliate finial from the top of an architectural canopy gable, in reserve. F8, 4G, 19·5cm² (*Fig.224*)

S31   Fragment from a crocketed pinnacle with beading in stickwork. F1, ¬, 11cm² (*Fig.224*)

S32   Painted with a masonry pattern and curved architectural arch, decorated with same beading as *S31*. F2, ¬, 14cm² (*Fig.224*)

S33   Painted with a masonry pattern and one horizontal beaded border in reserve and stickwork. F2, ¬, 14cm² (*Fig.224*)

S34   Yellow pot-metal. Painted with masonry pattern in reserve, a quatrefoil with pointed lobes. F2, 3G, 11cm² (*Fig.225*)

S35   Painted canopy finial, possibly from a repeated border pattern in reserve. F8, ¬, 14cm² (*Fig.225*)

S36   Painted canopy finial, possibly from a repeated border pattern. F8, ¬, 19cm² (*Fig.225*)

S37   Opaque glass, painted with 3-dimensional architectural feature, probably a base or pedestal. Possible foliate decoration beneath in reserve. F4, 1G, 18cm² (*Fig.225*)

S38   White glass. Border of rosettes, highlighted in yellow stain, encircled with parallel lines for an edge. Multi-lobate design beyond the edge. F, 2G, 17cm² (*Fig.225*)

S39   White glass. Border of rosettes, highlighted in yellow stain, encircled with parallel lines for an edge. An unknown design in outline and fine wash at one edge. A line is picked out as highlight. Possibly architectural. F, 1G, 12cm² (*Fig.225*)

S40   White glass. Foliate design in outline. F, 1G, 6cm² (*Fig.225*)

S41   White glass. Geometric design in outline and cross-hatching highlighted in yellow stain. F, ¬, 5cm² (*Fig.225*)

Linear stickwork and geometric borders

S42   Opaque. Painted with encircled quatrefoils in reserve, with tiny circles in the interstices of the lobes. H17, 4G, 5·5cm² (*Fig.227*)

S43   Fragment of running trefoil edge painted in outline on pot-metal green. H, 2G, 7cm² (*Fig.227*)

S44   An ornate quatrefoil in the centre of a strapwork lozenge, placed within a regular pane with the spaces between the lozenge and frame decorated with semi-circular lobes and serrated edges (reconstructed). H, ¬, – (*Fig.226*)

S45   Opaque glass. Painted with a linear design in outline. Encircled quatrefoil interspersed with circles. H14, 2G, 12cm² (*Fig.227*)

S46   Yellow pot-metal. Painted with a linear design in outline. Alternate cross-hatched circles and encircled quatrefoils interspersed with trefoils. H, 4G, 18cm² (*Fig.227*)

Heraldic and miscellaneous painted fragments

S47   Two fragments of an heraldic lion passant guardant, in reserve with internal detail. J, 3G, 13·5cm² (*Fig.227*)

S48   Possibly white glass. Roundel painted with five-pointed star with wavy arms in reserve. M1, 1G, 20cm² (*Fig.227*)

S49   Fragment painted with a large leaf in reserve. E, 4G, 8cm² (*Fig.227*)

S50   White glass, painted with black letter script '*na*' or '*ma*' (broken). Outlined with painted lines. M1, 1G, 10cm² (*Fig.227*)

Haverholme, Lincolnshire (1961–4)

Each entry ends with a 1961–4 excavation glass number (bold) and DOE D drawing sheet number.

Hav1   Fragment painted with an edging pattern of saltires. H23, –, 11cm² (**117– PVA/61– D10 u/s** DOE D 628) (*Fig.230*)

Hav2   Painted with a cross-hatched ground contained within a strapwork border, suggesting a trellis arangement of a grisaille quarry. B5, –, 13cm² (**25–59 B12e 2** DOE D 620) (*Fig.230*)

Hav3   Fragment painted with two trefoil heads side by side, probably from an edging pattern. A1, –, 11cm² (**15–13–B12c 1** DOE D 642) (*Fig.230*)

Hav4   Painted with a trefoil stem in reserve that has a curving cut-line to fit the design. A5, 2G, 17cm², (**30–0–B12e 1** DOE D 637) (*Fig.230*)

Hav5   Painted with a leaf design in reserve from a solid ground. Possibly used as part of a foliate border, probably side-alternating, or as a background diaper. D8, –, 9cm² (**2–8–B12b 2** DOE D 629) (*Fig.230*)

Quantification of Glass from St Andrew's by Period and Phase

Phase and context are given, followed by the type of glass present in cm^2. This quantification includes all glass found at St Andrew's. Further details of the phasing may be found on pp.559–60. Note that the stickwork category (H) is not broken down into sub-types in this quantification.

Period 6a

319, 3283	A10, $6cm^2$; H, $6cm^2$; L7, $26cm^2$; M1, $11\cdot5cm^2$; M2, $18cm^2$
321, 3236	M2, $3cm^2$
410, 4694	M2, $1cm^2$
413, 4432	M2, $2\cdot5cm^2$

Period 6b

215, 2162	L6, $3\cdot5cm^2$
322, 3194	L4, $31cm^2$; M2, $179cm^2$
417, 4053	M2, $1\cdot5cm^2$

Period 6b/c

220, 2092	M2, $1cm^2$

Period 6c

216, 2155	M2, $6cm^2$
216, 2158	A1, $20cm^2$
216, 2166	L4, $10cm^2$; M1, $16cm^2$; M2, $113cm^2$
216, 2202	M2, $1cm^2$
217, 2015	A3, $2cm^2$; M2, $10cm^2$
217, 2113	M1, $4\cdot5cm^2$
325, 3174	A1, $2cm^2$; A3, $36cm^2$; A7, $3\cdot5cm^2$; G2, $3\cdot5cm^2$; H, $8cm^2$; M1, $8cm^2$; M2, $68\cdot5cm^2$
486, 4103	M2, $2cm^2$
519, 5103	A7, $2cm^2$
519, 5110	M2, $3cm^2$
519, 5113	A1, $4cm^2$
519, 5131	G1, $6cm^2$; M1, $93cm^2$; M2, $118cm^2$

Period 6d

222, 2120	H, $4\cdot5cm^2$; M2, $13cm^2$
222, 2304	M1, $3cm^2$
327, 3181	L4, $10cm^2$
327, 3200	M1, $6\cdot5cm^2$; M2, $6cm^2$
432, 4530	M2, $5\cdot5cm^2$

Period 6e

130, 1386	M1, $2\cdot5cm^2$; M2, $13cm^2$
131, 1385	A1, $11cm^2$; B4, $4cm^2$; B6, $5cm^2$; G1, $6cm^2$; G5, $3cm^2$; H, $1\cdot5cm^2$; L4, $9cm^2$; M1, $16cm^2$; M2, $43cm^2$

Period 6f

439, 4402	M2, $7cm^2$

Period 6z

022, 10007	B6, $3cm^2$
132, 1468	L3, $18cm^2$

Period 7a

137, 1384	L4, $4cm^2$; L6, $6cm^2$; M2, $7\cdot5cm^2$
137, 1395	A3, $4cm^2$; E, $12cm^2$
137, 1448	M2, $20cm^2$
137, 6051	M2, $10\cdot5cm^2$
225, 2001	A3, $691cm^2$; B2, $580cm^2$; B3, $86\cdot5cm^2$; B4, $29cm^2$; B5, $53cm^2$; C1, $35\cdot5cm^2$; C2, $7\cdot5cm^2$; C3, $6cm^2$; C4, $8\cdot5cm^2$; C5, $20cm^2$; C6, $8cm^2$; D1, $40cm^2$;

Period 7a, 225 2001 (*contd*)

D2, 16cm^2; D5, 83cm^2;
D7, 28cm^2; D8, 21cm^2;
D9, 3·5cm^2; D10, 3·5cm^2;
D11, 3cm^2; D12, 2cm^2;
D13, 2·5cm^2; D14, 7cm^2;
E, 148cm^2; F1, 7·5cm^2;
F2, 8cm^2; F3, 22cm^2;
F4, 20cm^2; F5, 43·5cm^2;
F6, 26cm^2; F7, 2·5cm^2;
F8, 6·5cm^2; F9, 17cm^2;
G1, 39·5cm^2; G2, 38cm^2;
G5, 2cm^2; H, 129·5cm^2;
I, 5·5cm^2; K1, 111cm^2;
K2, 79·5cm^2; K3, 48cm^2;
K4, 74cm^2; K5, 26·5cm^2;
L1, 60·5cm^2; L3, 312cm^2;
L4, 1585cm^2; L5, 6·5cm^2;
L6, 203cm^2; L7, 78cm^2;
L8, 254cm^2; M1, 892cm^2;
M2, 11069·5cm^2

225, 2003 A3, 20cm^2; L4, 13cm^2;
M1, 13cm^2; M2, 36cm^2

225, 2005 A3, 18·5cm^2; F1, 6cm^2;
M2, 12cm^2

225, 2008 B6, 4cm^2; E, 3·5cm^2;
L4, 10·5cm^2; M2, 1·5cm^2

225, 2029 M2, 30cm^2
225, 2050 M2, 13cm^2
225, 2061 A1, 3cm^2; A3, 31cm^2;
E, 6cm2; M1, 1cm^2;
M2, 25·5cm^2

225, 2062 A3, 15·5cm^2; C2, 2cm^2;
C5, 1·5cm^2; C6, 14·5cm^2;
D5, 13cm^2; D7, 2cm^2;
E, 4·5cm^2; F8, 4·5cm^2;
G1, 1cm^2; H, 5cm^2;
J, 21·5cm^2; L4, 4·5cm^2;
M1, 53·5cm^2; M2, 73·5cm^2

225, 2063 A1, 1cm^2; A3, 2cm^2;
B2, 2cm^2; K4, 4·5cm^2;
L3, 19cm^2; L4, 33·5cm^2;
L6, 10cm^2; M1, 20cm^2;
M2, 182·5cm^2

225, 2064 A1, 3cm^2; M2, 10·5cm^2

225, 2069 M1, 1cm^2
225, 2071 M2, 6·5cm^2
225, 2074 M1, 3cm^2; M2, 6cm^2
225, 2075 A1, 6cm^2
225, 2078 M1, 5·5cm^2
225, 2079 M2, 10cm^2
225, 2080 K3, 1·5cm^2
225, 2081 B6, 2cm^2; C1, 1·5cm^2;
C2, 2·5cm^2; D7, 1cm^2;
E, 5·5cm^2; F3, 5cm^2;
G5, 5cm^2; L4, 5·5cm^2;
L7, 5cm^2; M1, 66cm^2;
M2, 86·5cm^2

225, 2082 A1, 9cm^2; M2, 15cm^2
225, 2083 L3, 5cm^2; M2, 1·5cm^2
225, 2084 M2, 1·5cm^2
225, 2109 A1, 3cm^2; B2, 6cm^2;
C5, 1·5cm^2; F8, 19cm^2;
M1, 13cm^2; M2, 52·5cm^2

225, 2114 A1, 4705cm^2; A3, 255cm^2;
A6, 14cm^2; A10, 1cm^2;
B2, 177·5cm^2; B3, 2cm^2;
B4, 412cm^2; B5, 6cm^2;
B6, 35cm^2; B6, 16cm^2;
B7, 18cm^2; B8, 14cm^2;
C1, 5cm^2; C3, 2·5cm^2;
C5, 43·5cm^2; C6, 2·5cm^2;
D1, 11·5cm^2; D2, 10cm^2;
D3, 4cm^2; D4, 2cm^2;
D5, 44·5cm^2; D6, 6·5cm^2;
D7, 5cm^2; D8, 28cm^2;
D14, 2cm^2; E, 162cm^2;
F4, 20cm^2; F5, 13cm^2;
F6, 3·5cm^2; F7, 20·5cm^2;
F8, 14·5cm^2; F9, 8·5cm^2;
G1, 14·5cm^2; G2, 62cm^2;
G3, 16cm^2; G4, 4cm^2;
H, 88·5cm^2; J, 30·5cm^2;
K1, 40·5cm^2; K2, 81·5cm^2;
K3, 99cm^2; K4, 54·5cm^2;
K5, 32·5cm^2; L1, 25cm^2;
L3, 94cm^2; L4, 746·5cm^2;
L5, 23cm^2; L8, 36cm^2;
M1, 792cm^2;
M2, 10696·5cm^2

Period 7a, 225 2114 (*contd*)

225, 6060	L4, 9cm^2
329, 2028	A3, 6cm^2; M2, 12cm^2
329, 2039	F4, 8cm^2
329, 3143	L4, 14cm^2; M1, 1cm^2
329, 3185	A3, 3cm^2; M2, 3·5cm^2
329, 3518	M1, 7cm^2
331, 3002	A1, 13cm^2; A2, 11·5cm^2; A3, 184·5cm^2; B3, 18·5cm^2; B4 7·5cm^2; J, 61cm^2; K1, 18cm^2; K2, 25cm^2; K4, 31cm^2; L1, 49·5cm^2; L3, 37cm^2; L4, 199cm^2; L5,114cm^2; L6, 106cm^2; L7, 32cm^2; M1, 107cm^2; M2, 1348·5cm^2
331, 3003	A3, 16cm^2; M1, 9cm^2; M2, 9·5cm^2
331, 3007	A3, 16cm^2; M1, 3cm^2; M2, 1·5cm^2
331, 3009	A1, 7cm^2; A3, 46cm^2; B5, 2cm^2; E, 19·5cm^2; H, 4cm^2; J, 27cm^2; K1, 5cm^2; K2, 6·5cm^2; L3, 9cm^2; L5, 54cm^2; L6, 22cm^2; M1, 13·5cm^2; M2, 136·5cm^2
331, 3010	A3, 5·5cm^2; L3, 9cm^2; M2, 53cm^2
331, 3012	A3, 20cm^2; B4, 4cm^2; H, 3cm^2; L1, 23cm^2; L4, 12cm^2; L5, 33cm^2; M1, 15cm^2; M2, 68cm^2
331, 3040	K1, 1cm^2; M1, 3cm^2; M2, 2cm^2
331, 3048	M1, 3cm^2; M2, 8cm^2
331, 3050	A3, 10cm^2; M2, 4cm^2
331, 3118	M2, 5·5cm^2
331, 3161	A1, 8cm^2; A3, 4cm^2; M1, 35cm^2; M2, 36cm^2
331, 3163	A1 8cm^2; A3, 1335cm^2; A5, 98cm^2; B2, 21cm^2; B4, 4cm^2; B5, 1cm^2; B6, 293·5cm^2; B6, 23cm^2; B7, 94cm^2; C2, 5·5cm^2; C5, 14·5cm^2; D4, 10cm^2; D5, 60·5cm^2; D8, 3·5cm^2; E, 42·5cm^2; F2, 5cm^2; F3, 25cm^2; G1, 7cm^2; G2, 75cm^2; G3, 10cm^2; G5, 8·5cm^2; H, 86cm^2; J, 10.6·5cm^2; K1, 101cm^2; K2, 90cm^2,K3, 144cm^2; K4, 34·5cm^2; K5, 15cm^2; L1, 3·5cm^2;L3, 16cm^2; L4, 290cm^2; L5, 24·5cm^2; L6, 25cm^2; L8, 5·5cm^2; M1, 475·5cm^2; M2, 2620cm^2
331, 3180	A3, 733cm^2; B4, 185cm^2; B5, 10cm^2; B6, 2cm^2; D4, 2cm^2; D5, 18·5cm^2; D8, 3cm^2; E, 20cm^2; G1, 58·5cm^2; G2, 4·5cm^2; G3, 5·5cm^2; G6, 3cm^2; H, 52·5cm^2; K1, 137·5cm^2; K2, 95·5cm^2; K3, 46·5cm^2; K4, 90cm^2; K5, 6·5cm^2; L1, 4cm^2;L3, 15·5cm^2; L4, 65cm^2; M1, 247cm^2; M2, 1034cm^2
331, 3215	A3, 193cm^2; K1, 17cm^2; K2, 4cm^2; M2, 65cm^2
331, 3282	A1, 4cm^2
331, 3532	M2, 8cm^2
331, 3538	M2, 6cm^2
443, 4070	A3, 44cm^2; L3, 5cm^2; M1, 3cm^2
443, 4096	A3, 7·5cm^2
710, 7002	M2, 2cm^2
710, 7054	M2, 4·5cm^2

Period 7b

444, 4016	E, 1cm^2
444, 4019	A3, 6cm^2
444, 4023	M2, 2cm^2
444, 4048	K3, 16cm^2; L3, 10cm^2; M2, 19·5cm^2
446, 4429	M2, 15cm^2
446, 4448	A3, 19cm^2; M1, 4cm^2
446, 4666	M2, 2cm^2

Period 7c

804, 8016	M2, 17cm^2
804, 8023	E, 13cm^2; M2, 7·5cm^2
804, 8024	M1, 10cm^2; M2, 1·5cm^2
806, 8003	A1, 4cm^2; L4, 8cm^2; M1, 3cm^2; M2, 14·5cm^2

Period 8

2060	A3, 44·5cm^2; B2, 15cm^2; C1, 17cm^2; C2, 12cm^2; C5, 6cm^2; D5, 4cm^2; E, 2cm^2; F3, 10·5cm^2 F8, 27cm^2; K1, 3cm^2; K3, 17cm^2; K4, 13·5cm^2; L4, 62cm^2; L8, 16cm^2; M1, 150cm^2; M2, 357cm^2
3001	M1, 2cm^2; M2, 29cm^2
3019	A1, 5·5cm^2
3029	L4, 10cm^2
3030	A1, 12·5cm^2; A3, 111·5cm^2; B3, 100cm^2; B6, 28·5cm^2; H, 19cm^2; J, 54·5cm^2; K1, 28cm^2; K2, 35cm^2; K4, 5·5cm^2; L1, 67cm^2; L2, 86·5cm^2; L3, 46cm^2; L4, 239·5cm^2; L5, 245·5cm^2; L6, 127cm^2; L8, 47cm^2; M1, 29cm^2; M2, 662·5cm^2
3031	H, 2cm^2; L5, 10·5cm^2; M2, 1cm^2
5059	M1, 5cm^2
5060	G1, 4cm^2
5088	M1, 1·5cm^2

Period 9

1023	K3, 4cm^2
4002	L5, 7·5cm^2; M1, 3cm^2; M2, 36·5cm^2

Period 10

1397	M1, 3·5cm^2
3025	F2, 8cm^2
3026	A3, 19·5cm^2; E, 2cm^2; M2, 79cm^2
6080	M2, 15cm^2

Unstratified

2000	A2, 3cm^2, A3, 17·5cm^2; B6, 8cm^2; C5, 1cm^2; E, 12cm^2; F2, 10cm^2; F6, 18cm^2; F7, 9cm^2; F8, 90cm^2; G1, 5cm^2; K4, 3cm^2; L3, 13·5cm^2; L4, 14cm^2; L8, 10cm^2; M1, 8cm^2; M2, 246·5cm^2
3000	A3, 383cm^2; B4, 4cm^2; B6, 27·5cm^2; D2, 5cm^2; E, 2cm^2; J, 12cm^2; K2, 6·5cm^2; K3, 16cm^2; K4, 6cm^2; L4, 17·5cm^2; M1, 14cm^2; M2, 272·5cm^2
4000	L3, 12cm^2; M2, 7cm^2
5000	A3, 16cm^2; M1, 36cm^2; M2, 13cm^2
7000	A3, 14cm^2; M2, 20cm^2
8000	A1, 3·5cm^2; D5, 4cm^2; D8, 2·5cm^2; E, 8cm^2; H, 2·5cm^2; K1, 1cm^2; K2, 6·5cm^2; K3, 7cm^2; M1, 6cm^2; M2, 12·5cm^2
10000	L7, 8cm^2; L8, 8cm^2; M2, 2cm^2

List of Phases Containing Glass Fragments

Phase   Description

Period 6: The Gilbertine priory, 12th–16th century

Period 6a: Original Gilbertine priory

319	Construction of east alley (Passage K)
321	Burials in east alley
410	Soil dumped to level site for construction
413	Construction of north-east part of dormitory and latrine

Period 6b: First modifications to the priory

215	Burials within nave
220	Burials within nave (Period 6b or 6c)
322	Reconstruction of east alley
416–19	Sequence of construction deposits and post-holes in north alley indicating continued repair and maintenance

Period 6c: Major reconstruction of the priory

216	Demolition of original nave and construction of new church
217–19	Burials within new nave
325	Reconstruction of east range (dormitory and former chapter house)
485–7	Filling of northern drain
519	Demolition of eastern arm of original church

Period 6d: Further modifcations to the priory

222	Modifications within the church
327	Modifications within east range
431–2	Modifications within north range

Period 6e: Continued use and modification of the priory

129–30	Construction and use of well and pit south of church
131	Final fill of pit south of church

Period 6f: Final modifications to the priory

439	Partitions at east end of north range

Period 6z: Features not related to the stratified sequence

132–4	Burials south of nave
022	Pits and other features east of priory buildings

Phase   Description

Period 7: The demolition of the priory, 16th century
Period 7a: Demolition of south and east ranges
137   Demolition and robbing of church
225   Demolition and robbing of church
329   Demolition and robbing of east alley
331   Demolition and robbing of east range
443   Demolition and robbing of east end of church
710   Construction and use of limekiln in cloister garth and other demolition-
             related activities

Period 7b: Demolition of north range
444   Demolition of north range
446   Robbing pits east of north range

Period 7c: Demolition period occupation
803–6   Pits and occupation deposits at west end of north range

Acknowledgements

York Archaeological Trust and the principal author wish to express their thanks to all who have co-operated in the compilation of this fascicule.

The following people are thanked for their patience in answering persistent questions and for allowing access to glass for study. These include Keith Barley, stained glass craftsman; Peter Gibson, formerly the Secretary of the York Glaziers' Trust, Penny Winton, Secretary of the York Glaziers' Trust; Evelyn Baker, Senior Archaeological Field Officer, Dr Holly Duncan and Teresa Jackman of Bedfordshire County Planning Department Archaeological Service; Martin Allfrey, Curator for the North, English Heritage, for access to the Rievaulx glass; Anna Eavis, Archivist, CVMA Archive, for correspondence and photographs; and Alistair Chisholm and D. Hooley.

The author would also like to thank Mark Bennet, Lincolnshire County Council Sites and Monuments Record; Clive Cheesman, Rouge Dragon Pursuivant, The College of Arms, for advice on heraldry; David King and Dr D. O'Connor for information and advice on various aspects of medieval glass. She is also grateful to her friends and colleagues at Durham, Dr S.J. Lucy, Dr A.R. Millard and Dr P.A. Rowley-Conwy for reading and commenting on the text during the latter stages of production.

The principal author is grateful to the Fishergate team, including R.L. Kemp, who directed the excavations, site supervisors J. Lilley and M. Whyman, and post-excavation assistant K. Jones.

The authors of the conservation report wish especially to thank the conservation staff of the York Archaeological Trust; Dr Dafydd Griffiths and the Institute of Archaeology at the University of London. The following individuals are also thanked: A. Ballantyne, S. Bradley, J. Cronyn, S. Davidson, J. Dinsmore, D. Ellam, P. Gibson, C. Gregson, S. Hanna, M.E. Hutchinson, B. Knight, D. March, R. Newton, S.N. Reisman, S. Service, J. Shepherd, P. Shorer, K. Starling, K. Tubb and J. Vint.

Dr G.A. Cox wishes to thank Mr S. Moehr of the University of York for kindly polishing the sectioned samples used in the technical examination of the glass from Fishergate. His former colleague Dr G.I. Cooper carried out the infrared investigations reported here; he expresses his thanks and appreciation for his contribution to this research.

York Archaeological Trust is very grateful to the successive owners of the site at 46–54 Fishergate, particularly Redfearn National Glass plc and Costain Homes (North-Eastern) Limited, for permission to excavate the site. Funding for the excavation was provided by English Heritage, the City of York and Costain Homes (North-Eastern) Limited. The entire post-excavation project was funded by English Heritage.

The project has been managed at the Trust by W. Sherlock and D. Petts, and by Dr P. Wilson for English Heritage.

Thanks are expressed to Christine McDonnell, Bev Shaw, Renée Gajowskyj, Gill Woolrich and Karen Adams of the Trust Finds Department who provided ready access to the material.

The majority of the glass fragments were drawn by C. Bentley, with the remainder by P. Chew. The reconstructed quarries, borders and windows were produced by P. Chew, who also prepared the maps, distribution plots, X-ray emission spectrum and the purse from Coppergate. The Fishergate site location plan was prepared by C. Bentley; the plans of St Andrew's Priory, Fishergate, and of Sempringham Priory were produced by S. Chew. Photographs were taken by S.I. Hill, except where separately acknowledged: Fig.186a is reproduced by courtesy of Batsford Ltd, © The Victoria and Albert Museum; Fig.188 is reproduced by courtesy of the Board of Trustees of The Victoria and Albert Museum; Fig.208 is reproduced by courtesy of The Colonial Williamsburg Foundation; Fig.215 is reproduced by courtesy of The British Library; Fig.229 is reproduced by courtesy of Selby Abbey, © Judges Postcards Ltd.

The summary was translated into French by C. Sheil-Small and into German by K. Aberg. Latin translations on pp.457 and 504 were provided by Victoria Thompson. This fascicule has been under the editorial supervision of W. Sherlock, D. Petts and F. Mee, who also prepared the text for publication. It is published with the assistance of a generous subvention by English Heritage.

Summary

The report aims to explore the relationship between a set of material culture and the social context of its use, re-use, changes in its form and deposition. Art-historical, archaeological and literary evidence are all brought to bear, in conjunction with scientific analysis and experimental conservation work.

The excavations on the site of the Gilbertine Priory at Fishergate, York, uncovered the largest quantity of window glass from any house of this peculiarly English medieval monastic order. It is the only assemblage of any size to come from a modern, controlled excavation. Research on this glass provided the opportunity to study all other known assemblages of window glass associated with the Gilbertines, and the results are presented here for the first time.

The Fishergate glass can be divided into two main periods of glazing: one relating to the original early to mid 13th century church and claustral buildings, the other relating to an early 14th century rebuild and contraction of the priory. An aesthetic difference was apparent between these two episodes. In the first, figural glass was hardly represented at all and there was little use of colour. In the second episode of building there was evidence for extensive use of figural glass, colour and even some heraldry. It is argued that this difference is evidence for an intentional aesthetic and ascetic choice made at the time of the founding of the first priory followed by the changing economic and spiritual fortunes of the priory in the 14th century which forced the canons to accept the rather more worldly aesthetic preferences of a wealthy and influential external patron.

The most important of the other remaining Gilbertine window glass assemblages come from the mother house of the order, Sempringham Priory, Lincolnshire, and a lesser house, Ellerton Priory, North Yorkshire. These revealed high-quality glazing of the first half of the 14th century and a small number of complete heraldic shields, respectively. It is argued that the latter in particular may also reflect the contemporary trend for expressions of secular patronage within monastic contexts.

The report includes a discussion of the innovative conservation and storage solutions developed for excavated medieval window glass, and analyses of the chemical composition and deterioration of the Fishergate glass.

Résumé

Ce rapport a pour but d'explorer les interconnections entre un ensemble d'objets façonnés et le contexte social de leur utilisation, de leur réutilisation, des changements de leur forme et de leur déposition. Les indices littéraires et archéologiques, les indices relevant de l'histoire de l'art sont tous utilisés, conjointement avec l'analyse scientifique et le travail de conservation expérimental.

Les fouilles menées sur le site du Prieuré des Gilbertins à Fishergate, York, ont révélé la plus importante quantité de verre de vitres jamais découverte dans une maison de cet ordre monastique médiéval de type spécifiquement anglais. C'est le seul ensemble, de quelque taille qu'il soit, provenant de fouilles modernes contrôlées. Les recherches sur ce verre ont donné l'occasion d'étudier tous les autres ensembles connus de verre de vitres associés aux Gilbertins, et les résultats sont présentés ici pour la première fois.

Le verre de Fishergate peut être divisé en deux grandes périodes de vitrerie: l'une relative à l'église et aux bâtiments monastiques d'origine, datant du début au milieu du 13ème siècle, l'autre relative à une contraction du prieuré et à une reconstruction du début du 14ème siècle. Une différence esthétique était également apparente entre ces deux périodes. Dans la première, il n'y avait pratiquement pas de verre figuratif et la couleur était fort peu utilisé. Dans la seconde période de construction, il y avait des indices d'une grande utilisation de verre figuratif, de couleur et même de quelques blasons. On soutient que cette différence prouve qu'il y eut un choix intentionnellement esthétique et austère lors de la fondation du premier prieuré, suivi d'un changement de la fortune économique et spirituelle du prieuré au 14ème siècle qui força les chanoines à accepter les préférences esthétiques plutôt plus matérielles d'un donateur extérieur riche et influent.

Les plus importants des autres ensembles de verre de vitres Gilbertins qui restent encore proviennent de la maison mère de l'ordre, le Prieuré de Sempringham, Lincolnshire, et d'une plus petite maison, le Prieuré d'Ellerton, Yorkshire. Ces prieurés ont révélé l'un, du vitrage de haute qualité datant de la première moitié du 14ème siècle, et l'autre, un petit nombre de blasons héraldiques parfaitement conservés. Cela peut prouver que ces derniers en particulier peuvent aussi refléter la tendance contemporaine vers l'expression du patronage séculaire dans des contextes monastiques.

Le rapport comprend une discussion des solutions novatrices de conservation et de stockage développées pour le verre de vitres médiéval découvert lors de fouilles, et des analyses de la composition chimique et de la détérioration du verre de Fishergate.

Zusammenfassung

Das Ziel dieses Berichtes ist es, das Verhältnis einer Kategorie materieller Kultur mit der sozialen Einbettung ihres Gebrauches sowie den Wandlungen in ihrer Form und Ablagerungsweise zu erforschen. Kunsthistorische, archäologische und literarische Hinweise werden hierzu in Zusammenhang mit wissenschaftlicher Analyse und experimenteller Konservierungsarbeit herangezogen.

Die Ausgrabung auf dem Areal der gilbertinischen Priorei in der Fishergate in York haben die bisher größte Menge an Fensterglas aus einer Niederlassung dieses ausschließlich englischen mittelalterlichen Ordens erbracht. Es ist das einzige Assemble von gewissem Ausmaß, das einer modernen, kontrollierten Ausgrabung entstammt. Forschungsarbeiten an diesem Glas bieten die Möglichkeit alle anderen bekannten Assembles an Fensterglas, die mit den Gilbertinern in Verbindung stehen zu untersuchen; die Ergebnisse werden hier zum ersten Mal vorgelegt.

Das Glas aus der Fishergate kann zwei Hauptzeiträumen der Verglasung zugeordnet werden: der erste bezieht sich auf die ursprüngliche Kirche und Klausur des frühen 13. Jahrhunderts, der zweite steht im Zusammenhang mit dem Neubau und der Verkleinerung der Priorei im frühen 14. Jahrhundert. Es zeigt sich außerdem ein deutlicher ästethischer Unterschied zwischen diesen beiden Zeiträumen. Im ersten Zeitabschnitt war figürliches Glas kaum vertreten;ebenso war wenig Gebrauch von Farbe gemacht worden. Im zweiten Bauabschnitt zeigt sich Befund für einen weitreichenden Gebrauch von figürlichem Glas, von Farbe und sogar einigen Wappen. Es wird argumentiert, daß sich in diesem Unterschied eine mit Absicht getroffene, ästethische und asketische Wahl zur Zeit der Gründung der ersten Priorei aufzeigt, die dann gefolgt wird von veränderten wirtschaftlichen und spirituellen Umständen der Priorei im 14. Jahrhundert, die die Kanoniker zwingen die mehr weltlich ästhetischen Wünsche eines reichen und externen Patrons zu berücksichtigen.

Die anderen wichtigen überkommenen gilbertinischen Fensterglasassembles stammen aus dem Mutterhaus des Ordens, der Priorei Sempringham in Lincolnshire und einem Tochterhaus, der Priorei Ellerton in North Yorkshire. Diese weisen hochwertiges Glas einschließlich einer kleinen Anzahl von vollständigen Wappenschildern für die erste Hälfte des 14. Jahrhunderts auf. Es wird argumentiert, daß im besonderen die letzteren den zeitgemäßen Trend für die Darstellung von sekularem Patronat innerhalb des klösterlichen Kontextes zum Ausdruck bringen.

Der Bericht enthält abschließend eine Diskussion der innovativen Konservierungs- und Aufbewahrungslösungen, die für ausgegrabenes mittelalterliches Fensterglas entwickelt wurden sowie die Analysen der chemischen Zusammensetzung und des Zerfalls des Glases aus der Fishergate.

Glossary

abrade: to scrape or grind away flashing to expose the base glass.

annealing (art-historical definition, as opposed to technical): a method of applying 'jewels' of different coloured glass to a base colour; the coloured and base (substrate) glass are soldered together by applying a layer of ground white glass between them and then fired.

back-painting: painting on the exterior face of the glass, often to create depth of tone.

came: the lead framework for the individual panes of glass in the stained window. They consist of lead rods, H-shaped in section, which are bent to shape around the glass and cut to the required length (see also *core* and *leaves*).

cartoon: a full-scale design for a window.

core: the cross-bar of a *came* is called the core.

crocket: foliate decoration on a roof or canopy gable.

crown/spun: method of window glass production in which a bulb is blown, pierced and spun out into a disc.

cut-line: full-sized pattern painted on the table or board showing all the lines which are to be cut from the glass to create the design.

cylinder/muff: method of window glass production in which a cylinder is blown, cut and flattened out.

diaper: a background design of regularly repeated motifs.

ferramenta: collective noun for ironwork supporting a window.

flash: a thin coat of coloured glass on a base glass. Flashed ruby is most commonly found.

forest glass: see *potash*.

geet: black lead glass.

grisaille: geometric or leaf patterns of regular design painted on or leaded into white glass (usually with little or no pot-metal); decorative patterns created by leading white glass.

grozing: the method of shaping by means of a metal tool with a hooked end which makes a characteristic 'bitten' edge.

half-tone: a dilute form of *paint*. As the paint itself can be different in shade, the half-tones can be varied as well. Mostly the later medieval paint is reddish-brown and the half-tones vary through pale, matt browns to white. Half-tones may be used for shading, or for thin washes often with *stickwork* or scratched decoration.

jewel: small, discrete piece of glass either inserted into, or attached to the surface of, a glass panel.

leaves: the long sides of the came.

Lorraine glass: name given to improved *cylinder* method of manufacture, or glass from this area.

matting: heavy, fairly even application of *paint.*

melt: the molten glass mixture.

merlon: upright section of wall forming battlements.

multi-layered glasses: 12th and 13th century *ruby* often made this way. Perhaps as many as 50 layers which bent back on each other in the manner of hairpins (Newton and Davison 1989, 95). Some 12th century glasses multi-layered in about half their thickness.

murrey: a deep, warm rose purple.

Normandy glass: name given to *spun* method of manufacture, or glass from this area.

paint: a mixture of finely ground glass, iron or copper oxide, and a flux, applied to the glass and fired.

pontil: a glass maker's tool in the form of an iron rod used to hold glass for manipulation.

potash: glass made with a flux of potassium oxide (K_2O) alkali, used predominantly in medieval window production in the 12th–16th centuries.

pot-metal: glass coloured throughout when molten with one or more metallic oxides.

quarry: a small pane of glass, usually diamond shaped.

reserve: portion of surface of glass left unpainted.

rinceau: a background design of flowing or curling foliage.

ruby: red glass, either *pot-metal* or *flashed.*

sabatons: laminated or otherwise constructed protection for the feet in armour.

saddle-bars: horizontal or shaped iron bars sunk into the stonework of a window and used to brace the glass panels.

seeds: the air or gas bubbles trapped in fired glass, produced during the melting process.

smear shading: an application of thin *paint* on the glass, applied directly with a soft brush or mop to the areas of shadow. A wider brush of badger hair was used to stroke the paint in alternate directions to give an even or matt appearance (Newton and Davison 1989, 98). Under a microscope the brush strokes will be plainly seen. Often used on the exterior of the glass rather than over the trace lines.

stickwork: removal of paint with a stick before firing; also scratching when done with a needle point.

stippling: a method of shading by dabbing *paint*; the paint is first applied as an even layer then lightly stippled with a badger hair brush before dry. The stippling can be controlled to create a graduated effect as required and can be quite fine. The paint can be carefully brushed away from the glass once dry, to form highlights. Used both on the exterior and the interior surface of the glass.

strapwork: parallel lines painted at the edge of a *quarry*, often crossing at the apex, so that when leaded into a regular pattern they give the impression of a trellis.

ties: strips of metal which would be soldered to the inside of completed panels in place in windows. The strips were often made from short lengths of lead, often lead cames which had been split longitudinally. Copper alloy might also be used.

trace lines: the lines of detail painted on the glass, traced through from the *cartoon*.

vesica: a pointed oval shape, often used to enclose figures of Christ, the Virgin, etc.

yellow stain: a stain ranging from pale lemon to orange, produced by applying a solution of a silver compound (silver nitrate or silver sulphide) to the surface of the glass which, when fired, turns yellow. It is nearly always found on the exterior of the glass.

Notes

The scanning electron microscope (SEM) used in this investigation was a Cambridge Instruments model 90B. It was operated at a voltage of 15kV and a beam current of 0·65nA. The SEM was equipped with a Si(Li) X-ray detector (resolution 150eV at 5·9keV) to permit quantitative electron-probe microanalysis (EPMA) of samples to be carried out. A ZAF correction program was used to eliminate matrix and other disturbing effects (Scott and Love 1983). For the purpose of analysing glass, an area of approximately 50μm × 40μm was scanned by the electron beam and the net intensities of the characteristic X-rays emitted by elements of interest were measured; a representative X-ray spectrum for a potash glass is shown in Fig.236 (p.539). With one exception, each of the peaks in Fig.236 is a Kα peak. The exposure time was 100s. Each sample was analysed three times and the mean composition computed to produce the data given in Table 9 (pp.532–3). 'Spot' analyses were carried out using a stationary electron beam; the spatial resolution of the instrument when used in this mode was approximately 5μm.

The Fourier transform-infrared spectrometer was a Mattson Galaxy Series 6020 instrument interfaced to a Specta-tech IR Plan microscope. This permitted IR reflection spectra of surface areas as small as 20μm × 20μm to be obtained. These were converted into the corresponding absorption spectra by means of a Kramers-Kronig transformation routine.

Abbreviations

Most abbreviations are those recommended by the Council for British Archaeology but the following are used in addition. Bibliographic brief references used in the text are explained in the Bibliography.

BI   Borthwick Institute of Historical Research, University of York
BL   British Library
CVMA   Corpus Vitrearum Medii Aevi
DBA   Dictionary of British Arms
LAO   Lincolnshire Archives Office
PRO   Public Record Office
YML   York Minster Library

Manuscripts consulted

Brescia, Biblioteca Queriniana MS AV17
Cambridge, Corpus Christi MS
Lincoln, LAO Reg.5
London. BL Add. MS 35211
—— BL Add. 38116
—— BL Arundel MS83
—— BL Cotton MS Cleopatra Eiv
—— PRO C 66/185
—— PRO SC6/Henry VIII 7452
—— PRO SP5/3 (Suppression Papers)
York. BI, Prob. Reg. 2 (Probate Registers)
—— YML D/C Wills 1
—— YML E3. 9 m.1
—— YML E.3.25 m.2
—— YML Ms L1 (7)

Printed works

Adams, P.B., 1984. 'Glass corrosion', *Journ. Non-Crystalline Solids* 67, 193–205

Alexander, J. and Binski, P. (eds), 1987. *Age of Chivalry: Art in Plantagenet England 1200–1400*, Royal Academy of Arts (London)

Alexander, J. and Crossley, P., 1976. *Medieval and Early Renaissance Treasures in the North West*, Whitworth Art Gallery Exhibition catalogue, University of Manchester (Manchester)

Allen, T., 1828. *A New and Complete History of York* (London)

Alten, H., 1986. (unpublished) *The Conservation of Archaeological Medieval Glass*, undergraduate dissertation, Institute of Archaeology, London

—— 1988. 'Changes in waterlogged medieval window glass', *Material Research Soc. Symp. Proc.* **123**, 279–84

Archer, M., 1985. *An Introduction to English Stained Glass* (London)

Armstrong, P., Tomlinson, D. and Evans, D., 1991. *Excavations at Lurk Lane Beverley, 1979–82*, Sheffield Excavation Report **1** (Sheffield)

Asad, T., 1987. 'On ritual and discipline in medieval Christian monasticism', *Economy and Society* **16**/2, 159–203

—— 1993. *Genealogies of Religion: Discipline and Reasons of Power in Christianity and Islam* (Baltimore)

Ashurst, N. and Kelly, J. 1989. *Analysis and investigation of mortar samples from the Gilbertine priory of St Andrew's, Fishergate, York*, unpublished specialist report, YAT archive

Asmus, J.F., 1975. 'Use of lasers in the conservation of stained glass' in D. Leigh (ed.), *Archaeology and the Applied Arts, IIC Congress, Stockholm 1975* (London), 139–41

Aston, M., 1988. *England's Iconoclasts: Laws Against Images* (Oxford)

—— 1989. 'Iconoclasm in England: Official and Clandestine' in C. Davidson and A.E. Nichols (eds), *Iconoclasm versus Art and Drama*, Early Drama, Art and Music Monograph Series **11**, Western Michigan Univ. (Kalamazoo), 47–91

Axworthy Rutter, J.A., 1990. 'Window lead' in S.W. Ward (ed.), *Excavations at Chester: the Lesser Medieval Religious Houses, Sites Investigated 1964–83*, Grosvenor Museum Archaeological Excavation and Survey Reports **6** (Chester), 118–19

AY. Addyman, P.V. (ed.). *The Archaeology of York*
7   *Anglian York (AD 410–876):*
    1 R.L. Kemp, 1996. *Anglian Settlement at 46–54 Fishergate, York*
11   *The Medieval Defences and Suburbs:*
    2 R.L. Kemp and C.P. Graves, 1996. *The Church and Gilbertine Priory of St Andrew, Fishergate*
12   *The Medieval Cemeteries:*
    2 G. Stroud and R.L. Kemp, 1993. *The Cemetery of the Church and Priory of St Andrew, Fishergate*
15   *The Animal Bones:*
    4 T.P. O'Connor, 1991. *Bones from 46–54 Fishergate*
16   *The Pottery:*
    6 A.J. Mainman, 1993. *Pottery from 46–54 Fishergate*
17   *The Small Finds:*
    9 N.S.H. Rogers, 1993. *Anglian and Other Finds from Fishergate*
    12 A. MacGregor, A.J. Mainman and N.S.H. Rogers, 1999. *Craft, Industry and Everyday Life: Bone, Antler, Ivory and Horn from Anglo-Scandinavian and Medieval York*
    15 P. Ottaway and N.S.H. Rogers in prep. *Craft, Industry and Everyday Life: Finds from Medieval York*
    16 I. Carlisle, Q. Mould and E. Cameron, in prep. *Craft, Industry and Everyday Life: Leather and Leatherworking from Anglo-Scandinavian and Medieval York*

Baines, T., 1871–7. *Yorkshire, Past and Present: a history and description of the Three Ridings of the Great County of York* (London)

Baker, D. (ed.), 1978. *Medieval Women*, Studies in Church History Subsidia 1 (Oxford)

Baker, J., 1978. *English Stained Glass* (London)

Bettembourg, J.-M., 1976. 'Composition et alteration des verres vitraux anciens', *Verres et Réfractaires* 30(1), 36–42

Biddle, M. and Hunter, J., 1990. 'Early medieval window glass' in M. Biddle (ed.), *Object and Economy in Medieval Winchester* 1, Winchester Studies 7 (Oxford), 350–86

Binski, P., 1991. *Medieval Craftsmen: Painters* (London)

Brault, G.J. (ed.), 1997. *Rolls of Arms, Edward I (1272–1307)* (London)

Brooke-Little, J.P. 1970. *Boutell's Heraldry*, revised edition (London)

Brown, S. and O'Connor, D.E., 1991. *Medieval Craftsmen: Glass-painters* (London)

Browne, J., 1847. *The History of the Metropolitan Church of St Peter, York* (London)

—— 1859. 'A description of the representations and arms on the glass in the windows of York Minster, also the arms on stone, Leeds', YML Ms Add.20

Burgoyne, I. and Scoble, R., 1989. *Two Thousand Years of Flat Glass Making* (Pilkington)

Burton, J.E., 1979. *The Yorkshire Nunneries in the Twelfth and Thirteenth Centuries*, Borthwick Paper 56 (York)

Cal. Papal Letters. Calendar of Entries in the Papal Registers Relating to Great Britain and Ireland, Papal Letters (London)

Cal. Fine. Calendar of the Fine Rolls 1461–71; 1485–1509 (London)

Cal. Pat. Calendar of Patent Rolls 1334–8; 1358–61 (London)

Campbell, M., 1987. '585 Triptych' in Alexander and Binski (eds) 1987, 460–1

Caviness, M.H., 1973. 'De convenientia et cohaerentia antiqui et novi operis: medieval conservation, restoration, pastiche and forgery' in P. Bloch, T. Buddensieg, A. Hentzen and T. Muller (eds), *Intuition und Kunstwissenschaft: Festschrift fur Hanns Swarzenski* (Berlin), 205–22

Charleston, R.J., 1991. 'Vessel glass' in J. Blair and N. Ramsay (eds), *English Medieval Industries: Craftsmen, Techniques, Products* (London), 237–64

Charlesworth, D., 1978. 'The Roman glass' in A. Down, *Chichester Excavations III* (Chichester), 267–73

Chesshyre, D.H.B. and Woodcock, T., 1992. *Dictionary of British Arms. Vol 1: Medieval Ordinary* (London)

Clay, C.T., 1944–7. 'Notes on the early archdeacons in the church of York', *Yorks. Archaeol. J.* 36, 269–87, 409–34

Clay, J.W. (ed.), 1912. *Yorkshire Monasteries: Suppression Papers*, Yorks. Archaeol. Soc. Record Series 48

Collins, J.F. and Buol, S.W., 1970. 'Effects of fluctuations in the eH-pH environment of iron and/or manganese equilibria', *Soil Science* 110(2), 111–17

Collongues, R. and Perez y Jorba, M., 1973. 'Sur le phénomène de corrosion des vitraux, Part 1', *Conversion Ecole Nationale Supérieur de Chemie* (Paris)

—— 1974. 'Sur le phénomène de corrosion des vitraux, Part 2', *Conversion Ecole Nationale Supérieur de Chemie* (Paris)

Collongues, R., Perez y Jorba, M., Tilloca, G. and Dallas, J.-P., 1976. 'Nouveaux aspects du phénomène de corrosion des vitraux anciens des églises francaises', *Verres et Refractaires* 30(1), 43–55

Constable, G., 1978. 'Aelred of Rievaulx and the nun of Watton: an episode in the early history of the Gilbertine Order' in D. Baker (ed.) 1978, 205–26

Cooper, G.I., Cox, G.A. and Perutz, R.N., 1993. 'Infrared microspectroscopy as a complementary technique to electron-probe microanalysis for the investigation of natural corrosion on potash glasses', *J. Microscopy* 170 (2), 111–18

Coppack, G., 1986. 'Some descriptions of Rievaulx Abbey in 1538–9: the disposition of a major Cistercian precinct in the early sixteenth century', *J. Brit. Archaeol. Assoc.* 139, 100–33

Courty, M.A., Goldberg, P. and Macphail, R., 1989. *Soils and Micromorphology in Archaeology* (Cambridge)

Cowan, I.B. and Easson, D.E. (eds), 1976. *Medieval Religious Houses, Scotland* (London)

Cox, G.A. and Cooper, G.I., 1995. 'Stained glass in York in the mid-sixteenth century: analytical evidence for its decay', *Glass Technology* 36(4), 129–34

Cox, G.A. and Ford, B.A., 1989. 'The corrosion of glass on the sea bed', *J. Materials Sci.* 24, 3146–53

—— 1993. 'The long-term corrosion of glass by groundwater', *J. Materials Sci.* 28, 5637–47

Cox, G.A. and Gillies, K.J.S., 1986. 'The X-ray fluorescence analysis of medieval blue glass from York Minster', *Archaeometry* 28(1), 57–68

Cox, G.A., Heavens, O.S., Newton, R.G. and Pollard, A.M., 1979. 'A study of the weathering behaviour of medieval glass from York Minster', *J. Glass Stud.* 21, 54–75

Cramp, R., 1970. 'Decorated window-glass and millefiori from Monkwearmouth', *Antiq. J.* 50, 327–35

Crewe, S., 1987. *Stained Glass in England c.1180–c.1540* (London)

Croft, R.A. and Mynard, D.C., 1986. 'A late 13th century grisaille window panel from Bradwell Abbey, Milton Keynes, Bucks.', *Medieval Archaeol.* 30, 110–11

Cross, C. and Vickers, N. (eds), 1995. *Monks, Friars and Nuns in Sixteenth Century Yorkshire*, Yorks. Archaeol. Soc. Research Series 150

Crossley, D.W. and Aberg., F., 1972. 'Sixteenth-century Glassmaking in Yorkshire. Excavations at Furnaces at Hutton and Rosedale, North Riding, 1968–71', *Post-Medieval Archaeol.* 6, 107–59

Crowfoot, E., Pritchard, F. and Staniland, K., 1992. *Textiles and Clothing c.1150–1450*, Medieval Finds from Excavations in London 4 (London)

D'Alessandro, L., 1984. (unpublished) *The Application of Silanes in the Treatment of Archaeological Material*, undergraduate dissertation, Institute of Archaeology, University of London

Davidson, C. and O'Connor, D.E., 1978. *York Art: A Subject List of Extant and Lost Art* (Kalamazoo)

Davies, I., 1973. 'Window glass in eighteenth-century Williamsburg' in A. Hume (ed.), *Colonial Williamsburg Occasional Papers in Archaeology 1: Five Artifact Studies* (Williamsburg), 78–99

Day, L.F., 1909. *Windows: A Book about Stained and Painted Glass* (London)

Dekòwna, M., 1974. 'Problème de l'éxistence d'un atelier à Szczecin au haut moyen age' in *Annales du 6ième Congrès de l'Association Internationale pour l'Histoire du Verre*, Centre des Publications de l'AIHV (Liège), 143–58

Dodwell, C.R., 1961. *Theophilus: De Diversis Artibus* (London)

Doremus, R.H., 1975. 'Interdiffusion of hydrogen and alkali ions in a glass surface', *J. Non-crystalline Solids* 19, 137–44

Drake, F., 1736. *Eboracum: or the History and Antiquities of the City of York* (London)

Drury, P.J., 1974. 'Chelmsford Dominican priory; the excavation of the reredorter, 1973', *Essex Archaeol. Hist.* 6, 40–81

Dugdale, W., 1846. *Monasticon Anglicanum*, 6 vols (London)

Dunning, G.C., 1952. 'A lead ingot at Rievaulx Abbey', *Antiq. J.* 32, 199–202

Eales, J., 1895. *St. Bernard of Clairvaux. Cantica Canticorum: eighty-five sermons on the Song of Solomon* (London)

Eames, E. in R. Poulton (ed.) 1985. *Archaeological Investigations on the Site of Chertsey Abbey*, Research Volume of the Surrey Archaeol. Soc., No.11 (Guildford)

Eco, U., 1986. *Art and Beauty in the Middle Ages* (London)

Eighth Report. Eighth Report of the Deputy Keeper of the Public Records (1847)

Elkins, S.K., 1984. 'The emergence of a Gilbertine identity' in J.A. Nichols and L.T. Shank (eds), *Distant Echoes: Medieval Religious Women 1*, Cistercian Studies Series 71 (Kalamazoo), 169–82

Ellis, R.H., 1986. *Catalogue of Seals in the Public Record Office 1, Monastic Seals* (London)

El-Shamy, T.M., Lewins, J. and Douglas, R.W., 1972. 'The dependence on the pH of the decomposition of glass by aqueous solutions', *Glass Technology* 13, 81–7

Ernsberger, F.M., 1980. 'The role of molecular water in the diffusive transport of protons in glasses', *Physics and Chemistry of Glasses* 21(4), 146–9

Errett, R.F., Lynn, M. and Brill, R.H., 1984. 'The use of silanes in glass conservation' in N.S. Bromelle, E.M. Pye, P. Smith and G. Thompson (eds), *Adhesives and Consolidants*, Preprints of the Contributions to the IIC Paris Congress, 2–8 September 1984 (London), 185–90

Fitz, S., 1981. 'A new method of cleaning browned medieval glass', *ICOM Committee for Conservation, 6th Triennial Meeting, Ottawa 1981*, Working Group: Easel Paintings (Ottawa), 81/20/5–1 to 81/20/5–6

Fitz, S., Fitz-Ulrich, E. and Frenzel, G., 1984. *Die Einwirkung von Luftverunreinigungen auf ausgewälte Kunstwerke mittelalterliche Glasmalerei*. Forschungsbericht 10608002. Bundesministerium des Innern. E. Schmidt (Berlin)

Fletcher, W.W., 1972. 'The chemical durability of glass — a burial experiment at Ballidon in Derbyshire', *J. Glass Stud.* 14, 149–51

Foreville, R. and Keir, G. (eds), 1987. *The Book of St Gilbert* (Oxford)

Foucault, M., 1988. 'Technologies of the self' in L. Martin, H. Gutman and P. Hutton (eds), *Technologies of the Self: A Seminar with Michel Foucault* (Massachusetts), 16–49

Frank, S., 1982. *Glass and Archaeology* (London)

French, T.W., 1971. 'Observations on some medieval glass in York Minster', *Antiq. J.* 51, 86–93

—— 1975, 'The west windows of York Minster', *Yorks. Archaeol. J.* **47**, 81–5

French, T.W. and O'Connor, D.E., 1987. *York Minster, A Catalogue of Medieval Stained Glass: the West Windows of the Nave*, CVMA Great Britain 3/1 (Oxford)

Friar, S. (ed), 1987. *A New Dictionary of Heraldry* (London)

Frodl-Kraft, E., 1965. 'Das "Flechtwerk" der Fruhen Zisterzienserfenster, versuch einer Ableitung', *Wiener Jahrbuch fur Kunstgeschicte* 20/24, 7–26

Gage, J., 1982. 'Gothic Glass: Two Aspects of Dionysian Aesthetic', *Art History* **5**:1, 36–58

—— 1995. *Colour and Culture: Practice and Meaning from Antiquity to Abstraction* (London)

Gamlen, St. J. O., 1975. 'Some local medieval window glass affinities', *J. Brit. Soc. Master Glass Painters* **15**/3, 8–16

Gee, E.A., 1969. 'The Painted Glass of All Saints' Church, North Street, York', *Archaeologia* **102**, 151–201

Geilmann, W. von, 1956. 'Beiträge zur Kenntnis alter Gläser IV, Die Zersetzung der Gläser im Boden', *Glastechnische Berichte* 29(1), 144–68

Geilmann, W. von, Bertold, H.T. and Tolg, G., 1960. 'Beiträge zur Kenntnis alter Gläser V, Die Verwitterungsprodukte auf Fensterscheiben', *Glastechnische Berichte* 33(6), 213–19

Gent, T., 1730. *The Ancient and Modern History of the Famous City of York* (York)

Gibson, P., 1972. 'The stained and painted glass of York' in A. Stacpoole, *The Noble City of York* (York), 67–223

——1979. *The Stained and Painted Glass of York Minster* (Norwich)

——1989. 'Architectural Glass' in Newton and Davison 1989, 241–74

—— n.d. (unpublished).'Notes on the window glass from Ellerton', York Glaziers' Trust

Gillies, K.J.S. and Cox, G.A., 1982. 'Medieval Window Glass: Its Composition and Decay', *Proc. 22nd Symposium on Archaeometry, University of Bradford, U.K. March 30th–April 3rd 1982* (Bradford),181–3

—— 1988a. 'Decay of medieval stained glass at York, Canterbury and Carlisle. Part 1: Composition of the glass and its weathering products', *Glastechnische Berichte* 61(3), 75–84

—— 1988b. 'Decay of medieval stained glass at York, Canterbury and Carlisle. Part 2: Relationship between the composition of the glass, its durability and the weathering products', *Glastechnische Berichte* 61(4), 101–7

Golding, B., 1995. *Gilbert of Sempringham and the Gilbertine Order, c.1130–c.1300* (Oxford)

Graham, R., 1901. *S. Gilbert of Sempringham and the Gilbertines: A history of the only English Monastic Order* (London)

—— 1940. 'Excavations on the site of Sempringham Priory', *J. Brit. Archaeol. Assoc.* **5**, 73–101

Graves, C.P., 1995. 'Window glass' in G. Ewart and J. Lewis (eds) *Jedburgh Abbey: The Architecture and Archaeology of a Border Abbey*, Soc. Antiq. Scot. Monogr. Ser. (Edinburgh)

—— 1996. 'The window glass' in M. Foreman, *Further Excavation at the Dominican Priory, Beverley, 1986–89*, Sheffield Excavation Reports **4** (Sheffield), 126–44

Grissom, C.A. and Wessen, N.R. 1976. 'A new method for the preservation of waterlogged archaeological remains: use of teraethyl orthosilicate' in *Pacific Northwest Wet Site Wood Conservation Conference, 19–22 September 1976* (Washington), 49–59

Harden, D.B., 1959. 'New light on Roman and early medieval window-glass', *Glastechnische Berichte* **32** (8), 8–15

—— 1961. 'Domestic window glass: Roman, Saxon and medieval' in E.M. Jope (ed.), *Studies in Building History. Essays in Recognition of the Work of B.H. St J. O'Neil* (London), 39–63

Harrison, F., 1922. 'The west choir clerestory windows in York Minster', *Yorks. Archaeol. J.* **26**, 353–73

Harrison, F. 1927. *The Painted Glass of York* (London)

Hawthorne, J.G. and Smith, C.S. (eds), 1963. *On Divers Arts. The Treatise of Theophilus* (Chicago)

Hebgin-Barnes, P., 1996. *The Medieavl Stained Glass of the County of Lincolnshire*, CVMA, Great Britain, volume 3 (Oxford)

Heslop, D. and Harbottle, B. 1999. 'Chillingham Church, Northumberland: the South Chapel and the Grey Tomb', *Archaeologia Aeliana* (5) **27**, 123–34

Holden, A., 1990. 'Barcelona '90: 1st International Stained Glass Symposium, May 1990', *Stained Glass* Autumn 1990, 9

Hone, W., n.d. *Ancient Mysteries Described, especially the English Miracle plays founded on Apocryphal New Testament Story, extant among unpublished manuscripts in the British Museum* (London)

Horne, E., 1930. 'A crucifixion panel at Wells', *J. Brit. Soc. Master Glass-Painters* **3**, 12

—— 1935. *Downside Review* **53**, 48–51

Horton, A., 1975. *The Child Jesus* (New York)

Hufgard, M.K., 1989. *Saint Bernard of Clairvaux: A Theory of Art Formulated from His Writings and Illustrated in Twelfth-Century Works of Art* (Lewiston)

Hunter, J.R., 1981. 'The medieval glass industry' in D.W. Crossley (ed.), *Medieval Industry*, Council Brit. Archaeol. Research Report **40** (York), 143–50

Irvine, J.L., 1892. 'Notes on specimens of interlacing ornament which occur at Kirkstall Abbey, near Leeds, Yorkshire', *J. Brit. Archaeol. Assoc.* **48**, 26–30

James, M.R., 1926. 'The Drawings of Matthew Paris', *Walpole Society* **14**, 1–42

Kenyon, G.H., 1967. *The Glass Industry of the Weald* (Leicester)

Kerr, J., 1983. 'Window glass' in A. Streeten, *Bayham Abbey*, Sussex Archaeol. Soc. Monogr. 2 (Lewes), 56–70

—— 1985. 'The Window Glass' in J.N. Hare (ed.), *Battle Abbey: The Eastern Range and the Excavations of 1978–80*, English Heritage/HBMCE Archaeological Reports 2, 127–38

—— 1986. 'Historical discussion' in Croft and Mynard 1986, 110–11

Kerr, J. and Biddle, M., 1990. 'Later medieval window glass' in M. Biddle (ed.), *Object and Economy in Medieval Winchester*, Winchester Studies 7 i (Oxford), 386–423

King, A.A., 1955. 'Appendix: Gilbertine Rite' in *Liturgies of the Religous Orders* (London), 396–410

Knight, B., 1989. 'Imaging the design on corroded medieval window glass by beta-backscattering radiography', *Studies in Conservation* 34/4, 207–11

Knight, C.B., 1944. *A History of the City of York* (York)

Knowles, J.A., 1936. *Essays in the History of the York School of Glass-Painting* (London)

—— 1956. 'Notes on some windows in the Choir and Lady Chapel of York Minster', *Yorks. Archaeol. J.* 39, 91–118.

Knowles, D. and Jadcock, R.N., 1953. *Medieval Religious Houses: England and Wales* London

L and P Henry VIII. Brewer, J.S., Gairdner, J. and Brodie, R.H. (eds), 1864–1932. *Calendar of Letters and Papers, Foreign and Domestic, of the Reign of Henry VIII* (London)

LMMC 1940. *London Museum Medieval Catalogue* (London)

Lafond, J., 1969. 'Was crown glass discovered in Normandy in 1330?', *J. Glass Stud.* 11, 37–8

Lee, L., Seddon, G. and Stephens, F., 1982. *Stained Glass* (London)

Leff, G., 1958. *Medieval Thought: St Augustine to Ockham* (Harmondsworth)

Lillich, M.P. (ed.), 1982. 'Studies in Cistercian Art and Architecture Vol.2', *Cistercian Stud.* 66

—— 1984. 'Monastic stained glass: patronage and style' in T.G. Verdon (ed.), *Monasticism and the Arts* (Syracuse), 207–54

Little, M., 1988. (unpublished) *York Archaeological Trust Conservation Report* 27

Lutze, W., 1988. 'Silicate glasses' in W. Lutze and R.C. Ewing (eds), *Radioactive Waste Forms for the Future* (Amsterdam), 93–130

McAvoy, F., 1989. 'Sempringham Priory' in J.B. Kerr (ed.), *English Heritage: The Work of the Central Excavation Unit 1987–88* (London), 19–20

Maish, J.P., 1987. (unpublished) *York Archaeological Trust Conservation Report* 13

Marks, R., 1976. 'Medieval Stained Glass in Bedfordshire', *Bedfordshire Magazine* 15, 179–84, 228–33

—— 1986. 'Cistercian window glass in England and Wales' in Norton and Park (eds) 1986, 211–27

—— 1987. 'Stained glass, c.1200–1400', '734 Ornamental window' and '737 Figures in grisaille' in Alexander and Binski (eds) 1987, 529–31

—— 1991. 'Window Glass' in J. Blair and N. Ramsay (eds), *English Medieval Industries: Craftsmen, Techniques, Products* (London), 265–94

—— 1993. *Stained Glass in England during the Middle Ages* (London)

Marschner, H., 1985. 'Verwitterung und Konservierung von historischen Fensterglas. Bericht über Arbeiten am Zentrallabor des Bayerischen Landesamt für Denkmalpflege 1981–84' in H. Marschner and Y. Langenstein (eds), *Glaskonservierung, historische Glasfenster und ihre Erhaltung*, Arbeitsheft 32 des Bayerisches Landesamt für Denkmalpflege (Munich), 44–55

Marshall, K.C., 1979. 'Biogeochemistry of manganese minerals' in P.A. Trudinger and D.J. Swaine (eds), *Biogeochemical Cycling of Mineral-Forming Elements* (Amsterdam), 253–292

Martindale, A., 1992. 'Patrons and minders: the intrusion of the secular into sacred spaces in the late Middle Ages' in D. Wood (ed.), *The Church and the Arts*, Studies in Church History 28 (London), 143–78

Metford, J.C.J., 1983. *Dictionary of Christian Lore and Legend* (London)

Miller, D., 1985. *Artefacts as Categories* (Cambridge)

Milner-White, E., 1952. 'The resurrection of a fourteenth-century window', *Burlington Magazine* 94, 108–12

—— 1959. *York Minster: An Index and Guide to the Ancient Windows of the Nave* (York)

Morgan, N.J., 1983. *The Medieval Painted Glass of Lincoln Cathedral*, CVMA, Great Britain, Occasional Paper 3 (London)

—— 1988. *Early Gothic Manuscripts* 2 vols, A Survey of Manuscripts Illustrated in the British Isles (London)

Newton, P.A., 1961. (unpublished) 'Schools of glass painting in the Midlands, 1275–1430', Ph.D. thesis, University of London

—— 1975. 'The weathering of medieval glass', *J. Glass Stud.* 17, 161–168

—— 1978. 'The Medieval Window Glass' in J.H. Williams, 'Excavations on Greyfriars, Northampton, 1972', *Northamptonshire Archaeology* 13, 129–30

Newton, P.A. and Kerr, J., 1980. 'Window Glass' in N. Palmer, 'A Beaker Burial and Medieval Tenements in the Hamel, Oxford', *Oxoniensia* 45, 197; Fiche 2 EO1–2

—— 1979. *The County of Oxford*, CVMA, Great Britain, vol.1 (London)

Newton, R.G., 1977. 'More 12th-century blue soda glass', *CVMA News Letter* 24, 3–4

—— 1981. 'A summary of the progress of the Ballidon glass burial experiment', *Glass Technology* 22, 42–5

—— 1985. 'The durability of glass —a review', *Glass Technology* 26, 21–38

Newton, R.G. and Davison, S. (eds), 1989. *Conservation of Glass* (London)

Norton, C., 1983. '*Varietates Pavimentorum*: Contribution a l'etude de l'art cistercien en France', *Cahiers Archaeologiques* 31, 69–113

—— 1986a. 'Early Cistercian tile pavements' in Norton and Park (eds) 1986, 228–55

—— 1986b. 'Table of Cistercian legislation on art and architecture' in Norton and Park (eds) 1986, 315–93

Norton, C. and Park, D. (eds), 1986. *Cistercian Art and Architecture in the British Isles* (Cambridge)

Norton, E.C., Park, D. and Binski, P., 1987. *Dominican Painting in East Anglia: the Thornham Parva Retable and the Musée de Cluny Frontal* (Woodbridge)

O'Connor, D.E., 1975. 'Debris from a medieval glazier's workshop', *Interim: Bulletin of the York Archaeological Trust* 3/1, 11–17

—— 1987. '472 Virgin and Child' and '473 Virgin and Child' in Alexander and Binski (eds) 1987, 404–5

—— 1989. 'The Medieval Stained Glass of Beverley Minster' in C. Wilson (ed.), *Medieval Art and Architecture in the East Riding of Yorkshire*, Brit. Assoc. Archaeol. Conference Trans. for the year 1983 (London), 62–90

O'Connor, D.E. and Haselock, J., 1977. 'The Stained and Painted Glass' in G.E. Aylmer and R. Cant (eds), *A History of York Minster* (Oxford), 313–95

Owen, D., 1975. 'Medieval Chapels in Lincolnshire', *Lincs. Hist. and Archaeol.* 10, 15–22

Palliser, D.M., 1971. *The Reformation in York, 1534–1553*, Borthwick Paper 40 (York)

—— 1979. *Tudor York*, Oxford Historical Monographs (Oxford)

Park, D., 1987. '564 Retable with Crucifixion and (from left) Sts Dominic, Catherine, John the Baptist, Peter, Paul, Edmond, Margaret and Peter Martyr', catalogue entry in Alexander and Binski (eds) 1987, 447–9

Paul, A., 1990. 'Chemical durability of glass' in A. Paul (ed.), *Chemistry of Glasses* (2nd ed.) (London), 179–218

Pedrick, G., 1902. *Monastic Seals of the Thirteenth Century* (London)

Perez y Jorba, M., Dallas, J-P., Bauer, C., Bahezre, C. and Martin, J.C., 1980. 'Deterioration of stained glass by atmospheric corrosion and microorganisms', *J. Materials Sci.* 15, 1640–7

Pevsner, N., 1968. *The Buildings of England: Bedfordshire* (Harmondsworth)

Phillips, D., 1985. *Excavations of York Minster* 2, (London)

Platts, G., 1985. 'The decline and demise of Sempringham Village', *Lincs. History and Archaeology* 20, 45–57

Plueddemann, E.P., 1982. *Silane Coupling Agents* (New York)

Raine, J. (ed.), 1858. *The Fabric Rolls of York Minster*, Surtees Society 35

Raw, F., 1955. 'The long-continued action of water on window glass: weathering of the medieval glass of Weoley Castle, Birmingham', *J. Soc. Glass Technol.* 39, 128–33

RCHMY. Royal Commission on Historical Monuments (England). *An Inventory of the Historical Monuments in the City of York*. 2: The Defences (1972); 3: *South-West of the Ouse* (1972); 4: *Outside the City Walls East of the Ouse* (1972) 5: *The Central Area* (1981), (London)

Reisman, S.N. and Lucas, D., undated a. *Basic laboratory recommendation for the treatment of glass retrieved from an underwater environment*

—— undated b. *Recommendations for the treatment of glass objects retrieved from underwater*

Reyntiens, P., 1977. *The Technique of Stained Glass* (London)

Roberts, J.D., 1984. 'Acrylic colloidal dispersions as pre-consolidants for waterlogged archaeological glass', *Preprints of the ICOM Committee for Conservation, 7th Triennial Meeting, Copenhagen, 10–14 September 1984* (Copenhagen), 84.20.21–22

Robinson, D. (ed.), 1978. *The Register of William Melton, Archbishop of York, 1317–1340* (Torquay)

Robinson, W., Vos, P. and Jutte, B.A.H.G., 1985. 'Preservation and conservation at Hastings' in J. Gawronski et al. (eds), *Report of the Voc Ship Amsterdam: Foundation, 1984* (Amsterdam)

Routh, P.E.S., 1986. 'A gift and its giver: John Walker and the East Window of Holy Trinity, Goodramgate, York', *Yorks. Archaeol. J.* 58, 109–21

Rudolph, C., 1990. *The 'Things of Greater Importance': Bernard of Clairvaux's Apologia and the Medieval Attitude Toward Art* (Philadelphia)

St John Hope, W.H., 1900. 'Watton Priory, Yorkshire', *Transactions of the East Riding Antiq. Soc.* 8, 70–107

—— 1901. 'The Gilbertine Priory of Watton, in the East Riding of Yorkshire', *Archaeol. J.* 58, 1–34

Salzman, L.F., 1928. 'Medieval Glazing Accounts', *J. Brit. Soc. Master Glass-Painters* 2, 116–20

—— 1967. *Building in England Down to 1540. A Document History* (Oxford)

Sandler, L.F., 1986. *Gothic Manuscripts, 1285–1385*, 2 vols, A Survey of Manuscripts Illuminated in the British Isles (Oxford)

—— 1987. '10 Genealogical roll of kings of Britain' in Alexander and Binski (eds) 1987, 200–1

Scholtze, H., 1991. 'Chemical resistance' in H. Scholtze (ed.), *Glass, Nature, Structure and Properties* (Berlin), 328–55

Schreiner, M., 1988. 'Deterioration of stained medieval glass by atmospheric attack. Part 1: Scanning electron microscopic investigations of the weathering phenomena', *Glastechnische Berichte* 61(7), 197–204

Scot, V.D. and Love, G. (eds), 1983. *Quantitative Electron-Probe Microanalysis* (Chichester)

Shaw, H. (ed.), 1848. *A Booke of Sundry Draughtes* (London)

Silane Coupling Agents: Their Function, Chemistry, Mechanics, and Methods of Use, Product literature, 3–14, 33–4

Spitzer-Aronson, M., 1974. 'La distribution du cuivre dans les verres rouges des vitraux médiévaux', *Compt. Rend. de l'Académie des Sciences* C278, 1437–40

—— 1975. 'Contribution à la connaissance des vitraux du Moyen-Age. La présence du plomb et du cuivre et leur diffusion sélective dans les vitraux rouges des cathédrales francaises', *Compt. Rend. de l'Académie des Sciences* C280, 207–9.

—— 1976. 'Contribution à la connaissance des vitraux du Moyen Age. Insuffisance de la diffusion pour expliquer la non-concordance stricte entre la présence de cuivre et la couleur à l'intérieur des verres des vitraux rouges', *Verres et Réfractaires* 30(1), 56–61

—— 1977. 'La répartition "initiale" du cuivre, retrouvée et calculée, dans certains vitraux rouges médiévaux', *Compt. Rend. de l'Académie des Sciences* C285, 269–72

—— 1979. 'Prècisions sur les techniques mediévales des vitraux par des recherches en physique', *Verres et Réfractaires* 33, 26–34

Spriggs, J., 1980. 'The Recovery and Storage of Materials from Waterlogged Sites in York', *The Conservator* 4, 19–24

Steane, J., 1985. *The Archaeology of Medieval England* (London)

Stephenson, M., 1900. 'Monumental Brasses in the West Riding', *Yorks. Archaeol. J.* 15, 10–13

Stiegman, E., 1984. 'Saint Bernard: the Aesthetics of Authenticity' in M. Lillich (ed.) 1984, 1–13

Swanson, H., 1980. (unpublished) *Craftsmen and Industry in Late Medieval York*, D.Phil. thesis, University of York

—— 1983. *Building Crafstmen in Late Medieval York*, Borthwick Paper 63 (York)

—— 1989. *Medieval Artisans: An Urban Class in Late Medieval England* (London)

Taxatio. Taxatio Ecclesiastica Angliae et Walliae auctoritate P. Nicholai, circa AD 1291, Record Commission, 1802

Torre, J., 1690–1. 'York Minster 1690–1', YML Ms L1 (7)

Toulmin Smith, L. (ed.), 1907. *The Itinerary of John Leland in or about the Years 1535–1543* 1 (London)

Tudor-Craig, P., 1987. 'Panel painting' in Alexander and Binski (eds) 1987, 131–6

Tummala, R., 1976. 'Stress corrosion resistance compared with thermal expansion and chemical durability of glasses', *Glass Technology* 17, 145–6

Turner, W.E.S., 1956. 'Studies in ancient glasses and glassmaking processes. Part 5. Raw materials and melting processes', *J. Soc. Glass Technol.* 40, 277–300

VCHB. Page, W. (ed.), 1904: *Victoria County History for the county of Bedford*, Vol. 2 (London)

VCHL. Page, W. (ed.), 1906 *Victoria History of the County of Lincolnshire* (London)

VCHN. Page, W. (ed.), 1906. *Victoria History of the County of Nottinghamshire* (London)

VCHN 2. Page, W. (ed.), 1910. *Victoria History of the County of Nottignhamshire. Volume 2* (London)

VCHY. Tillott, P.M. (ed.), 1961. *Victoria History of the County of Yorkshire: The City of York* (London)

VCH Yorks. Page, W. (ed.), 1914. *Victoria History of the County of Yorkshire: North Riding* (London)

VCH Yorks. Allison, K.J. (ed.), 1969. *Victoria History of the County of Yorkshire: East Riding* (London)

Vogel, G.E., Johansson, O.K., Stark, F.O. and Fleishman, R.M., n.d. *The Chemical Nature of the Glass-Coupling Agent Interface.* Unpublished preliminary copy of a report to be presented at the 22nd Annual Meeting of the Reinforced Plastics Division, The Society of the Plastics Industry, Inc. Sections 13–B, 1–10

Warner, M., 1985. *Alone of All Her Sex: The Myth and the Cult of the Virgin Mary* (London)

Wells, W. 1975. *Treasures from the Burrell Collection* (London), 49–51

Westlake, N.H.J., 1882. *A History of Design in Painted Glass* (London)

Willis, R. and Clark, J.W., 1886. *The Architectural History of the University of Cambridge and of the Colleges of Cambridge and Eton* (Cambridge)

Winston, C., 1848. 'On the Painted Glass in the Cathedral and Churches of York, Memoirs Illustrative of the History and Antiquities of the County and City of York' reprinted in Winston, C., 1865, *Memoirs Illustrative of the Art of Glass Painting* (London)

—— 1867. *An Inquiry into the Difference of Style observable in Ancient Glass Paintings, especially in England, with Hints on Glass Painting* (2 vols) (Oxford)

Wood, E.S., 1965. 'A medieval glasshouse at Blunden's Wood, Hambledon, Surrey', *Surrey Archaeol. Coll.* 52, 54–79

Woodcocke, T., Grant, J. and Graham, I. 1996. *Dictionary of British Arms. Medieval Ordinary. Volume 2* (London)

Woodforde, C., 1946. *Stained Glass in Somerset, 1250–1830* (Bath)

—— 1954. *English Stained and Painted Glass* (Oxford)

Woolley, R.M., 1921. *The Gilbertine Rite*, Henry Bradshaw Society 59 (London)

YMF. Clay, C.T. (ed.), 1958–9. *York Minster Fasti* 1, 2, *Yorks. Archaeol. Soc. Research Series* 123–4

Zakin, H.J., 1979. *Cistercian Grisaille Glass*, Harvard PhD, Garland Publishing

Index

By Susan Vaughan

Illustrations are denoted by page numbers in *italics* or by *illus* where figures are scattered throughout the text. Places are in York unless indicated otherwise. The following abbreviations have been used in this index: C - century, E- East, N - North, S - South, W - West